Living Virtuously: A Wife's Complete Guide to Keeping Her Heart and Home

ISBN Print: 978-0-9906945-0-2
ISBN eBook: 978-0-9906945-1-9
ISBN ePub: 978-0-9906945-2-6
Library of Congress Control Number: 2014916850

Living Virtuously may be purchased at special quantity discounts. Resale opportunities are available for Bible Studies, Sunday School, Churches, gifts, fund raising, book clubs, and premiums.
Visit http://www.keeperofthehomestead.com/ for information on this and other products produced by Homesteading Productions LLC

Requests for special discounts or general information can be emailed to Mark Harrison homesteadproductions@gmail.com. Written requests to:

Mark Harrison
Homesteading Productions LLC
2632 Lower Cane Creek Rd
Pleasantville, TN 37033

All scripture quotations are taken from the King James Holy Bible.

This publication is designed to provide accurate and authoritative information in regard to the subject matter covered. It is sold with the understanding that the author, contributing writers or the publisher is not engaged in rendering counseling, or any other type of professional services. If counseling or other expert assistance is required, the services of a competent professional should be sought.

1. Homemaking 2. Homesteading 3. Encouragement 4. Virtuous Living 5. Learning 6. Frugality 7. Teaching 8. Christianity 9. Religion

I. Harrison, Erin II. Living Virtuously: A Wife's Complete Guide to Keeping Her Heart and Home

Cover design by Erin Harrison
Cover photos by Erin Harrison
Interior design and layout by Erin Harrison
Publishing Consultant: Mel Cohen of Inspired Authors Press LLC
Editing by Mel Cohen and Aaron Aprile
Printed in the United States of America

Living Virtuously

A Wife's Complete Guide to Keeping Her Heart and Home

Erin Harrison
Keeper of the Homestead

Table of Contents

Acknowledgments

I want to give all the glory to God. He has truly saved me to the uttermost. Without Him I would never had the opportunity to have such joy and virtue. It is because of Him that I have been able to have victory in my life.

I want to take the time to thank my husband for being such a solid rock in my life. Thank you for encouraging me to overcome and be thankful in all things. Thank you for being patient through the times when I was a bad wife. Thank you for loving me when I was hard to love, for standing by my side, and for carrying me through the times when I was too weak to stand on my own. You are my best friend.

I want to thank my children for being my buddies in all that I do and for being such precious people who care about others. I love you guys more than life itself, and I pray the Lord will use you in a marvelous way someday.

I want to thank my mom and dad for teaching me to love others and to have integrity in all I do. Thank you, Mom, for being a good wife to Dad and a good example of sacrificial giving. You taught me how to be good cleaner even though I used to drive you crazy because I was a slob. Thank you, Dad, for teaching me how to work hard, and do what needs to be done to the best of my ability. Thank you for always teaching me to learn from my mistakes and from people who are difficult. They are sometimes our best teachers.

A special thank you to my brother in the Lord, Michael Hoff. He never let being sick, in a wheelchair, or in pain stop him from praising God and reaching out to the lost. He challenged me to rise above my disabilities and make them into my greatest teaching abilities in Christ. He taught me to be thankful in all things.

Forward

I had the privilege of getting to watch Erin develop from the moment God brought her into this world to what she has become today. It continues to be an amazing experience to see and share in all that she is as a daughter, mother, teacher, artist, musician, photographer, keeper of the home, student of the scripture, and minister of what is true as well as what is good for us all. She relentlessly strives to encourage everyone she touches to accomplish learning and understanding of what it means to become a complete human being in a very complicated world.

She utilizes the many struggles she has had through her life, together with what she has learned from her parents and mentors, and combines that with what she has researched and studied herself to guide others into understanding for themselves how they can rise above any challenge life may throw their way. She frequently thinks of creative ways she can get her children, herself, and everyone else to get motivated to do all the things we all should be doing in our daily lives. She realizes, as should we all, that life deals us a continuous flow of choices that we need to make, and what choices we make forms us into who we become. Never before in history have the people on this planet been given as many choices as there are today. And our choices increase exponentially each day. Erin has recognized that right at that pivotal moment of choosing which way to proceed a person can make the right decision for themselves. They just need that necessary nudge in the right direction to proceed.

She teaches us, with joy, that there are many advantages and benefits to committing to this lifestyle which she endorses. It most certainly isn't what's being promoted by the mainstream nor will it be the most popular. Her methods of dealing with life's trials and tribulations will prove to be the most gratifying and rewarding. She has mastered the trick that the best way for anyone to learn is to try to get others to learn what you need to understand. When the student is ready, the teacher appears. I know that I have learned a lot from her in trying to be a good father. There can never be a father more proud of a daughter as much as I am of Erin.

I feel so blessed to be one of Erin's best students.

~Steve Mereness, Erin's Dad

Introduction

My first of many miracles

I was not raised in a Christian home, nor did I have a picture perfect childhood. I had some pretty hard things happen in my life, from sexual abuse to total rejection. At my lowest points in life, I felt that the world would be a better place without me. I struggled with depression and anxiety, fear and loneliness, hopelessness and confusion. These were things that led me to bad thought patterns until I became a slave to sin and shame. One night as I crawled around the floor moaning and crying into my pillow because I felt so utterly alone, something inside me cried out to God. I raised my arms in all my brokenness before a mighty God and asked Him to save me. I did not have a Bible. I was not evangelized. I did not go to church. I knew no one who knew Jesus, yet somehow I knew He was real. That night, my life changed forever. It was the night I was given a new beginning. I repented towards God. His spirit came to live in me and I was a NEW creature! There was a desire to learn more about Christ. I wanted a Bible and I wanted to share this newness I had experienced with others.

Reading page after page in my Bible, highlighting verse after verse, I found out what happened to me that night. It was real and His word was real also, washing me with each word I read. The journey had just begun. I kept a diary; In it I wrote love letters to God. I begged Him to use me, and to teach me how to be more like Him each day. Not understanding doctrine at the time proved to lead me into strange teachings and wild goose chases. I was like a wave of the sea, tossed to and fro. God was faithful to always bring me back to where I needed to be. Having a desire to learn has come in handy. I have never been too stubborn to admit when I was on the wrong path. I look back and see that God took my willingness to learn seriously. He allowed me to walk paths that nearly broke me, paths that lead me straight back to Him and His Mercy. Every time I broke, more of His light shone through. Every hard knock was a special gift. It was a way I could understand more of God's love and in turn God uses me to give others hope.

I attribute all grounding to my husband. While I have a personality that can get lost in the clouds, he grounds me and helps hold my sails from flying away. It is a miracle that God gave me a good husband amidst all of my many, many times of wandering and wavering.

When my husband first met me, I do not think he could have known what was in store for him–the roller coaster rides, the coldness, and hard work it would take to keep me from drifting away. Yet, to this day, he tells me I was worth the fight. He saw something that I could not see; he saw my willingness to get back up every time. I never stayed in the pit. I fought to keep from drowning, to keep my head above the water. He could see my deep faith in God through every circumstance life brought.

I was a terrible wife to start with. I was a terrible cook; I burned everything from macaroni and cheese to frozen pizza. I was a packrat and a slob. My life was a mess. I did not know how to fix it nor how to find balance in my sea of chaos. To top it all off, I was not a welcoming bride. Because of all my shame from abuse, I transferred all my guilt onto him. I withheld my affection, because I could not bear my own brokenness. He remained faithful through it all. His love and patience, more than anything has allowed me to grow. He was constantly pushing me to rise to the high calling God had in my life, to use all the talents God has given me.

Now I enjoy a glorious marriage, an orderly home, a precious relationship with each of my children, and most importantly a life full of joy. I did not get there all at once. It took years of turning sadness into gladness. Little by little, I learned to choose joy. In this book you will see little pictures of perspective, many perspectives of women who have chosen joy, and have a heart to share the things they have learned. It is our prayer to meet you right where you are, give you hope and encouragement in your marriage, in your mothering, and in bringing a level of joy into your home.

My second miracle

When my husband and I met, he had no idea I was a scarred and broken young girl. He only saw a funny person who shared his hopes and dreams of wanting a large family, a small homestead, and a way to serve God. He was an honorable young man who had walked with integrity while waiting for his one true love. I, on the other hand, was a used and abused child. Several family members and friends had taken liberties with me when I was young. As a bride standing in my bright finery, it never occurred to me that what had happened to me as a little girl would come raging through my life and remain there, crippling both me and my beloved for more than eight horrible years. But it did.

Each day was a cloud of tears as I begged him not to go to work, phoning him repeatedly over some minor issue until he despaired of not getting his work done, or worse, losing his job. There were nights when I would curl up into a tight ball and weep as far away from him as the bed would allow. I avoided him so much it is amazing that I did conceive each year. As one baby after another came, my emotional state worsened. My days were filled with crying babies, fighting toddlers, cooking, big messes, piles of laundry, cows to milk, and all the other chores of a homestead.

I was overwhelmed and thought I would surely die. But for my Beloved it was worse. He worked long days in the bitter cold only to come home to a distraught wife and five children under five years old who were crying, hungry, and demanding. There was firewood to chop and bring in, animals to attend, and a thousand other odd chores. And when he climbed exhausted into his cold bed with his even colder wife, he stared into the darkness and wondered why.

This man needed a miracle. He needed divine wisdom to set his home in order. He needed a way to lead his wife to overcome and find her life. My husband is a simple man—slow, steady, hardworking, and steadfast. But after all the years of sacrificial giving, he was running out of hope. Why would God allow this to be his lot? Had he not honored God in his youth? Had he not sought to do the right thing? Had he not had a vision of ministry? There seemed to be no end to misery, and there certainly were no loving arms to help ease his daily toil.

One day he told me to get out my mom's old camera and start taking pictures. Somewhere in this simple man's heart God had planted an idea. Woman was not only meant to be a help meet and mother, she was meant to be a person who had dreams, challenges, and drives. She was meant to be a Proverbs 31 lady who was full of enterprising adventures and money-making ideas. My husband knew my interest was in art, so what came to his mind was photography. Maybe I would find an outlet to distract me long enough for him to work ten hours a day so he could make a living for our growing family.

Let the miracle unfold! This busy homesteading mom got busier! I rushed through my chores, assigning my children small chores to ease the load. For the rest of the day I took lots of photographs of loved ones. I loved taking photos, and people loved my work. I loved art in every form, whether it was painting, printmaking, drawing, sculpting, or taking photographs. My creativity was explosive. I started a photography business after taking a risk to buy a digital SLR camera. Instead of pulling my hair out in bitterness as I had been doing, suddenly every day was spent taking hundreds of photos. I got a secondhand computer from my dad and started learning Photoshop. It was hard, but a challenge that I knew I had to master.

The kids and I would play all day, deciding what kinds of pictures we could take next, pictures that would be added to my portfolio. Pictures like my oldest child wearing a straw hat or climbing up the big tree in the front yard, the girls dressed in their pretty dresses looking out the window, teddy bears clutched under tiny arms; and wonder of wonders, I stopped calling their daddy every hour. I stopped with the tears and frustrations. I built a good schedule so that I could have a couple of hours early in the morning to focus on the computer work before the kids woke up, and a couple of hours while they napped. And when Daddy came home, we would run to tell him what we did that day, and show him all the pretty pictures Mommy took.

I was satisfied as a human being; I was successful, creative, and fulfilled. I stopped dwelling on my fears, hurts, frustration, boredom, and anger; I was too busy growing and changing. Within that one year the sad, broken girl was gone and in her place was a vibrant young woman, a loving wife, a happy mother, and a money-making entrepreneur. Instead of pulling my husband's soul down, I was giving back. It was a miracle. I fell into my husband's arms with joy and thanksgiving. Finally the good man was being rewarded for being so loving, kind, and patient.

Just like what happened to the virtuous lady in Proverbs 31, money started flowing into our home. The first year I made $12,000 taking photos of children, families, school graduations, and weddings. The second year it doubled. The third year it again doubled. I would get referrals from people who had their photos taken by me and loved my work. I would set up an appointment to meet their family at a park and take my children along for the fun. They would help carry bags and pack the minivan as we would plan out a picnic and play time around my work. My children had fun meeting other kids their age, and when the other kids would throw fits, we had fun talking about how silly it was. It trained them so much better than if I had stayed home all day fighting against my mind and discontentment. A few years later, the business grew to a six-figure income and my husband learned how to take videos at the weddings so we could work as a team. We both worked from home and went to a wedding once a week together, just the two of us. It was like a date. We would talk on the way there as we planned the event.

One morning I woke up before daybreak, as I usually do. It is a time I set aside for work that does not interfere with mealtime, homeschooling, and spending time with family. I opened my computer and started looking through hundreds of old photos. Tears began to flow as I thought about the past and how fleeting life can be. There was one photo of the kids toddling across my bare wood floors with mischievous smiles on their faces. Other photos told the stories of the babies smashing birthday cakes with their tiny fists and then stuffing their little mouths. I rejoiced, knowing that I had finally come to appreciate the good that God had given me, and that I had let go of the evil the devil had sent.

During those black years I felt it would never end. Maybe you didn't bring the baggage into your marriage that I did, and maybe your husband is a mean, lazy jerk or even a pervert; but pity, despair and bitterness will not set you free from your own state of nothingness, lack of productivity, wanting of challenge, nor any real rewards. Do you know what I am talking about—working and never seeing the end of it? It is the everyday grind, the repetitive tasks, the thankless labors, and being tired of just living. I remember how desperate and lonely I was. I lived in blame toward those who had hurt me, or criticizing others who hadn't rescued me. I was un-settled all the time. I felt as if I was sinking on a vast ship of five screaming, demanding passengers, with no life vests to save us. None of the children could possibly understand how tired I really was. They could not help me, and they could not carry on an intelligent conversation, as I so craved.

I piled all my needs onto my poor husband, who had no clue what to do to make me happy. He would come home to a frumpy, crabby woman in tears, desperate to take whatever he had left to give at the end of the day, and I would draw out whatever bit of life was left in him until he could give no more.

Before my husband encouraged me to work harder, I was a young mother handicapped by her own mind. I had no idea that my mind was self-absorbed in pity and frustration and that my energy was being drained by my bitterness. All those years are gone forever. I am sad that I did not enjoy my babies and the husband of my youth as I should have. It is a miracle that my husband did not pack his bags and leave me. I know I would have, if I had been treated the way I treated him.

I am ashamed of that time, yet I am thankful that my husband loved me through it. He came to see that all I needed was more to do, not less. And he was right. How could a mother give more? How could she possibly stretch her wings farther than the children she was working so hard to tuck under the safety of her wing? I needed structure. I needed something to pour myself into so I would not get consumed with myself.

Proverbs 31 is written for us ladies to take note and follow. It is an instruction manual written to show us how to find our way as wives and mothers who are created in HIS image. We were created to excel. We were created to be VIRTUOUS! To be busy in something productive instead of busy moping around like a frump.

My children are almost grown, with my oldest only three short years from adulthood. As my children move on with their lives, it is humbling to look back on those years and see how fast they flew by. Each child was given to me as a blank slate. I could have continued sowing frustration and discontentment into the pages of their lives, blaming everyone, bitter at my lot, and putting pressure on my husband to meet my demands.

Thank God HE freed me from all that. Instead, I worked and taught my children about work. Thankfully, they only remember a hardworking, happy mom who taught them the trade of photography among other things.

Years have passed and I have not lost a vision for virtue in all that I do. I strive for victory over every circumstance, staring at each one with a smile on my face, knowing I will never let myself back into the pit. Every piece of life has been precious, every season a gift. God supplies the grace, and I am grateful I did not give up.

Lately, I had a nice conversation with my very mature, sober-minded eleven-year-old daughter, who is now taller than I am. I told her about my early morning tears as I looked at the photos of her as a wee baby. I mentioned that many of those years I worked so hard that it seemed as if I did not get to cherish every little mundane thing of life. She looked back at me and said, "Mom, you worked so hard that it makes me want to work hard, and you always said 'working hard is a good thing.' I think we had a lot of fun together, working hard." That glorious answer will ring in my mind fifty years from now when I am all wound down from life, and it will always give me a sense of real accomplishment.

That was one of many stories that make up my choice for virtue. My story is a story unique to me. Each chapter in this book will contain an encouraging word, a Keeper Tip, or a Lesson on Etiquette, bridging the gap between keeping our heart and keeping our home. The 31st chapter of Proverbs can be applied to our lives today in our modern world. God is always complete when He gives wisdom, and Proverbs 31 is no exception. He carefully and perfectly lays out every aspect of life for a woman. And now, take a journey with me and countless other women as we aspire to be a Virtuous Woman—a woman after God's heart.

A Good Woman is Virtuous

Proverbs 31 is a record of a king reflecting back on some important things that his mother had taught him. He called this wisdom, "the prophecy that his mother taught him." His mother admonished him to refrain from certain lewd women. She warned him of the evil of the use of alcohol and how it would pervert a king's judgment. She encouraged him to speak for the man who cannot speak for himself, and to plead the case of the poor and needy. Then, his mother expressed her concerns that he find a good woman for a wife. She started by telling him that a virtuous woman is rare and precious. And, so he would know what to look for, she described at length how a really good woman spends her time and what she gets accomplished. It was as if she were telling her son, who would soon be king, "You will know her, son, by what she DOES."

A Good Woman is a Doing Woman

All the key words in Proverbs 31 are action words. She is a creative merchant. She is a worker. Almost every verse describes daily chores or a new enterprising task she is involved in. No one, not even her enemy, would call this woman lazy or slothful. She is diligent in her work, both when it is convenient and when she does not feel like working. In the end, it is this woman's work that speaks of her worth.

How does God rate one wife good and the next wife bad? The opposite of diligence is slothfulness, and "He also that is slothful in his work is brother to him that is a great waster" (Proverbs 18:9). A great waster is a loser. A slothful woman is wasteful by not taking care of things in a timely manner, therefore causing her goods to be damaged. A slothful woman wastes her time and often the time of her friends. A lazy woman puts off a job, saying it can be done tomorrow. God chose to add to his written Word the description of a virtuous woman so we would clearly know one when we meet her. The portrait painted here of this good woman, whom God says is worth much more than priceless jewels, far above the value of the average wife, is that of a diligent worker.

A virtuous woman is busy doing constructive activities. She explores business opportunities. She is saving money, making money, and investing money. I came to greatly admire this woman as I studied through her day-to-day activities. I stopped and asked myself over and over, "What could I start doing that would make me more of an active help meet for my husband?"

~Debi Pearl

Chapter One
What is Virtue?

"Who can find a virtuous woman? for her price is far above rubies."
Proverbs 31:10

Nearly an entire chapter of the Bible is devoted to this virtuous woman, so you know it is important for every woman to read and ponder.

First, let us examine the word virtue. Virtue is defined as having or showing high moral standards, but I like to compare virtue with integrity. When I think of virtue I see *integrity,* which is the quality of having strong moral principles while being whole and undivided.

Nothing can stop a person of integrity and virtue from doing what they know to be right and true. We live in a society that blends the lines of morality, where good is evil and evil is good. We are now in a time where we condone things that 100 years ago would have been a black-and-white case of sin. As times change, like a forceful raging current, we find ourselves riding with the current of moral deprivation instead of grabbing onto something solid to gain a footing so we can reach the moral high ground. The pull of that current takes such a struggle to fight against that we begin to feel weary, like we might drown in it.

Who can find a virtuous woman, a person of integrity? It is rare. Most people do not have integrity anymore. There is a lot of good intention but a lack of follow-through. Today, promises are made for the breaking.

My word is my bond

This is an old saying. It used to be that you could take someone at their word. If they said they would be somewhere, you could trust that you would find them there when they said they would be there. If a person said they would help you, you could count on them. Too many times people offer great things but never have the integrity or virtue to make these great things happen. Where there is no action, intentions are but a puff of air in a vacuum.

Many times I have heard a friend say, "We have to get together sometime." In my mind I am thinking, "Really? *Sometime* will never come." It is just too easy to say that phrase. Easy to roll off the tongue—*sometime.* It satisfies the need to be niçe for the sake of being nice. It qualifies a person as caring. My response is, "When? When would you like to get together?" People are not ready for *when.* They like *sometime.* When you ask for a date, they fumble around and say, "We'll have to get in touch next week and see what the week brings." That is as good as saying, "I am busy; if I get around to thinking of you next week, I may even be able to say *sometime* again and give you enough 'nice' to go on for another week until you get the point that I have no intention of getting together with you."

It is fun for me to actually set the date and see what happens. Nine out of ten times something will come up for others that causes them to cancel. I have that feeling myself sometimes. I make a plan to get together or to help someone and then when the clock is staring me right in the face while I am busy doing something else, I get that same temptation to call and cancel. It takes a great measure of integrity to drop my project and just go and do as I promised, to keep my word. I guess that is more important to me than to finish what ever I was doing. Whatever I was doing will be there when I get home.

The trick is to never make commitments if you cannot keep them. I do not fault a person if they never offered in the first place. To the one who makes a vain offer but fails to follow through, I see this as a lack of virtue and integrity. Most times I have learned to figure that people will not show up at all, and when they do I am amazed. That is how bad it has gotten in our present society!

Integrity is not something that a person can wear as a badge on their sleeve; it is something that defines a person. When a person has virtue, you will see a trail of integrity in all to which they put their hands and hearts. Neither is it a series of unfinished dreams and projects or a life filled with broken promises; it is something as sure as the sun shining even when it is behind the clouds. It is always there, giving light and warmth to the life of every person it touches.

Integrity is rare and something that carries value, like a ruby. Rubies are jewels that are found within rocks of the earth. They are chiseled out of rough and dirty ground. The value of the ruby depends on several qualities. The color, cut, clarity, and carat weight gives the ruby its value. I find it interesting that the most valuable rubies on earth have the deepest color of blood red. Interesting because our value as a Christian is not by what we have done, it is through the blood of Christ that we can be viewed as righteous.

I like to think of my life as dirt and rock with a shining ruby peeking through. The vast crumbling rock reveals the glorious ruby. The first thing you see is the beautiful red glistening back—so clear you can see your refection. It is just like how God sees the blood applied to one of His children and His reflection as He gazes upon its precious luster.

For God to compare the value of a virtuous woman to that of a price far above rubies is special. The most expensive ruby in the world is worth over six million dollars! If we are virtuous and have integrity our worth is far above that of the most prized rubies this earth has to yield. We are precious first because of His blood but also because we stand for what is right even when it is inconvenient. When we are shamed or reviled we continue to have the integrity to stand, undivided, holding to the truth we know in our hearts. Our pureness is that of a precious ruby, clear and true.

Recipe to be a GOOD WOMAN

Proverbs 31:10—A good woman as described here is very valuable. There are not many like her.

"Who can find a virtuous woman?
for her price is far above rubies."

Key words: *far above*

Rare, uncommon, unusually excellent, unique, precious, matchless.

Virtues of Charity
LOVE

As a wife and mother, the very essence of my existence is to love and to be loved by those in my own household first, and then to those that are not in my household—my neighbors. More importantly, I must grasp the meaning of love by the one who designed it—God.

Charity is a word we find in the Bible, and is often referred to as "love." This is the definition of charity: the practice of benevolent giving and caring. From a biblical standpoint, charity is a virtue of unlimited love and kindness. What is unlimited love? Unlimited love is a love that loves without bounds. It is an adjective meaning; not limited or restricted in terms of number, quantity, or extent. That means it is something you can count on. It is a love and kindness that never ends, no matter the circumstances. Chapter 13 of 1 Corinthians takes us to the heart of this concept of unlimited love and kindness.

> *"Though I speak with the tongues of men and of angels,*
> *and have not charity, I am become as a sounding brass,*
> *or a tinkling cymbal."*
> ***1 Corinthians 13:1***

Okay, if you are like me and have boys, you know what loud obnoxious noises are. They tear through the room with thunderous footsteps. They barrel down the stairs; it sounds much like a stampede of elephants running for their lives. They are created to conquer, so any small matter requires a battle cry to magnify its importance. There are days that I feel so tired after teaching lesson after lesson while homeschooling, that my eyelids become heavy. I take the risk to shut them and attempt to get a little nap in on the sofa. After just dozing off, in comes a boy with the loud bang of a slammed door and the kick of a chore boot zinging through the air, hitting the wall with a crack. I jolt back into consciousness, wondering why. Why could they not just learn to close the door softly and tip toe into the room like I did when they were small and napping? So when people do not have charity (unlimited love and kindness), their spoken words are like an obnoxious sound. To me the most obnoxious sound is that of finger-nails scratching a chalkboard. Imagine how many people send the sounds of clamoring crashes and shrieking scratches when their words pour forth from a heart void of unlimited love and kindness.

"And though I have the gift of prophecy, and understand
all mysteries, and all knowledge; and though I have all faith,
so that I could remove mountains, and have not charity,
I am nothing."
1 Corinthians 13:2

Harsh. So I could have great faith, so great that I could remove a mountain, and if I do not have charity, I am nothing. I could know every-thing, understand everything, but if I do not have unlimited love and kind-ness, I am NOTHING? How many people do you run into that seem so smart, so together, so spiritual but yet they are selfish or unkind to others? I have met many self-proclaimed children of God that when I hear their great swelling words, their little religious plug-ins every other sentence and then I see how they set themselves apart, I cringe inside because I see something missing.

One lady comes to my mind—an old friend of mine. She was so much larger than life. She could outwit the finest Bible scholar. She could outrun the entire church with her devotion to God. She was uncompro-mising in her grand faith and sure to nail you to the cross if she caught you compromising in your walk with God. She would not "put up with that." Prayer was done like a sounding trumpet for all to hear and admire. "Come all, come around; listen to her devotion, her authenticity." I was under the thumb of her teaching, and the command to exhort one another in truth was one-sided. There was nothing she would learn from my immature understanding of God's word. It was like her words were that of the Holy Spirit. I would nod my head and listen to the clamor of her many words for hours, knowing that there was nothing I could say to refute her. She was blinded by the smokescreen she masterfully created with her many religious words. As a self-proclaimed evangelist, she would prowl after every human like a lion prowls after its prey, digging in her claws. I would watch her, just wishing I wasn't there, hoping these poor people would come away not completely confused.

At her home I observed a very conditional sort of love. If you do as she says, you are on her good side. Anything other than agreement is anarchy to God himself. Her husband shrinks under the constant bullying. When I stood up to her, that was "it" for me. She threw me out of her life. Unlimited love and kindness was not her song. Without this charity, all her pomp and circumstance, all her swelling words of wisdom, her endless faith—it amounts to nothing.

I am thankful for her witness in my life because I learned more from her example than I could have learned being around someone who was easy to be around. I learned what I do not want to become. I strive to always esteem others greater than myself. I want to always be teachable, and my faith to soar within the bounds of unlimited love and kindness.

"And though I bestow all my goods to feed the poor,
and though I give my body to be burned,
and have not charity, it profiteth me nothing."
1 Corinthians 13:3

Hello philanthropists! It is amazing how many people in the media brag about how much money they gave to this or that charitable organization. You see them holding an orphaned child who is smiling. Even everyday people like to brag about themselves—how they went and brought a meal to this person, or how they gave to this missionary, or how they helped with a homeless shelter feeding the poor. It is good to help, but God sees the heart. You can do all these things, but if your motivation is to be seen of men, to get some kind of glory out of being a grand example of a benevolent Christian, you get your reward—here, not in heaven. I have seen people give to the needy, yet cringe when a dirty bum sits beside them on a bench. What's worse is when people give to have a "hold" on you. They expect you to listen to them because they have done "oh so much for you."

Strings are attached to every little gift. You know you are in trouble after you have been given a bag of groceries when you were down and out, and then later that same person gets mad at you because you did nothing for them. It profits us nothing if we do not give in a pure heart filled with unlimited love and kindness, expecting nothing in return.

When I think of these three verses, I think of motherhood. I think of the unlimited love I naturally have for my children. They could be screaming their heads off, acting like total lunatics in public so that I look like a terrible parent, but I still love them. They could walk away from my grand words of encouragement on loving one another to slapping their sibling across the head for no good reason. The wars break out, things get ugly, and yet I love them. They break many of the things we work hard to buy. They stare up with these cute little eyes, saying, "I thought it was a horse, mommy." The frustration mounts; but that remark was so cute, so I love. They could whine and fuss until my ears feel like they will fall off, and I just keep plugging away with my love towards them. I could never stop loving my children. No matter what they do, no matter how many messes they make, no matter how many times they are not thankful for the sacrifices I have made, I still love.

A story comes to mind

I remember a day 14 years ago when Miles was about 18 months old. He asked me for a piece of cheese, so I turned away from him and walked toward the refrigerator. I proceeded to open the door and look for the cheese. I placed it on a cutting board that I had on the counter top. Miles tugged my pant leg as he whined, "Mama, cheese; Mama, cheese!" I patiently continued toward the drawer where I found a knife. Slowly, I sliced the cheese, and by this time Miles was laying on the floor, crying his eyes out. I thought to myself, wow, this must be how it feels to God. We pray, and when nothing happens we immediately feel that God has turned His back on us and walked away. Instead, just like I was busy preparing something for my child that he was too small to see and understand, God is busy lining the circumstances up in His own good timing.

Miles, in his small understanding, thought I was forsaking him when I turned away. He lost faith when I was steadfastly stuck to the counter-top doing something other than handing him the cheese. His heart fainted as he saw me pick up a knife. Impatience got the better of him as he wailed, not knowing that I was preparing something wonderful for him. And yet God loves us when we are His children, born again into his family. As our father in heaven, He still gives good gifts to us even though we behave selfishly, even when we throw fits, and even when He sees that our love has a limit. His good gifts don't always come as fast as we want them, nor sometimes in the way we asked for them; but one thing is for certain— our whining is obnoxious in the sight of God. We whine so loudly in the form of disappointment, ungratefulness, and discontentment. His charity is unlimited, His kindness never ceases, and He remains full of mercy toward us even though we do not deserve it. I am thanking God today for His Charity toward my life. I could cry every time I try to fathom why He is good to me even when I fail. Wow, it is amazing to be loved by God!

"Charity suffereth long, and is kind;"
1 Corinthians 13:4

To suffer is to endure something unpleasant or to be subjected to something bad. Suffering comes in many different forms:
Pain, Loss of a loved one, Hunger, Poverty, Abuse, or Disease.
We have all suffered one or more of these to varying degrees. Some of us survive and learn patience, while others become bitter because of it. One person can believe God allowed the suffering so they could grow and overcome, thus becoming a stronger person. Yet, another person will shake their fist at God with anger, and wonder why.

When I think of suffering long, I think of when I had my nerve injury. The pain was constant. I would lay awake all day and night, rocking back and forth as I cried loudly. I had a bedpan beside me, dozens of pills, and only the cold dark corners of the room to comfort me all the day long. My husband would walk past with his hands over his ears because it killed him to hear my cries of pain. My children were scared to come near me, for fear of hurting me. I threw up a lot, and laid in the bed beside my dirty bedpan. I would beg God to give me mercy and grace for each passing minute. I lived minute by minute, for I could not bear to know that pain another second. And the torturous pain went on for nine months. Yet, all I could fathom was that the burning in my foot could not compare to what hell would be like. It did feel like an eternity, as I look back. Every minute seemed like an hour, my days like years. I patiently endured each minute I was given. When people would ask, I could not bear to complain; I would utter these few words, "I am better than I deserve." I know there are so many worse situations. To keep my mind pure, I would sit there and thank God for the things I did have, counting my blessings one by one. I knew that I could endure the intense pain if it was only temporary—temporary in an eternal sense. I held fast to my heavenly home where I would one day walk on streets of gold.

When intense suffering ceases, you appreciate the breaks you have all the more. It prepares your heart for other disappointments that may come in life. I have a friend who buried two of her children at a young age. I can't imagine the suffering of loss that she has to endure on a daily basis. You begin to see that things could always be worse. The suffering of pain I endured was actually nothing compared to real suffering that is unjust.

Christ suffered death on the cross for our sins. He patiently endured the cross of shame to give us new life. He did not defend himself. Instead he showed charity towards us when we were yet sinners.

Enduring people patiently

To "suffereth long" in charity means something different than patiently enduring pain in life. It is patiently enduring others with unlimited love and kindness. After all, there is a plug of the word *kind* after *suffereth*. Some people are very hard to be around; so much so, that you feel you actually suffer them. God calls us to be different than the rest of society. Normal human love will love those who are good to them. Even an evil, murderous person is good to his buddies, and will lay his life down for them. The trick comes when you love someone who is not so nice to you. You return good for evil when nature tempt you to return evil for evil.

In our own homes, we sometimes have difficult people to live with. Do we patiently endure them? Do we practice the law of unlimited love and kindness when we are treated badly by our spouse or children? Instead, we often snap back or shrink in disappointment. We become indignant or we ignore. To be longsuffering we must not be quick in getting angry and frustrated. We must not be quick to offer the cold shoulder. I know I fail here. I do quickly get frustrated when the kids are acting foolish or disobedient. I am not always kind to them as I should be.

The Bible says…
"A soft answer turneth away wrath: but grievous words stir up anger."
Proverbs 15:1

"…charity envieth not: charity vaunteth not itself, is not puffed up,"
1 Corinthians 13:4

If we have charity, that is, an unlimited amount of love and kindness towards others, we are happy for them when they excel. We will not envy their wealth, beauty, or success. Most of the time we are sitting on the other side of the fence, perhaps in pain or in need. You may look longingly at their joyous smiles and envy. You might see that they have a better husband who lets them do the things they desire, while you are stuck with a Mr. No. How many of us can say this is true about ourselves? If our lives are a mess because of choices we made, we must love others enough to rejoice in their good fortune, not comparing ourselves among ourselves. We should only compare ourselves to Christ.

And when we do rightly, and experience some blessings out of charity, we do not flash our success like a braggart. If we have charity, we do not vaunt ourselves, which means to brag about ourselves or exalt ourselves above others. Like a mother who has 12 children and vaunteth about her growing number of children to the barren woman who has no children, it is not showing charity. We ought to be sensitive to others around us if we are to love fully. If our husband is wrong on some matter, we do not have charity toward him if we say, "I told you so."

Charity is not puffed up. A puff is a short, explosive burst of wind and when driven into something, it expands. In short, it puffs up. I like to think of the puffer fish. As a protective instinct, the puffer fish puffs its body up until it becomes a prickly ball of spines. Any creature that would try to eat it will be sorry they tried after they have spines sticking into the roof of their mouth.

When we puff up, we protect our pride. We build walls instead of tying strings of trust with those we love. It is a stubborn pride that will not give in and let the other person be right. Many marriages are ruined because of puffing up. People have a tendency to protect themselves. They do not want to be hurt or taken advantage of. It is to risk something sacred to them to be transparent. It is hard to say to your spouse, after you make a fool of yourself by having a childish fit, that you were out of line. I have sat for hours in silence on a car ride staring out the window because I was puffed up. Pouting and prideful, I'd inch my way as close to the window as possible. When I bring my thoughts back into the captivity of Christ, I see how foolish I was. What if we got into a car wreck, and the last thing I saw was my pouting face staring back at myself? What a pitiful sight! That would be a foolish way to end my days. Quickly I unpuff and look to my husband. I let my wall down and smile, telling him how much he means to me. How foolish I was to be so puffed up and bitter. How I know it is wrong to waste my minutes staring out the car window, separating myself from his steadfast, unwavering charity towards me. Instead of clinging to my pride, I hold his hand. He is ready to forgive his prodigal wife every time. What a blessing.

> *"Charity suffereth long, and is kind; charity envieth not;*
> *charity vaunteth not itself, is not puffed up."*
> **1 Corinthians 13:4**

The light of truth shines into my heart today, exposing the areas that are dark and full of cobwebs. I want to display this kind of unlimited love that is always kind, always patiently enduring. My days will be sweeter the more I practice. And the days of my husband and children will be sweeter if I can walk in charity toward them. Today I choose charity.

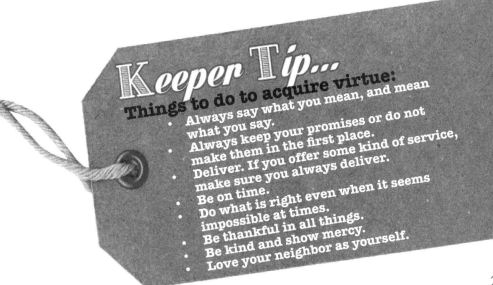

Keeper Tip...

Things to do to acquire virtue:

- Always say what you mean, and mean what you say.
- Always keep your promises or do not make them in the first place.
- Deliver. If you offer some kind of service, make sure you always deliver.
- Be on time.
- Do what is right even when it seems impossible at times.
- Be thankful in all things.
- Be kind and show mercy.
- Love your neighbor as yourself.

Tales of Victory...

Why the Gospel Changes Marriage

When I first got married, we received this lovely wooden box, and written inside was a beautiful poem. It said that marriage was like a box and most people getting married believed a myth. They believed love, romance, and companionship were things found in marriage, when in fact these things are actually found in people, and people infused these things into their marriage. Eventually if you took out more then you put in, your box would be empty.

I would daily look at that box and it would serve as a reminder to daily pour into my marriage. When I would take out, there was a sense of entitlement, after all I had infused whatever I took out into my marriage so I had every right to take out my fair share.

I remember keeping a running tab and account on how much my husband was infusing and putting it. It was terrible. Can you imagine the kind of wife my husband had to endure? Just thinking about how I behaved makes me sick.

I remember if he wanted to be intimate sexually, I would check our marriage box to see if he had infused romance lately and it had to be in the form that I approved. If he didn't read or pray with me, then he had no right to tell me how to behave spiritually. If he didn't listen to me then I wouldn't listen to him.

Our marriage became this "you scratch my back, I'll scratch your back" kind of love. The only problem was that I was so quick to point out when he wasn't scratching my back and therefore I would withhold scratching his.

How horrible to live this way. I was so judgmental, always pointing out his faults and failures as a man and leader of our home. We were both miserable.

I knew the scripture, "Love the Lord your God with all your heart, mind, soul and strength and love thy neighbor as thy self." You see, it was not a love issue for me; I loved my husband. I loved him the same way and as much as he loved me.

Then one day, I was reading and the words of Jesus to His disciples really penetrated my heart deeply. They were the words in John

13:34-35 "A new commandment I give unto you, That ye love one another; as I have loved you, that ye also love one another. By this shall all men know that ye are my disciples, if ye have love one to another."

I was hit with the pondering truth of the love of Jesus. Jesus was calling me to a different kind of love, a gospel kind of love, and if I was going to love my husband the way Jesus said to, then I would need to think about how he loved me.

This led me to the cross. The cross is where love was demonstrated and ultimately on display for all to see. While we were yet sinners Christ died for us. Scarcely would one die for a righteous man, but Jesus laid his life down willingly for the joy that was set before him.

He showed us what love is. He loves without condition, without reservation, and without wanting anything in return. His love is unconditional. This is gospel-centered love.

Jesus' love isn't an "if you do this or that then I will love you," but rather, nothing can separate us from the love of God, neither death, nor life, nor angels, nor principalities, nor powers, nor things present, nor things to come, Nor height, nor depth, nor any other creature, shall be able to separate us from the love of God, which is in Christ Jesus our Lord.

What a glorious love indeed! I remember, after reading and thinking about the way Jesus loved me, the next question was, "Is this enough for me?" Was the way Jesus loved me enough to compel me to love my husband the same way, or would I continue to love my way, the way I had been, the "if you scratch my back, I'll scratch your back" kind of way? Was Jesus enough for me?

This is what it boils down to in marriage: It isn't about putting in in order to take out; it isn't about serving to be served, loving to be loved, nor giving to get; it's about sacrificially laying down your life, saying, "My life is yours." Marriage represents Christ and the Church; we wives represent the bride of Christ to an unsaved world. Therefore, the way we love our husbands shows the world our love for Christ.

The gospel in marriage changes our attitudes from a "serve me" attitude to a "glorify God and love my spouse" attitude.

The gospel is enough and until Jesus satisfies you, you will continue to love selfishly.

~Darlene Lopez

Chapter Two
Virtuous Conduct

"The heart of her husband doth safely trust in her,
so that he shall have no need of spoil."
Proverbs 31:11

What does it mean to have the heart of your husband safely trusting in you? There are several ways we can spoil his trust and confidence in us by our...

- **Conduct**
- **Conversation**
- **Commitment**

In this chapter I will share about...

Virtuous conduct

How can our husbands trust in our conduct? Do we behave in a manner that brings disgrace upon our husbands? Maybe I am the Lone Ranger here, but I have been guilty of this myself. Early in my marriage I conducted myself in a manner that embarrassed my husband. I behaved unseemly both as a fool and a flirt.

The fool

When we would get into group settings, I would get hyper and foolish. It was not uncommon for me to start showing off with my Tae Kwon Do, or doing impersonations of different funny characters. All the people would laugh so hard they would nearly cry. It made me feel really good because I love to see people laughing and having a good time. My husband, on the other hand, would feel horrified. He would bury his head into his hands and just wish for it to be over.

For many years, I continued in this foolish conduct because I felt he was overreacting and that he should not care about what others think. Because he was the head of our home, he felt my conduct was influencing foolish behavior in our children, and it was making others have less respect for me. He would say, "Do you want our kids to be fools? When you act like a fool, you give people the impression that you do not take anything seriously." It took me years to see the fruits of my poor conduct and even more years to understand the shame I had brought on my husband. I was acting in a manner that gave him need of spoil. Being one in marriage means more than an agreement on a slip of paper. It means you are one in your success, one in your joy, one in your failings, and also one in your shame. Unknowingly, I caused my husband to not trust me.

The flirt

A married woman who is flirtatious with other men can cause her husband to spoil. He will always wonder if he is the apple of her eye or if she is longing for another. A woman can destroy her husband's trust by how she acts in front of other men. If she dresses in a way that shows off her goods, she is sharing something that is for her husband's eyes alone. Many women fail to realize that a husband, although he may love to see his wife looking seductive, would rather not share her seductive look with others.

If you can believe it, I used to be a bit of a flirt around other men by the way I dressed, combined with my actions. I liked to be noticed and enjoyed the positive attention that I received. I would curl my hair, paint my nails, wear gobs of makeup, and even use fake eyelashes. I wore tight pants and high-heeled boots, low-cut tops and lots of jewelry. This was about six years ago, and yes, I had all five of my children and it was while I was taking wedding photos. To the men, I looked available and I knew they were interested because they would ask for my number. I had lots of offers. I did not realize how serious my conduct was. Not only was I a disgrace to my husband and family, I was a stumbling block to many other men. I had no business behaving in that manner. My husband said, "Why are you trying to look like a teenager? You are 32 years old with a family; why do you want other men to desire you?" I tell you, I have made a lot of foolish choices; but I thank God that He is patient with me.

Some people argue that it was my bubbly, friendly personality. To prove my point, I did an experiment. I wore a long black skirt, put my hair in a ponytail, and wore a black modest top. I acted the same. No offers. No men chasing after me and checking me out. Then I had my accident in the midst of this unseemly behavior. It was the best thing that ever happened to me. I was headed on a wrong path, and the crippling pain I endured saved me from my own destruction. As I lay there day and night in utter agony, I pondered my ways. I could do nothing but scream in pain and pray for God to help me bear another minute. In that time of great suffering, God was all I had to lean on and it was then that I repented from my foolish ways.

I will never forget this one cold, dark night, a night that I could not sleep. I could see my life flash before my eyes, and see my children helping work on the homestead. I knew that was where I belonged. God gave me a vision to minister alongside my family to teach the skills of the land He created. As tears poured forth as a river, I knew I had strayed from my calling and God loved me so much that He would not allow me to go too far. The pale glimmer of the world was no longer important with all its vain glory, so I became steadfast from that moment forth. I will never desire the strange and empty attention of the world. No more compromise.

What a blessing to be an ornament of praise and honor to the Lord and to my husband! When I started dressing in a more discreet manner, my husband was so relieved. It took such a burden off him knowing that I was not a stumbling block. My husband will tell me to change my shirt if it is too snug. I am not offended; I feel special that he does not want to share his prize with others.

There are other women that would take offense at this. Some women are completely naive and do not have husbands who trust them enough to tell them how they feel about their conduct. I have seen a lot of flirtatious women dress ridiculously seductive. They either act like they do not have a clue or they make an excuse that their husband is fine with it. Sure. He is fine with whatever you say as long as he is afraid of the ramifications he will have if he says anything against you. Some women are master manipulators. They manipulate their husbands into agreeing with something which is totally against right and good. A man is no match against a woman who will make his life miserable if he defies her wishes. He has to walk on eggshells to keep the peace in her presence. If he says the shirt is too tight, she may fly off the handle or ignore him for days. What can he do? He cannot safely trust in her. The moment he tries to lead or tell her how he feels, she will trample the trust he had in their relationship.

Women do not realize how important it is for a man to safely trust in her. Keep in mind, I am addressing women. I realize men have many faults and can act inappropriately as well. I speak to you from my own experiences and from the perspective of a wife who desires to be a virtuous woman. May God bless you as you seek him each day. Let us be that jewel to adorn our Lord and our husband. Let us be a reflection and glory of our God each day.

Lord, help us be all we can be by the grace and mercy of the blood you poured out to cleanse and purify our souls. It is the only way we can be prized far above the ruby.

Lessons in *Etiquette*
Modesty

Charity "doth not behave itself unseemly..."
1 Corinthians 13:5

To behave unseemly, you would be acting inappropriately, against good womanly etiquette. If you have the law of charity inscribed on your heart, you will practice good etiquette. Etiquette for women has changed throughout history, in many ways. When I was a little girl, I learned a lot from my grandmother about etiquette. I would stay at her home some weekends. My grandmother would snap at me if I put my feet on the sofa, "You dassant do that!" I was not allowed to put my elbows on the table nor ask for anything to eat. You would just patiently wait your turn. Grandma Isla was born in the early 1900s. The era in which she was brought up was very different from what we know today. I think my grandmother would be utterly disgusted at the unraveling of our society. There are some contrasts of what was appropriate in her time from what is appropriate to our society today, such as the code of dress for women of the early 1900s. Women always wore long skirts with petticoats under them. They wore long stockings and laced shoes. Corsettes were used to help with proper posture. The hair was grown long and often pulled back. Women wore hats if they were to appear in public. It was a disgrace to have anyone see you in your pajamas.

Modern dress etiquette

In contrast, there is no code of dress today. You can see women in Walmart dressed in their pajamas, and sometimes in their underwear. There are things I see women wearing that I am embarrassed to even look at. Their breasts pop out of their low-cut tops, and I have to fight against the pull of my eyes from looking down. I can't even imagine how difficult it would be for a man to stop from staring. Women have wild hair styles, piercings, tattoos, gobs of dark makeup, and dress in a way that appears so inappropriate you wonder if they are a hooker. Bellies are visible, pants are so tight they look as though they are painted on the leg. And it is all worn with pride. Not even a blush of the cheeks. It feels wrong and inappropriate, very unseemly.

Practice charity in modesty

If you want to practice charity in your dress, you will dress with discretion. I am not saying you need to have a dress code like that of the early 1900s, but not to behave unseemly by revealing so much of your body that it forces others to gawk at you. The line of discretion is blurred with each passing year in the evolution of fashion. A person can dress modestly and still be fashionable. It takes effort to find appropriate-looking attire these days, but many ladies can pull it off.

Modesty is a touchy subject for many women. They feel offended if you mention it. I heard a young man once say that he felt safe around a woman who dresses more modestly. As women, we have power with our bodies. We can tempt or shield temptation. And yet there are men that are so far gone, that you could wear a tent and they will somehow find pleasure in their twisted imagination. For the most part, to dress unseemly would be in the intent of the heart, whether you are trying to get that attention you seek. Some of us are dense. I sometimes wear something that I think

Time-Tested Wisdom...

Taken from Created To Be His Help Meet by Debi Pearl

A Virtuous Woman is a Modest woman.

God speaks of a woman maintaining her chastity and purity by the clothes she wears. "In like manner also, that women adorn themselves in <u>modest apparel</u>, with <u>shamefacedness</u> and <u>sobriety</u>; not with broided hair, or gold, or pearls, or costly array; But (which becometh women <u>professing godliness</u>) with good works" (I Timothy 2:9-10). God says that a woman's apparel should profess godliness. Her clothes, hair, and adornments—not just her mouth—make a loud profession to all who see her that she is modest and godly, <u>or</u> that she is immodest and ungodly. Our Heavenly Father has dress standards! Would you employ the standard argument and dismiss God as "legalistic" when he tells us that there is a proper way to dress and there is an improper way? Clothes speak to all who see us. Clothes make a constant profession. That is, they declare out loud—drowning out our words—our true heart condition and our attitude toward ourselves and toward those who see us. When I want to tease or entice my husband, a slight change in my clothes, hair, or demeanor is all that it takes to arouse him. Men are very much different from women. Jesus warned men, not women, when he said, "Whosoever looketh on a woman to lust after her hath committed adultery with her already in his heart" (Matthew 5:28). Then God tells a man what to do about it if he cannot keep from looking and lusting. "And if thy right eye offend thee, pluck it out, and cast it from thee: for it is profitable for thee that one of thy members should perish, and not that thy whole body should be cast into hell" (Matthew 5:29). This is very serious business!

It is impossible for a woman to understand a man's visual drive. She can only believe what an honest and candid man tells her, but few men are willing to admit to their weakness. A woman's body, moving within visual range of a man, unless it is modestly covered in a way that says to the man that you have no interest in him taking pleasure in your appearance, can be as stimulating to him as disrobing completely. He may be a better man than the woman who is dressing immodestly and may have the fortitude to deny his eyes the stimulation you offer, but it makes you a source of temptation to sin, rather than someone to whom he can relate.

If you find pleasure in being a source of temptation to men, you are definitely an ungodly woman and are in desperate need of repentance.

~Debi Pearl

is cute. I like the color of the top because it goes with my skirt perfectly. It still has to pass the HUB Test (husband test). My husband will send me back to the dressing room if I wear a shirt that is too snug or a shirt that displays cleavage when I bend over. He is a good discerner as to what is appropriate for me. Each family should judge for themselves what they agree is appropriate, since there is no code for dress in the modern world and no prescription of dress noted in the scriptures.

Teaching my girls about modesty

My mother brought us two pretty white dresses for the girls when they were only eight and nine years old, from another family. They were pretty and very long. My daughter Molly asked me, "Do you think white and peach go well together?" I said "Why?" She said, "Well, look up at the top. My skin is showing so much I just wondered if that looks good, white with peach?" I know that she was feeling uncomfortable with the spaghetti straps of the bodice, so I told her, "You know what, darling, you can put a white t-shirt under it if you feel better about that." And she was happy that I let her do that.

I would never want to make her feel half-naked. Most parents forget about the modesty issue. The churches forget to teach about it and the kids start looking just like the rest of the world, leaving it all hanging out. It is surprising to me how many Christians are oblivious to modesty. You go to the churches and see girls, young girls, looking half-dressed and ready to go out looking for a mate. It is nice to look nice but not so far as to cross the line of your own purity and integrity. I realize some people have been slowly leaning in that direction, so slowly that they realize it when it is already normal to their children. They are putting immodest attire on their little girls, and all of a sudden they realize their daughter is becoming a young lady who looks desirable! It would be hard to teach a young girl that it is not good to dress that way after she has grown accustomed to that way of dressing. She would not even be one bit ashamed to have a bikini on. Now that Molly and Megan are young ladies, they seem to keep the pattern I laid before them. They have their own convictions on dress. I do not tell them what to wear. They make their own decisions in that area and I trust them. They do not flaunt their bodies toward the boys. When other girls dress inappropriately, they are the first to notice. I just talk to them about it. I ask them questions on how they think about it, which is good because it allows them to articulate their own minds on the matter.

Unseemly behavior of a flirt

Flirting is to behave as though attracted to or trying to attract someone, but for amusement rather than with serious intentions. Beware: Flirting is definitely unseemly. When you flirt you are not acting with good etiquette or propriety. Flirting is a form of manipulation which is meant to draw the attention of men by way of moving the body and batting the eyes. It is not practicing good charity that embodies unlimited love and kindness if we lead others on. You could be the most modestly dressed woman, but if you behave unseemly, in a manner that leads men on, you are not concerned about their soul.

Pride in modesty

There are ladies who get so far bent to the extreme of conservative modesty that they forget they are a wife first. I went through a phase where I went out of my way to be modest. I like to call it my PLAIN PHASE. I slicked my hair back into a tight bun and put a headcovering over my entire head. I stopped wearing makeup and even my wedding ring. My dress was like a tent covering my shape until I looked more like a bag lady than a young bride. I took ultimate pride in my humility. Black socks and ugly clopping shoes were a part of my new look.

I started hanging around the Amish and wanted to fit in with them in every way. I wanted to learn to sew, bake, dress, and talk like them. I somehow felt that I would be better if I was WITH them. My husband hated every bit of it. He said I had "Amish Mennonitis"—a disease of my outward lack of adornment. He did not find me attractive. That was my goal; I wanted to be less attractive to men, so I would not be a stumbling block. It was not out of character for me to rush to the opposite extreme. I found out that modesty is a matter of the heart. One time I was grocery shopping at Walmart in my Amish getup, and my husband took another cart because he was embarrassed to be with his pretending Amish wife. I guess he thought it would be a bad witness—the driver holding hands with the Amish wife. (Since he looked normal, people would tend to think he was my driver. Makes sense to me now.) It is so funny how we women can

Letters from my Readers

Dear Erin,

     I am a 19-year-old single girl from TN. I was raised on a farm, along with my family of nine kids. I am probably more redneck and tomboyish than most girls, and I like it that way. But even though I was raised on a farm with lots of work and chores to do, my parents always stressed modesty. I can do in a dress what a lot of girls can't even do in pants. My dad has always said, "If you can't do it in a dress, then you shouldn't be doing it." So when I see girls {who call themselves Christians} dressing immodestly, it pains me. When the world looks at us, they should see something different than what they're used to. We should stick out. No, not like sore thumbs, but as different.

     At first, when we had gone to just wearing dresses, I felt odd. One time I overheard a girl asking another, "Why is that girl wearing a dress?" Now that I'm older, I see the difference that I didn't see then. I stick out, but in a good way!

     I am learning that, as children of God, our utmost purpose in life should be to love, praise, please and follow God, no matter what! It may be uncomfortable for a time; you may feel out of place, but what good does it do to be like everyone else? What does the opinion of others matter in the eyes of eternity? What we really should be worried about is, what does God think? Is He pleased with our actions? My choice of dress and attitude? I have found, when your main goal is to love and serve God no matter the cost, your life is full of adventure, blessings, peace and utmost joy in the Lord. It can't come thru anything else.

     My question to other young ladies out there is: What does God think about your dress? Do you show too much of your legs? Maybe too much of your breasts? Or are you emphasizing the fact that you have breasts or that you have a nice behind? Where is your chastity? Your discretion? People should see in you a chaste girl with her eyes focused on Christ, not one that lets her stuff hang out for all the men to see. They shouldn't have to look away from you to not be tempted by the things that are right at their eye level. I just want to tell other Christian ladies that it is not godly and it's not right. Thanks for listening. ~ Cameron get so self-righteous that we lose sight of reality. I looked silly, and I was be-having in a manner that was dishonoring my head. No headcovering could mask that one!

As I walked with my headcovering held high on top of my head and my long blue dress covering every square-inch of my flesh, an older man walked up to me. He told me how beautiful I was. I was flattered of course. Finally, a man appreciated my conservative look. I took pride in him think-ing I was an Amish woman. BUT, I was too forward to be an Amish lady. He somehow knew that and started to come onto me. I thought he was just an old guy that enjoyed seeing the Amish, but he actually wanted to have me, even though I was dressed completely modestly. My forward behavior gave him access to my heart. Giving him my complete attention and look-ing into his eyes was revealing something exciting to him. He did not care what I was wearing. He knew it could all come off anyhow. Sick! To think I was that dense is embarrassing to me now.

My mother was always very embarrassed by my crazy Plain Phase. I grew up wearing pants and t-shirts. It was just as normal in my home as it is normal for people to dress that way in our modern culture. When I start-ed sewing all these baggy plain dresses, it was a shock to my family and friends. It was like, what happened to Erin? Just like parents who raise their children to dress extremely modestly (boys in long pants and long shirts and girls in long double-covered dresses and headcoverings), the change is a shock, and it feels hurtful when they see their children breaking the mold they set for them. My mother felt embarrassed to go into public with me and my Amish-looking children. Oftentimes she would insult me for how horrible I looked. I chalked it up to "being persecuted for righteousness' sake." Yeah, right! My own form of it.

Backwards headcovering

It used to hurt me so badly that my mother was more embarrassed to go into public with me than with my sister-in-law who dressed like a gothic seductress. My issue was more an identity crisis than anything. My sister-in-law and I had a way to attract attention. I was deceived into thinking that by dressing more "humble" I was going to be viewed as more "meek." Wearing a headcovering would show the world that I was "submis-sive," and that I understood the headship order of Christ. If your husband wishes you to wear a headcovering, it would be fitting to do so. It was not a picture of order for my particular situation because I was wearing the headcovering even though my husband told me NOT TO. I was disobeying my head to wear one. My coveting heart wanted it so bad I was willing to do anything to have my way of righeousness. I almost killed myself two times over this. My attitude was so ugly and so nasty that it nearly drove my husband to leave me. To think a stinking headcovering could be that divisive!

My self-righteous stance on modesty was no different than a gold ring in a pig's snout. I was not fooling God. Just like a woman can be vain in how she dresses immodestly, a woman can also be vain by dressing hyper-modestly. In all things there is a cry for Balance. My husband wants me somewhere in the middle. "Don't dress like a whore, but please do not dress like a frumpy old woman." Thankfully, I have been able to strike a balance in that area. I try to look attractive but not too revealing. I certainly learned not to be too forward with men as well. I am still shaped like a woman, so you know I am a woman. I like to be clean, presentable, and attractive to my man as well.

Pants or skirts

What do I personally recommend? My opinion is that it should be something between you and your man. What does your husband like? What does he feel is appropriate for you? If you are in doubt, ask him. See if he has an opinion one way or the other. Some men would be horrified if their wife started wearing dresses or skirts all the time, while others would find it very feminine and lovely. Some husbands will want you to dress in a way you feel comfortable. They want it to be your choice. If that is the case, examine your own heart in this matter. Bottom line—there is no use in ruining your relationship with your husband over what you are wearing.

> **Keeper Tip...**
> **Modest Mirror Test.** Look in mirror while you bend over. Can you see your goods? If so, the shirt is too open at the top. Next, Raise your arms. Does your shirt go so far that you can see your bare belly? If so, your shirt is too short. Sit on a chair in front of mirror. If you can see up your skirt when sitting or shifiting in chair, your skirt is too short.

Time-Tested Wisdom...

Taken from Created To Be His Help Meet by Debi Pearl

What About Pants?

We cannot leave this subject without dealing with an issue that comes up over and over again. Is it permissible for a woman to wear pants? Deuteronomy 22:5 is cited as a prohibition against a woman wearing pants: "The woman shall not wear that which pertaineth unto a man, neither shall man put on a woman's garment: for all that do so are abomination unto the LORD thy God." To cite this verse as prohibition against women wearing pants, one must assume several doubtful concepts. Do pants pertain to men? What verse? According to the Bible, the common garment for a man is a skirt or cloak. Seventeen times the Bible speaks of men wearing skirts, such men as Boaz, King Saul, and Aaron. One time, the Bible speaks of a woman's skirt, and another time it speaks of God's skirt. So, even God wears a skirt, as did the Scottish men and the Roman and Greek men of old. American Indian men wore mini skirts. During Bible times, as far as secular history reveals, the only people who ever wore pants were Eastern women.

We want the Bible to be strictly our guide, but there is always a danger of reading something into it to suit our personal sense of propriety. Anyone with an open mind knows that the passage is speaking against transvestitism—cross-dressing so as to appear as the opposite sex. The manner of dress would differ from one culture to another and from one era to another. Men and women are not to pervert and besmear the Creator's designation of their sexuality, which essentially challenges God's "and it was very good" declaration of the distinctiveness of his crowning "male and female" creation. It is disturbing to see women blurring gender distinction in the way they dress, and it is absolutely disgusting to see a man dress effeminately. Males and females dressing out of their gender is clearly troubling to God, which is why he addressed the subject in his Word. It is an abomination to him, an affront to his sovereignty in the creation of mankind. Keep that in mind as you choose your wardrobe. Modesty is the principal rule of female dress. If you want to get provocative, do so in private with your husband. In fact, I recommend it, but when you come out of the bedroom and go to church or to the local store, dress as you would dress for the Judgment Seat of Christ.

~Debi Pearl

Tales of Victory...

Prudent but not a Prude

My parents were artists and did a lot of ministry with the military in Memphis, TN. I was born there and when I was three years old my parents decided to pack up and move all five of us kids to the country. We were outsiders, city slickers who bought a piece of property right in the middle of an Amish community. It was a beautiful place and we learned so much from their culture. We were not Amish, just Bible believers who bought a farm. Even though we did not have rules and regulations on dress code, we were raised to be respectful to the people around us. We were quite poor so we bought the clothes we did not make from the junk stores or yard sales. I learned to work hard and save money.

Dad and Mom had a wonderful marriage. People were always coming to them for counciling for marriage, family, and Bible teaching. Mom instilled in us girls that when we marry, that man will be our head and we will be his Help Meet. She showed us everyday what that looked like by the way she loved and worked along side my dad.

Fast forward to when I was 19. I married James Easling, a wonderful man from Washington state. We moved to Pennsylvania for a job and worked together restoring antique carnival rides. We made great money— better than my parents ever did. I remember one time going to the mall, and James wanted to buy me full-price clothes. It was against every cheap bone in my body. I tried to talk him out of it. I told him they were too expensive but he said since we are making the money, we can spend it. I cringed but chose the cheapest thing and told him I liked it best. He smiled and picked the nicest thing and bought it with the rest. It felt wrong to spend the money when I really did not need it. Not only were they expensive but not as conservative as I was used to.

Growing up in an Amish community, I naturally dressed more conservatively for the people I was around, and, without realizing it, I had built rules of modesty in my mind that were not in my husband's. Everything that he would buy me or compliment me on was quality, tailored clothes. I worked to be his Help Meet but he was not what I grew up with; my clothes had always been cheap and four sizes too big.

Little by little, I began to realize that I was his but that I was trying to dress for everyone but him. So if he bought something for me, I would wear it for him. He glowed, that I was his. He bought it for me. He picked it out. I looked amazing and I was his. I started to realize people were not looking at me, they were looking at us. "Look at that couple. They look so happy. That is so rare to see. What is different about them?" I had to let go of everyone else and decide to be His. It is funny because that is when people stopped seeing me, and saw us. We are so much more together.

I have found you can be prudent and not a prude. Money is just money and it will all burn. Clothes are just clothes and they will not last. My job is to be my husband's help meet. Not his leader but his lover. Not his conscience but his confidant. Not his boss but his friend. We work hard together. We play hard together. We love each other and we still go shopping together!

~Shoshanna Easling

Time-Tested Wisdom...

Thinking Before We Speak

It is difficult for me to not just blurt out what I am thinking or write a response to a comment without thinking. The only problem with this is that it is so easy to say or write things that I wish I could take back. However, words, once out, can cut like a knife, so I must continually learn how to ponder my words carefully before speaking or writing them.

God wants all of our words to be acceptable to him. "Let the words of my mouth, and the meditation of my heart, be acceptable in thy sight, O LORD, my strength, and my redeemer" (Psalm 19:14). He also commands, "Wherefore, my beloved brethren, let every man be swift to hear, slow to speak, slow to wrath" (James 1:19). This is a very difficult task for talkers like me!

What has helped me most is to quote Psalm 19:14 to myself before I even get out of bed and I also ask the Lord to give me wisdom in the words that I write. When someone asks me for advice, I try to ponder the question for awhile and even ask the Lord for wisdom in responding, trying to be sensitive to the feelings of those asking.

It is a difficult line to walk sometimes when you want to speak the Truth boldly but also be sensitive to other's feelings. Sometimes the Truth is harsh and needs to be said. I never want to water down God's Word, for my desire is to please the Lord rather than men. In this day and age, when so many pastors are preaching that Jesus wants all of us to live in a large house and have nice things, we must know the Word and teach it without fear.

Many people are broken and stumbling and so in need of the Truth, so we must continue to speak and write it, but we always need to do it in love. All of our words need to be carefully thought about before we speak, especially when we are angry. The more you practice this, the better you will get, especially with the God of the universe living inside of you giving you wisdom and strength.

***"Seek those things which are above, for you are dead to sin and your life is hid in Christ with God. Now believe it!

~Lori Alexander
From Blog: Always Learning

Chapter Three
Virtuous Conversation

"The heart of her husband doth safely trust in her,
so that he shall have no need of spoil."
Proverbs 31:11

Can your husband safely trust in your conversation? When he is gone will he wonder what you are saying about your private life or about him?

Backbiting

Talking bad about our husband to others can spoil his reputation among the brethren. When a wife does not get her way, telling other sisters about how unreasonable or controlling her husband is can make her feel better for the moment but it will spoil his good name.

I have had a couple of sisters in Christ which have continually cried to me about how horrible their husbands were to them. One wife would call me in desperation telling me that she could not take his controlling nature any longer. She felt she was not allowed to go anywhere or do anything but serve him. It did not matter that she had talents and dreams; she was forced to set her life aside to be at his beck and call. I listened, I cried with her, and I began to despise her husband. There were times I would get so angry for how poorly she was being treated that I would tell her to leave him. Wow. I know now that I was wrong to feed into her backbiting. The right thing would have been for my husband and me to have a meeting with her and her husband. Her husband deserved his day in court. He had no voice and I did not get to hear his heart as I judged him and condemned him.

The poor conversation pulled me into relating situations in my own marriage with which I was not happy, and so we began to commiserate. Our husbands were brought before the slaughter of our words. Every time I was around her husband, I would think he was such a jerk, even though he was kind to our family.

Years later, I saw myself as a wretched wife. I would see how trustworthy my husband was, how he would never go around telling people about how nasty I was to him. He did not tell people when I would slam a door in his face or tell him that I was leaving him when I did not get my way. I could act like a total unreasonable jerk to him, and trust that my good name would not be smeared. No one wants other people to know what happens behind closed doors. Even the people who have a great measure of self-control, can act nasty in their own seething, quiet way, and would not want others to find out about it. From then on, I knew it would spoil the trust we had in each other. I stopped my slanderous tongue against my dear husband.

When another wife came to me about her troubles with her unreasonable husband, I did not cater. I did not feel sorry for her. I saw my own past ugliness in her every word. When you know there are husbands out there who beat their wives, molest their children, commit adultery, watch porn, or are addicted to alcohol or drugs, what a blessing it is to be married to an honorable man who may be stern and controlling but who only wants to protect his family. He is generally like that because he feels a grave responsibility to the Lord for his children. This husband carries a heavy weight in his heart, making sure he provides the resources and protection that his family needs.

His wife goes around telling people all that he says behind closed doors in order to vent, instead of trusting the Lord to give her the grace to endure. When you put it into perspective, the beaten wife of a perverted husband would simply give anything to have such a protective man in whom she can trust. It is all in your perspective. I have learned not to tolerate this behavior. It is hard for me to not comfort and allow her that venting, but I know it is one-sided and it spoils the trust that he may have in her. If she were actually in a dangerous or abusive situation, I would have called the police and had him arrested. I do not mess around with things like that since I was abused myself. If you are in an abusive situation, I would suggest the same. It is a sin to enable such abuse to continue. In this woman's situation, she was simply not happy because her husband was being harsh and unkind towards her. She feels unappreciated and overlooked.

What can an unhappy wife do to keep her conversation pure?

- **She can pray.**
- **Try to treat her husband the way she would wish to be treated in all areas of life.**
- **Make a practice of writing down all the wonderful things about her husband.**
- **If she is faced with an opportunity to talk bad about her husband: stop talking, pray, and change the subject.**
- **Say something kind about her husband every opportunity she gets in public. It is better they think he is her hero for his protective ways than for him to be known as a tyrant.**

TMI (Too Much Information)

Are you telling intimate details of your married life? Can your husband trust in what you are telling others about his private life? His finances? This has caused my husband more frustration than almost anything else I have ever done. I tell people too much information. Recently, when my husband was having an ailment, I asked him why he did not tell me he was suffering for so long. He said that he was afraid to tell me because he thought I might broadcast such a thing. I had a terrible habit of just saying whatever came to my mind. Sometimes he would just shake his head in disbelief that I actually said a certain thing. He did not trust my mouth at all. He knew it was an untamed thing and could burst forth with just about anything at anytime. It takes years to regain confidence and trust in a person once it has been lost. I told him that I would never tell people about his personal issues and that it has literally been years since I have done such a thing. He looked back and me and said that he noticed I had been doing much better in recent years.

My training sessions

When I used to be around other people, I would become nervous if there was a space of time when no one was talking. I felt that it was my God-given responsibility to fill that void. Then the floodgates would open and I would tell all. To train me, he would have a slip of paper in his pocket on which he wrote "TMI." When we would be in a situation where I was talking and I started to give out too much information about private things such as our finances or other personal issues, he would flash that piece of paper in my direction. Even when I was on the phone he would pass by with that paper as a gentle reminder. That really worked for me. I wanted my husband to trust me again, so I really appreciated how he helped me overcome. My husband showed me these Bible verses:

"Whoso keepeth his mouth and his tongue keepeth his soul from troubles."
Proverbs 21:23

"But I say unto you, That every idle word that men shall speak, they shall give account thereof in the day of judgment."
Matthew 12:36

"Let the words of my mouth, and the meditation of my heart, be acceptable in thy sight, O LORD, my strength, and my redeemer."
Psalms 19:14

"Let no corrupt communication proceed out of your mouth, but that which is good to the use of edifying, that it may minister grace unto the hearers."
Ephesians 4:29

"Wherefore, my beloved brethren, let every man be swift to hear, slow to speak, slow to wrath:"
James 1:19

He did not show me these verses because he felt he was better than me; he showed me these verses based on his deep love for me and concern for my witness to others. I can see so much wisdom in his lack of words. My many words have gotten me into worlds of trouble throughout my life. I see this now, but there was a time that I was not so appreciative. The one thing that has driven me the craziest in our marriage is how little he talks. But in reality, it has become the best thing for me. I simply could not understand why he had almost nothing to say. What was he thinking? Was he thinking at all? On the flip side he once told me how much he loves to hear me talk to him. On long rides listening to all my stories, he actually enjoys my many words and feels empty if I stop talking to him. One day, he said to me, after I wondered why he did not talk very much, "You are like a babbling brook. Your voice is a comfort rolling over me. I am a deep well. It takes a lot of effort to draw the water up. It only gets drawn up when there is a need." Amazing! I love how his few words carry the meaning of my thousands. I have learned that the freshest water comes from the deepest wells within the Earth. Everyone knows it is unsafe to drink out of a stream unless it is flowing from a fresh spring. You can see how clean it is by the clarity of the water. If it is clear and cool, you know it is spring-fed and you can trust in it. The spring of life is Christ. If you are tapped into Him, pure words flow from your heart. Lord, please let our conversation be pure and undefiled. Let our words be healing and edifying to our husbands so that his heart can safely trust in us.

Virtues in Charity
TRUTH

"Rejoiceth not in iniquity, but rejoiceth in the truth;"
1 Corinthians 13:6

Rejoice:
To feel or show great joy or delight

Iniquity:
Immoral or grossly unfair behavior. Sins against God's word.

Truth
That which is true or in accordance with fact or reality. Faithfulness and constancy. Righteous virtue.

There are a few ways we can rejoice in iniquity:
- **If we are taking pleasure in our own sin.**
- **Taking pleasure in others sin.**

- **If we are happy when someone is getting their due.**
- **We enjoy hearing or sharing bad reports (gossip).**

For women, I see this as all too prevalent even among seasoned Christians. I have always struggled with bad reports. There is a point in every conversation where there is a space of time that develops. It is that point at which a topic has been concluded and we women move in for a juicy story.

There are two types of rejoicers in iniquity

1. **The Broadcaster:** The one who tells the bad report.
2. **The Responder:** The one who reacts to the report.

The broadcaster will say, "Did you hear so-and-so was doing this or that?" The responder will reply, "Oh, how horrible. That person deserves to pay for what they did!" Sound familiar?

I have only met one or two women in my entire lifetime who resist this pull. Both of these women were not Christians. Go figure! Why is it that we Christians cannot kick this bad habit?

About twelve years ago, I was talking with a cousin of mine. I had a bad situation come up and I decided to broadcast it to her (talebearing), which was normal for me to do. She looked at me and said, "I really do not want to hear bad reports about other people. I do not feel comfortable with things like that."

I can remember my heart pounding and my face feeling like it changed five shades of red. I was "trying to be a light" to my family and friends while my grandmother was dying. I was trying to be that Christian example and then I pull *that*? What is going on? Here, this older cousin of mine, who does not even trust fully in Jesus, shows me up in her virtue.

There is a passage in the book of James that really hits me between the eyes:

"And the tongue is a fire, a world of iniquity: so is the tongue among our members, that it defileth the whole body, and setteth on fire the course of nature; and it is set on fire of hell.
For every kind of beasts, and of birds, and of serpents, and of things in the sea, is tamed, and hath been tamed of mankind:
But the tongue can no man tame;

it is an unruly evil, full of deadly poison.
Therewith bless we God, even the Father; and therewith curse we men,
which are made after the similitude of God.
Out of the same mouth proceedeth blessing and cursing. My brethren, these
things ought not so to be."
James 3:6-10

This ought not to be so! But it is so. It is quite prevalent. I actually try to guard myself from it but even then it is hard, especially when you are around someone who is entrenched in this sin and they are someone you look up to. It is so funny to watch people at a church meeting. I have been to so many different types of churches, from stoic Baptist to raising-your-hands-and-falling-in-the-aisles Pentecostal. Each filled with their dedicated flocks. All of which seem so pious in their own right. They praise God with their mouths, raise their hands in holy dedication, and sing songs with their eyes closed in utter worship.

We then travel out to the parking lot or nursery and, oh my, the smiles fade and the bad reports start flying. I have been there and done that. Guilty. I am guilty of being the Broadcaster and the Responder. At times I would feel the race of my heart to share a bit of a juicy story about a person caught doing some sin. It is fun. You can get reactions and people enjoy the story. They want to hear more. It is kinda like a way of passage sometimes. You actually get the attention from the other person, and you can indulge in the story together as if you were best friends.

So, why do we broadcast?
- **It attracts the crowd.**
- **Gives a good filler for a dull conversation.**
- **It makes you look righteous.**
- **It causes you to feel better about yourself.**

I have also been a willing Responder to bad reports. I aid and abet the crime by driving the nails into the accused. I agree with the accusations and by so doing I:
- **Keep my friend by way of agreement.**
- **Make myself feel better by further putting others down.**

- **Give myself an advantage over others in the huddle of slander by voicing my disgust.**

How can we Christians do this? We boast about how we serve God here or there, minister to these people or those people, and then out comes poison! We just got done praising God and then we can't wait to curse man whom God loved so much and for whom he gave his Son to die. It is sad. We get on the phone and tell all kinds of bad reports to someone else. If only we could get caught. If only our sins would find us out. Then, and only then could we feel the heat of it as we get burned. I have been burned by my own mouth many times. It hurts badly to know you brought shame to another person by your words.

Here is an excuse for how we Christian women broadcast bad reports, as if this excuse is excusable in the sight of God: "I am telling you this for prayer." Oh, there. That makes it better. Not really. Or, "I am telling you this because I just needed to VENT." Nice try.

My children do it all the time. They love telling stories about others' bad behavior. Stories about kids who are mean, nasty, or selfish to them. They smile when the other child gets in trouble and is punished. So often I have to stop them and instruct them to find something nice to say about that person—to bless that person in some way. I have talked badly about people to my husband in front of the children, so I don't have to wonder where they picked up the habit.

Different times in my life I have been able to conquer this; but I find more and more as I age, that the best way to avoid this tendency is to avoid people. Where there are people, there is rejoicing in iniquity— whether it is a bad report or gladness in seeing the proud pulled down. We are happy when we see someone get their due. Sick. But true!

How do we overcome? Do we stick a piece of duct tape over our mouths and ears? Do we crawl into a hole and hide? NO! Certainly not! We overcome by doing the opposite:

By Rejoicing in the truth.

God gives us the antidote for our poison

He tells us in His word what we can focus on rather:

*"Rejoice in the Lord always: and again I say, Rejoice.
Let your moderation be known unto all men. The Lord is at hand.*

*Be careful for nothing; but in every thing by prayer and supplication with
thanksgiving let your requests be made known unto God.*

*And the peace of God, which passeth all understanding, shall keep your
hearts and minds through Christ Jesus.*

*Finally, brethren, whatsoever things are true, whatsoever things are honest,
whatsoever things are just, whatsoever things are pure, whatsoever things are
lovely, whatsoever things are of good report; if there be any virtue,
and if there be any praise, think on these things."*
Phillipians 4:4-8

If we can have the courage to stand up to people by saying what my cousin was brave enough to say, "I really do not want to hear bad reports," just think of how far-reaching our actions might become. It could influence our children to stop talking bad about others. When we thwart another believer from this bad behavior, it could encourage them to focus on the truth, the pure things of life, the good reports that edify others. The "Good Report Diet." If only we could let this be a kindly reminder of the power of our words—how our words either minister or tear down. I want my words to minister and to encourage, so I am going to put myself on a good report diet. We go on diets to improve our weight or health; why not go on a diet to improve our conversation? I hear of people all the time going on a gluten-free diet. They talk about it, they spend extra time and money to follow it through. They determine to cut all sugar and gluten out of their diet. People are actually successful in diets because they can stop addictions to food and starve the cravings.

It is amazing that people can be so good at conquering health in the body, but their words are still full of vile poison that tears people down. Why not be better at keeping our mind pure than merely our bellies? Keeping our mind pure is of eternal value. Keeping our belly pure is good practice but is not eternal. It may help you be stronger, feel better, or live longer but it will not keep you from the fires of hell. If we speak bad things, it comes out of our heart…

"Out of the abundance of the heart the mouth speaketh.
A good man out of the good treasure of the heart bringeth forth good things:
and an evil man out of the evil treasure bringeth forth evil things.
But I say unto you, That every idle word that men shall speak, they shall give
account thereof in the day of judgment.
For by thy words thou shalt be justified,
and by thy words thou shalt be condemned."
Matthew 12:34-37

Let us be a light to others today by sharing the truth instead of iniquity. Feasting on those things which are lovely and of good report will make our heart and our mind healthy.

Lessons in Etiquette
Telephone

Charity "doth not behave itself unseemly"
1 Corinthians 13:5

Calling hours

In the early 1900s women would have calling hours. Calling hours were the times set apart for people to drop in. Since there were no telephones or computers, calling hours were very special. It was improper to call upon a lady during her morning hours because everyone knew that was a time set aside for keeping the home. Washing, baking, and cleaning would all be done in the forenoon. In anticipation of a possible visitor, a woman would quilt, knit, or do needlework quietly in a chair with her home in order. If a call would come, her home would be tidy, she could offer a cup of tea, and set aside her handwork to visit her neighbor. The children knew that if someone is calling, they were to play in another room, staying completely quiet. If no one should call that day, she would have that time to work quietly with her hands, creating something beautiful or just relaxing for a bit before the evening chores. Calling hours were an unwritten but strictly-observed timeframe, for example, from 1:00–3:00 pm. The woman of the house could also make a call during that timeframe. There was also proper visiting etiquette on the part of the caller. The woman who would make the call would be gracious to bring a special treat to give to the lady she is visiting. If she brought her children, they were trained to never speak to the adults, but rather to sit quietly on the floor and play in another room so the adults could talk. They were to be seen, not heard.

With the invention of the telephone, people no longer had to make "house calls"—they could make a "call" from the comfort of their homes. What a liberation for women! Now you did not have to wait around all day for the dreaded "pop-in," so you could let the house go a little. People would call first.

Telephone etiquette

With the luxury of the telephone we must learn how to have good etiquette when using it. Women will pick up the phone to make a call, whenever they think of it. They may interrupt another lady homeschooling, or while they are busy tending their home and family. People call during meals. They call late in the evening when you are trying to spend time with your husband. There is no discretion and it is very unseemly. When you follow the law of Charity, you realize there is more to life than your need to talk with someone. You strive to be respectful of other people's family times. In my earlier days, I would not think of how my actions would affect others; I would visit a friend unannounced, with my children, without a dish to pass, and linger there for hours. It was rude. My Amish friends started to avoid me years ago, because I did not observe the old-fashioned rules of the calling hours. When one of the Amish men finally told me that I just talked too much, I was embarrassed that I had been so rude. I stayed too long. I wore out my welcome. He concluded that, "We Amish are busy. There are times we set aside each day to do all the things we Amish do. When you come, you keep the women from their chores." I was chastened by this, and it changed my practices. I was not behaving in a manner that was seemly nor in a way that showed I cared about their lives.

Figuring out what others do that frustrates me will help me change how I act toward others. Loving my neighbor as myself means I do to them what I would like done to me. I treat them the way I want to be treated. As

I started to examine my own life, I realized that I did not like it when a telemarketer would call during a meal. It made me angry when I had to stop what I was doing to RUN to the phone to answer only to find out it was some company trying to take a survey. Other times when I was just tucking my little ones into their beds, the horrid noise of the telephone would sound like a trumpet, and I would cringe with anger to answer the phone. I would tell the children I would be right back. By the time I listened to the many concerns of a friend, trying to be there for her, I would be on the phone long after the children were fast asleep. I have had to turn my phone off because people would call me while I was trying to teach my children in the morning. Even though you would tell people the right time to call, they would still call during the busy hours of the day. It was never an issue of not wanting to talk with them, because I never like to put people off as if they do not matter. The timing was the key factor. Now when I call, I try to call between 1:00–3:00 pm. 1:00 would be after lunch and school, and 3:00 would be the latest to call so as to not interfere with meal preparations and hubby homecoming.

Since I did not appreciate the calls at times when I was busy living life and tending to my flock, I started to make sure I was not guilty of crossing that line in others' lives.

First rule of phone etiquette

The first rule of phone etiquette would be to think of the other person's schedule. Ask them if it is a good time to call. If they say they are busy, then ask them when would be an appropriate time to call. Keep your conversations short. If the person says, "Well, I must be going…" do not bring up more things to talk about. I used to talk people's ears off, and keep them from their duties as a wife and mother. I would bring up more stories or ask more questions to make the conversation linger. Now, I try to practice charity by showing unlimited love and kindness in my actions toward others. Being courteous and respectful of their time is the new law written on my heart. In fact, I barely call anyone anymore. I went so far in the opposite direction that I have to retrain myself to call people again. I want to think of others and remember to keep in touch. It shows that I care about them.

Leaving Home by Phone, E-mail, and Chat Rooms

"I will therefore that the younger women marry, bear children, guide the house, give none occasion to the adversary to speak reproachfully" (I Timothy 5:14).

God's will for a young woman, according to the verse above, is that she guide the house and provide no occasion to bring reproach upon the family from Satan. In the previous verse, the apostle Paul tells what the young women were doing that enabled Satan to bring reproach upon the family. "...they learn to be idle, wandering about from house to house; and not only idle, but tattlers also and busybodies, speaking things which they ought not."

The sum of their sin was being idle instead of being industrious, visiting from house to house (phone to phone), tattlers (just talking about people) and repeating everything they heard, and giving their "righteous" opinions about everyone's business. The Scripture tells young women to be keepers at home because of their natural tendency to loaf around doing nothing except seeking entertainment.

Modern inventions have provided a way for a woman to stay at home and still not be a keeper at home. We can sit at home in body while traveling in spirit by means of the telephone and the computer. You cannot keep your home and everybody else's at the same time. More churches and individuals have been destroyed over the knitting table, the telephone, and now the computer, than by any other means. "A virtuous woman is a crown to her husband: but she that maketh ashamed is as rottenness in his bones" (Proverbs 12:4).

"Keeping the home" is more than staying at home; it is having a heart that is fixed on the home. A help meet will be engaged in creative enterprises that challenge and inspire the children. She will guard the home against outside influences, and she will always be on watch to protect the children from their own inventions of evil. She will not be idle and neither will her children. She will ease her husband's load by painting the hall and cutting the grass. She will be frugal in all her endeavors, and she will teach the children to love serving Daddy. She will keep the home so that when Daddy comes home, it is to a sanctuary of peace, love, and order.

A real help meet will make herself useful to her man instead of wasting her time.

~Debi Pearl

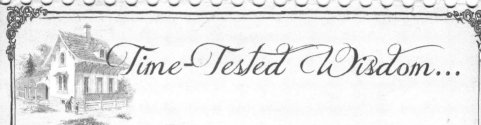

Time-Tested Wisdom...

Leaving the Activity-Filled Lifestyle

If you want to be a keeper at home, one of the first things you need to do is step back and honestly evaluate where you might be giving away too much of your time and energy. If the various activities and commitments in your life are leaving you too worn out to meet the needs of your husband, children and home, then something has got to go. Obviously, it's not going to be the husband, children and home!

Take a good look at your calendar. How many hours will you be away from home in a typical week? Can you remember the last time you spent at least two consecutive days at home? Are you cheerful every time you pack up the kids, walk out the door and head off to the next meeting, lesson, outing, appointment, practice, etc.? Are your kids happy? Or, do you look at your busy calendar with dread and your kids are crabby and cranky because you are out so much? Do you manage to keep your house in a reasonable state of order? Does your family sit together around the dinner table more than two times a year? Does your husband get enough of your time and attention?

These are all questions I stopped to ask myself many years ago because I was burned out and frustrated and I needed answers. I decided to take a hard look at what the Bible teaches about women. What I found was a portrait of quiet, humble commitment to excellence in domestic life. I finally admitted—to myself, my God and my peers—that I really didn't enjoy involving myself in dozens of outside activities. I realized that I needed to be home most of the time if I wanted to aspire to that biblical ideal.

And so, I began to disconnect from the activity-filled lifestyle which was modeled all around me. I had no idea up until that point the depth of satisfaction waiting for me in the daily work of the "homestead" life.

I have experienced real joy in the simple act of baking an apple pie, or gazing at a row of canning jars filled with variously-colored jams. I have heard the voice of the Spirit whisper in my heart while I did nothing more than quietly hang a load of laundry on a warm spring morning. There is a deep sense of purpose and contentment in this humble work which can be found nowhere else.

~Lori Alexander
From Blog: Always Learning

Chapter Four
Virtuous Commitments

"The heart of her husband doth safely trust in her,
so that he shall have no need of spoil."
Proverbs 31:11

Do you make commitments that involve your husband without getting his approval? Can he trust that you will not overcommit yourself or your family in things that cause him to stress? Do you keep the commitments you make to him, setting aside all else to serve in your home and family?

A hard time saying "NO"

Saying "NO" is something that has been hard for me to do my entire life. When someone asks me for something or to help them with something, my heart rejoices for the opportunity to serve and to love my neighbor as myself. I do not count the cost as I willingly abandon practical wisdom. Oftentimes I will not even tell my husband until the commitment is at hand. He always looks completely surprised and says, "What?! You have to do this now and you did not tell me?" It stresses him out when he has to bring things together that have not been thought out prior to the event. I figure it would be too much to tell him in advance, and he may freak out either way. What is my deal?! How could my husband ever trust that I will be careful about my planning? How many things can I do in one day?

When this happens, I get very frustrated because I have put too many irons in the fire. I race around the house and start getting short with him and with the children because I keep my commitments once I make them. I do not want to let others down when all along I am letting down the ones who need me the most—my family. This has been a serious problem for me for so long, and I am happy to announce, I finally "got it!" *I hate pickles!*

Okay, I must say, I get myself into some serious pickles with my commitments. I took on an older couple to care for and move from another state without my husband's full consent. He was not very keen on the idea and felt that it could be something that would turn into a lifelong commitment. It is something that you cannot abandon once you commit to it. I plowed through with the plans because I felt so sorry for the couple. I knew no one else would do it, and I felt that they needed us or they would die. My heart just could not turn them away.

He knew it was bad to let the poor people die, but wished we could help some other way than to have them living right next door. It is just that he felt we had too much already on our plate, with health issues, homeschooling, and businesses to take on another family. He was wise way beyond words. He practically killed himself moving them and paying nearly all the expense of the move as well. The man was accusing him of not spending enough time on the move, and he was upset that things had gotten broken or left behind. My husband felt so horrible because he did all he could do and it just was not enough to please the man. It broke my heart knowing it was my fault that he had to endure this.

That is not all; it turned into a constant need. The man needs fellowship, love, and help with many things, which is a real need. Mark has to take him places because he does not have transportation. And when I could no longer bear the daily three-hour visits (during my homeschooling or busy morning schedule), he had to try to keep him occupied. When I completely wore myself out, I had to point my finger at myself since I was the one who invited this into our lives. Beyond that, I committed to homeschooling other children and taking in another person to live with us. All without prior council with my husband. I just say, "Yes, yes, yes!" Pickles of pickles. I just pour myself into all these other people, and all the while I let my family go by the wayside.

Finally, I broke under the weight of my self-imposed burdens. Burdens I essentially created for myself. And none of these people are to blame. They had real needs and I love them all so much. All of the people have been so kind and wonderful but having too many at one time proved to break down my will to serve my family. You see, when I have others around, I have a genuine love for that person. I seek to please them and to fulfill their needs. It is real for me. I get emotionally wrapped up in that person's life. When they are sad, I am sad for them. If they are joyful, I rejoice with them.

It ends up becoming an emotional roller coaster ride for me. My husband is left with the after effects. He gets me after I spent all my energy and after I poured all I had into someone else's life. When I get burned out and weary, I run into his arms, broken and unsure of how to fix myself. I ask for answers and beg for help from a man who needs me to be there for him as well. I want him to fight the battles I started. It is not fair to him nor is it right for me. God has been teaching me that I need to protect my heart so that I can give it fully to my husband, my children, and to the Lord. I want my husband to trust that I will not get him into a pickle. It is good to be helpful, but I found out that there is an easy solution to making commitments with others…

Keeper Tip...

Ask your husband first! If someone asks me to help them with something, all I have to say is… "I would love to help, but I need to check with my husband first and then I will let you know."

WOW, THAT WAS EASY!

I make time to ask my husband and find out what he thinks and whether we have time for this new commitment. We can also figure out a solution together which may be more simple than me doing it for them. At the very least, we could pray for them and recommend other options.

Keeping commitments

It is very important to keep the commitments you have made with others and, most importantly, with your husband. As I have mentioned before, I was great at keeping my commitments to others, but lousy at keeping the commitments with my own family. I guess when you know you have unconditional love in your home, which is a very good thing, you know you have some flexibility. If you let your neighbor down, they will get mad and think you are irresponsible. If you let your husband or children down, you know they will still love you and will be there waiting for you.

When my husband asks me to take care of things that are important to him, I write them down and fully intend to complete them. When other people come calling, I set the list for my husband aside. When he asks me later if I was able to do those certain things, I would let him know that this person needed me. He always says, "Oh, that's okay; maybe you could try to get it done tomorrow." He has never once gotten upset with me, since he appreciates my giving heart towards others. He feels it is a rare quality and it is something he loves about me. But I know I have let him down in keeping my commitments to him and it is something I think I should work on.

I want him to trust that I will keep my commitments to him and give him my first fruits. He deserves my whole heart since we are one flesh. I do not want to have him asking someone else for help because I have overextended myself. If I can build his trust that I will not get him into a pickle and I will be there for him when he needs me, he will have no need of spoil. His heart will safely trust in me.

A recap of Proverbs 31:11

The meaning of "no need of spoil," biblically, is that he has no need to pursue gain or provision because his wife has been diligent to manage all the domestic affairs that he has committed into her care. He can trust that he will not have to worry about things while he is away for work each day. When we women get involved with inappropriate conduct, conversation that does not edify, or by over-committing ourselves so that we fail to have the energy to manage the affairs of our home in a wholehearted, joyful manner, we pull our entire family down. It takes energy to keep our focus on our home and family. Sadly, we tend to put our energy into things that do not matter. We get busy worrying about what he did not do, or what this or that person did, and about everything else but our first calling. Negative

Letters from my Readers

Dear Erin,

Sometimes sparks fly when iron sharpens iron but the end result is a tool fit for its purpose. I am always encouraged by your posts. A wise man/woman will love you and increase in learning from a wise rebuke and instruction.

I had a recent experience of swallowing my pride with my dear hubby who was wanting to hold me accountable in my area of struggle (consistency), and it was hard to hear. My pride was offended, but I knew he was right, and I knew I needed accountability. I didn't want to hear it. I was trying real hard not to be angry and irritated with him. I was well aware that it was my flesh warring against the Holy Spirit. I frankly told my hubby, "The truth is, I don't want your accountability; but I know I need it."

I reluctantly accepted the challenge, and am trusting the Lord with this area of my life. I am determined to get victory, though there are many days when I want to just throw in the towel. I love my husband for the way he sharpens my iron, even if sparks do fly. I'm thankful for you, and many others who help sharpen me and keep me pressing on toward the goal which is being perfected in Christ. Bless you, Erin!

With Love in Christ,
Hollie

energy will never make a family or marriage thrive the way it was meant to.

God's intent for women is for us to pour into our family first, keeping our homes a haven of peace, love, and joy. That means we behave in a way that brings honor and a level of dignity to our husband. Let us go forth, examining our own hearts, whether we are an ornament of praise or a gold ring in a pig's snout. Our actions, words, and appearance should line up together to emanate grace and virtue.

> *"Likewise, ye wives, be in subjection to your own husbands;*
> *that, if any obey not the word, they also may without*
> *the word be won by the conversation of the wives;"*
> **1 Peter 3:1**

Recipe to be a GOOD WOMAN

Proverbs 31:11—A good woman is honorable, faithful, and chaste. She doesn't do anything or say anything behind her husband's back.

"The heart of her husband doth safely trust in her, so that he shall have no need of spoil."

Key words: *safely trust*

Trustworthy, dependable, inspires confidence, reliable, honest, deserving.

~Debi Pearl

To Be Discreet

Titus 2:4-5: "That they may teach the young women to be sober, to love their husbands, to love their children, <u>To be discreet</u>...."

One usually thinks of discretion as the ability to avoid saying or doing that which is inappropriat—to know when and how to conduct oneself so as not to offend. If this is all that is intended by the text, then a person intending to commit fraud would always attempt to do so discreetly, but much more is obviously contained in this word. The Greek word that is translated discreet is also translated, in the Authorized Version, "taste" several times. In other instances, it is translated "behavior" and "judgment." Discretion, therefore, is having good tastes...good judgment...useful...to be of good understanding. God says that a woman who lacks discretion is like a jewel in a pig's nose. She is ridiculous, out of place, embarrassing, a joke. Something otherwise lovely is rendered ridiculous in the context of indiscretion. She might be pretty, a real jewel of a beauty, but if the jewel is in the nose of a pig, what good is it? "As a jewel of gold in a swine's snout, so is a fair woman which is without discretion" (Proverbs 11:22).

As I studied the word discreet, I realized how easy it is for us women to miss having the character trait of discretion, and I marveled that so many of us so often have been guilty of its lack in our character. Think about it. Let's carefully examine discretion in all its many aspects.

To be discreet: Prudent; wise in avoiding error and in selecting the best means to accomplish a purpose; circumspect; courteous, polite, honest dealings.

~Debi Pearl

Chapter Five
Virtuously Good

"She will do him good and not evil all the days of her life."
Proverbs 31:12

This verse is in reference to the way we treat our husbands on a daily basis.

What is Good? By definition…
- that which is morally right; righteousness
- benefit or advantage to someone or something

How do we DO GOOD and NOT EVIL to our husbands?

- **Being kind to him… even if he seems cross with you.**
- **Encouraging him in his strengths… not pointing out his short-comings.**
- **Smiling at him and being friendly towards him… not cold and distant.**
- **Praying for him daily… not talking badly about him to others.**
- **Seeking to please him… not seeking your way all the time.**
- **Finding ways to help him… not nagging him about all that he needs to do for you.**
- **Making meals or lunches for him… not forgetting to feed your man.**
- **Making the home a haven of rest when he returns home from work… not a messy, loud home filled with chaos.**
- **Spending money wisely… not impulsively or wastefully.**
- **Teaching the children to honor him by our actions… not talking down at him or questioning him in front of the children.**

- **Planning ahead... not springing things upon him at the last minute.**
- **Being his biggest fan... not his biggest critic.**
- **Appreciating the things he does for you... not disregarding his efforts.**
- **Allowing him the grace to grow... not forcing him to change for you.**
- **Being patient with him... not placing unreasonable expectations on him.**
- **Being trustworthy... not sharing his secrets or failings with others.**
- **Being willingly affectionate to him (intimacy)... not withholding.**

I know some of you out there have horrible marriages and cannot find the strength to do good to someone whom you find hard to like. You read the list above and say, "Why doesn't my husband do these good things for me?" If we treated everyone the way we are treated, this world would fall apart. The trick is to do Good and Not EVIL all the days of your life. God is not giving you a guarantee that your life will be better if you do Good, He is telling you to DO GOOD. Sometimes we just need to do what is right because it is the better way. God's ways are better than our ways.

For example, as we follow Christ's teachings we can see how he handles doing good:

"Ye have heard that it hath been said,
An eye for an eye, and a tooth for a tooth:
But I say unto you, That ye resist not evil: but whosoever shall smite thee on thy right cheek, turn to him the other also.
And if any man will sue thee at the law, and take away thy coat, let him have thy cloke also.
And whosoever shall compel thee to go a mile, go with him twain.
Give to him that asketh thee, and from him that would borrow of thee turn not thou away.
Ye have heard that it hath been said, Thou shalt love thy neighbour, and hate thine enemy.
But I say unto you, Love your enemies, bless them that curse you,

do good to them that hate you, and pray for them
which despitefully use you, and persecute you;
That ye may be the children of your Father which is in heaven:
for he maketh his sun to rise on the evil and on the good,
and sendeth rain on the just and on the unjust.
For if ye love them which love you, what reward have ye?
do not even the publicans the same?
And if ye salute your brethren only, what do ye more than others?
do not even the publicans so?
Be ye therefore perfect, even as your Father
which is in heaven is perfect."
Matthew 5:38-48

I want to be different than the rest of society. When other people want to *get back* at others, I want to *love*. I want to *love* because God told me to *love*. What reward is there for doing good to those that are good to you? There are four ways we can repay others. We can return…

1. Good for Good
2. Evil for Evil
3. Evil for Good
4. Good for Evil

The first two examples are the most common.

Good for good

Everyone likes to return good for good. Your husband was good to you so you will be kind in return. Easy. That is normal and very good. But even gangsters in the ghetto who murder and steal can return good for good. They are good to one another. They will die for each other. It does not take a righteous human to return good for good.

Evil for evil

This one is also easy. Your husband was short with you so it is only right that you react in a short, nasty manner. It feels right and good. It makes sense. Like a little child will say after slapping another child, "But, he hit me first!" It starts from early in life and is completely normal human nature to get someone back. "An eye for an eye" has been practiced all throughout history. This is how wars start, and there is nothing ever solved through this practice.

When my kids return evil for evil, which they do, I cringe. Two wrongs NEVER make a right. Even if one started it, the whole thing just gets uglier after the other one fights back.

I know it makes perfect sense to react to your husband by the way he treats you, but it won't end well. It never will. I would like to add; it is very childish to behave that way. You may sound more grown up with the vocabulary you have learned, but the same bickering back and forth is as immature as a couple of little kids fighting over the last piece of cake. Stop that!

Evil for good

This one is LOW DOWN. It happens all too often. I see it in my children as well. One of my children might color a pretty picture to give to another child, but the other child might say, "That picture is ugly! I do not want it!!" That is evil for good. The first child was trying to do a good thing but was treated horribly in return.

Bullies are good at this. They love to see others hurting. They revel in how they can tear others down who are doing something good. Some women treat their husbands horribly evil even though their husbands work all day to provide for their families and remain faithful. She just thinks of herself and does not care how she comes across to her husband. Likewise, husbands can return evil for good toward their wives. Even though their wives were working hard all day to please them, they point out all that she failed to do. Husbands and wives are good at this and it is LOW DOWN.

Good for evil

This is the most rare, because it does not make sense. The rest of society will say that we are weak if we are good to someone when they are bad to us. Instead, I say it is godly. Sometimes we can win the other's heart with our kindness, goodness, and love toward them when they surely do not deserve it. This is how God loves us.

"But God commendeth his love toward us, in that, while we were yet sinners, Christ died for us."
Romans 5:8

If your husband comes home cross, you can smile anyway and run to greet him. He may find it strange at first, but I bet he will soon learn to enjoy that welcoming spirit. God has taught us a different way, a way that is strange to us. I am not saying you need to be good to a husband who is abusing you or your children. Again, if there is abuse going on, the right thing to do is to get immediate help. I'm just talking in general about how we treat our husbands, because they're not perfect, just as we're not perfect.

Doing good and not evil all the days of your life may seem very hard for you today, but it is easy if you look at it in a different way— through Christ's sacrifice. If we are believers, we want to be more like Christ in all areas of our lives. If Christ could be so good to us even though we have either done a lot wrong in our lives, or forgotten Him altogether, why not try learning the art of doing good to our husband today? Seek out ways to do him good and not evil. If nothing else, start by praying daily for him and for your marriage.

Here is my prayer today: "Thank you Lord for giving me a husband. Thank you for all that he does to provide for our family. Bless him today and keep him safe while he is away from home. Help me encourage him in all his strengths and be a warm welcoming spirit towards him. Make this a special day for our marriage, one that is filled with hope and grace. Help heal any broken relationships that may be out there today and give them a miracle—the miracle of your divine love. Thank you for attending my prayer; in Jesus' precious name I pray, Amen!"

Keeper Tip...

3 ways to do good:
- Do good to your husband even though he doesn't deserve it. Serving is not about deserving.
- Smile often. Be a warm welcome to his day.
- Be beautiful inside and out—Don't get ugly behind closed doors. Pouting is very frumpy.

Letters from my Readers

Dear Erin,

I simply love this post! I have had anger in my spirit lately towards my husband. I wanted to keep the children home, safe with me, and he went out and sent them to school! They went to school this past year, and I have been harboring a lot of anger.

What are some things I can do to let go of this anger? Do you have any advice on convincing my husband to take the kids out of school and keep them home?

~ Ashleigh

Dear Ashleigh,

I have had those same feelings myself when my husband made big life decisions without my full consent in our past. I have learned to trust him through the things I do not understand as the head of our family. God has always given me the grace to walk through some pretty difficult things and eventually I was able to realize my husband did have a better understanding than what I did at the time.

I think to start with, you could try to notice all the good things that he has done to lead the family. That is what helped me when I was really angry. I would try to put things into perspective: "at least he is not cheating on me, or at least he is not a drunken reprobate," or things like that. It helped me see the bigger picture and appreciate his love for me. Listen to his reasons and share with him your feelings. Remember, a house divided against itself will not stand. These angry feelings will turn into bitterness and the walls will grow stronger between you.

Your relationship with your husband is more important than how the kids are schooled. I know how much you want them home but the damage that they could get from witnessing bitterness between their parents would leave far more scars than any public school. I don't consider myself an expert on advising in a professional way; I only know what I have observed of marriages that went bad and why they went bad, and also my own mistakes from which I have learned.

I will be praying for you in your situation. I hope that I have said something that was helpful in some way. I pray God to heal your anger in this and give you the grace to walk through this in faith.

In Christ, Erin

Virtuous Charity
BEING UNSELFISH

Charity "doth not behave itself unseemly, seeketh not her own"
1 Corinthians 13:5

How do these verses apply to women? We already know to behave unseemly is to behave inappropriately.

Seeketh not her own...

This is simple: **Do not be selfish!** When we seek our own, we worry about how everything affects us. Let me tell you my "ME MONSTER" story.

Behold the Me Monster

Long ago and far away, there was a pitiful young mother. I say long ago and far away because it is so foreign to me now to behave thus. I was that pitiful young mother. I was depressed all the time—ALL THE TIME. I looked back on my life at that time, and all I could see was what others did to hurt me. Why MEEEEEEE? All the rejection, all the shame, all the pain I endured.

Death was something I coveted, for I thought I was worthless. I thought the world would be happier without me in it. Struggling with the scars of abuse on a daily basis was hard for me and my little growing family. My husband tried to hold me—to heal me. He cried for my pain. When I was pregnant with Michael, my fourth baby, I was bedridden from a fall I had a year before that broke my pelvis. The pain was great. It was when I was trying to become like the Amish. I had my mind made up. I had my bonnet on, my black socks on, and did not care a thing about my husband's wisdom. I knew better than he. I was more spiritual. He would beg and plead with me to get ahold of my senses. And when he saw that I was completely mentally deranged, he put his foot down and told me NO! He felt that joining the Amish would be giving up the faith he had in Christ, and he could not do that.

This is embarrassing...I became so angry that I was willing to kill

A Merry Heart

The Bible tells us that the joy of the Lord is our strength. For this marriage-making journey you're on, you will need all the strength afforded by the joy of the Lord.

God says in Proverbs 17:22, "A merry heart doeth good like a medicine." A merry heart is the foundation of health and happiness. And the day you have a merry heart will be the first day of rebuilding your marriage into the heavenly gift it was meant to be.

I have listened to the longest-faced women trying to assure me that they do indeed have the joy of the Lord, and I would sit there wondering where in the world they were hiding it. The last part of the verse above says, "but a broken spirit drieth the bones." How are your bones doing? I mean your bones. The Bible is far more literal than you may think. A broken spirit and dry bones result from not having a merry heart. A merry heart is very good medicine. It is a love potion.

When he first fell in love with you, you were a sweet little thing, full of laughter and fun. From the very bottom of your soul you were thrilled with him. Every day you woke up planning some activity that involved you both. Is he still married to the same sweet little thing, or have you become a long-faced, sickly complainer? Love is like a flower: you can't expect it to grow without sunshine. Has your lover seen your sunshine lately? Is he still your lover? What would he say?

Proverbs 15:13 says, "A merry heart maketh a cheerful countenance..." Everyone is drawn to a smile. Who and what you are is reflected in your face. Does your husband see you as a happy, thankful woman? Does he smile when he looks at you, amused at the cheerful little grin on your face and the totally delightful things you think and say—even the dumb things? Learn to charm him with your mischievous "only for him" grin.

~Debi Pearl

myself. One cold evening, when I could hardly walk, I went outside to die! I jumped into a snowbank and offered my body to the subzero temperatures. My husband came searching for his wife, calling desperately for me. And when he found me there, he sat there nearly crying, begging me to live. I cry just thinking about this moment. I screamed, "NOOOO, leave me, let me die!" And he picked me up in his strong arms and carried me kicking and screaming back into the warmth of our home. He held me in his arms and said how much he loved me, how he would die to protect me, how he would lay there all night outside if he had to in order to keep me from freezing to death. He told me that my purpose in this life was not over. He was able to see me as something I was not: A pure and precious gem.

Later, I met this man, a guy who was working with Mark on a job. Something drew me to him. He looked at me and told me, even as I smiled, that there was a sadness in my eyes. It was like a gift. I opened up to this person I did not even know and he told me how sinful I was. ME, sinful? I was sinned against as an innocent child. I was rejected by nasty people. I was hurt and in pain. How could I be to blame in this? I was so mad at first.

He told me that I was so focused on "ME" that I actually put "MYSELF" over everything and on the throne. He said this because I was telling him, "I am home all day taking care of these kids, and my husband comes home and is too tired to help—what about me? I am tired! I want to raise my kids Amish and my husband won't allow me to do this—what about my dreams? What about how I feel; they are my kids! I have been through so much. I, I, I, and what about ME? ME, me, I, me, ME, ME, ME!" (Hint: ME MONSTER.)

That was my sin. Depression is selfish. When you are depressed, you are only thinking about yourself—about poor and unfortunate *you*. I was seeking my own. He forced me to look at my heart. I hated him for it,

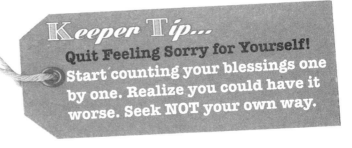

Keeper Tip...
Quit Feeling Sorry for Yourself! Start counting your blessings one by one. Realize you could have it worse. Seek NOT your own way.

but I realized later, as I really thought about it, that as a Christian, I am not here for ME. I am here for a purpose.

Christ did not come to die so that I could worry about me

Once I got my focus off myself, and onto what my purpose was, and onto Christ, it really made me get better. I had to start realizing that things could be worse. I had to start seeing things differently. I was really bad, you have no idea what grief I put my poor husband through. He never once made me feel bad about how I treated him. He took all my hatred and turned to me with Charity. I love him for that.

His mother despised me when we first fell in love. She was so wise. She could see that I was a mess, a broken vessel. She could see the baggage and the shame. And yet, most of us Christian mothers would do the same—we would want better for our sons, too. Which one of us would wish a wretched, broken, used-up girl to cling onto our sons? I hope I can see past the shame if it is staring me in the face, choose to take a broken vessel under my wing, and love her like Christ loves her and died for her. I want to be patient to endure the hard times and understand God's perfect will and timing in their lives.

God called my husband to complete me. He called him to save me from my own destruction. My husband understands Charity. He never seeks after his own. No matter how badly I treated him, threatened to leave him, cussed and fumed at him, and no matter how many mind games I played against him, he just loved me. He loved me, he loved me. When I did not deserve love, he loved me. When I was selfish and prideful, he loved me. And when I ask him, even today, "How did I ever deserve you?" He looks back every time, and he says, "How did I ever deserve you?"

Our relationship grew into something wonderful when I stopped looking at my glass as half-empty all the time. Now my joy is overflowing and it is because I compare myself to Christ, instead of trying to measure myself against my lot. My lot is not always favorable. Several years after my frigid crazy moment, I had a bad accident which crippled me with a four year uphill battle to get on my feet again.

You guessed it

My husband took care of me; he homeschooled our five little children, he cooked, he cleaned, he changed my bedpans, and carried me in his arms when I could not walk at all. It was very hard to fight against the "ME MONSTER" laying in a hospital bed, not being able to minister to my family the way I desired. I would often say to my husband, "I was created to be *your* HELP MEET, you weren't being created to be *my* help meet." This man of few words would say in response, "I was created to do whatever needs doing, and right now I am going to take care of you." He encouraged me to LIVE. He encouraged me to rise above my circumstances and choose LIFE, choose JOY.

He always wants me to be all I was created to be. While I shine and prosper, he hides in the background. He is a humble, quiet man. He never looks for glory or honor in any form. He humbly serves his family and his Lord.

100% of marriages that end are because of selfishness on the part of one or both sides. Wars start over selfishness. Abusers abuse because of selfishness. They do not care about how their actions affect others. When people are unkind, prideful, hateful, depressed, greedy, unthankful, or lazy it is due to selfishness and seeking their own. It is the opposite of charity.

Today, I get emails and phone calls from women who are utterly depressed. I finally figured out why. They are singing the same tune I sang those 10 years ago—"What about MEEEEEEE?" The chorus repeats after each sad refrain. The sentences always start the same…

"*I do this and I do that, but HE does nothing, or they never do this or that.*" I love the first part, the part where *she* does… The things we do for our family—the selfless laying down to serve each day. The second part of the sentence brings us down a sad path. BUT—meaning "I have no reward," or BUT—meaning, "No one looks out for me." It is a classic ME MONSTER situation.

Some of you will shake your fist at me as if I do not *get it.* I do not understand how bad it is for you. I do. Believe me, I was through the wringer, had tons of pity parties and I was the author of selfish thoughts! I'm not one to condemn the victim. I was a victim—I could remain a victim, or I could get up and start *living.* We all have a sad story. BUT, each of us has a choice. What are we going to do about it?

What can you do to change the circumstances? What are you going to do about HIM or THEY, or THIS or THAT? How is any of your depression or sadness going to change what happened?

When the answer is NOTHING or NO, then we need to accept it, learn from it, and do as Christ would do. Find a scripture that condones your negative thoughts, if there is one. You probably will not find one to support SELFISHness, but you will find countless verses to support SELF-LESSness. Therefore, we can learn Charity, the law of unlimited love and kindness, when we learn to NOT SEEK OUR OWN.

Here is a way to practice bringing your thoughts into the captivity of Christ. When you get a bad, negative, and selfish thought, write it down on one side of a journal. On the other side, take the time to find scripture to prove your thoughts godly, or if you can't prove that thought is right, you simply write down a verse that shows you a better way to think or behave. It is good practice to examine our motives and our words on a daily basis. Here is an example…

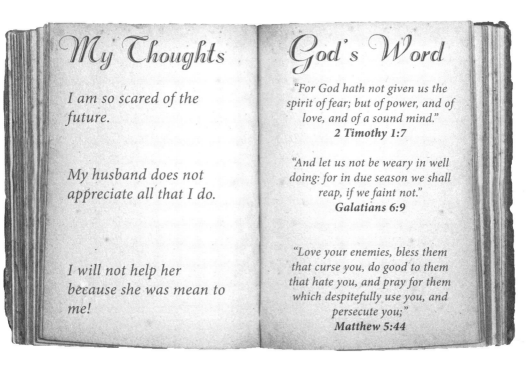

My Thoughts

I am so scared of the future.

My husband does not appreciate all that I do.

I will not help her because she was mean to me!

God's Word

"For God hath not given us the spirit of fear; but of power, and of love, and of a sound mind."
2 Timothy 1:7

"And let us not be weary in well doing: for in due season we shall reap, if we faint not."
Galatians 6:9

"Love your enemies, bless them that curse you, do good to them that hate you, and pray for them which despitefully use you, and persecute you;"
Matthew 5:44

Tales of Victory...

Interior Design of my Heart

It's been nearly four years that we have been living in our "handyman special" home. When we first bought our home, I remember telling my husband I didn't want to be part of picking out our house. I wanted him to choose. I would be thankful just to have a home to call our own. Having lived with his parents for a few months with our five small children, a place of our own was all that mattered at the time.

When he brought me to come look at the home he chose for us, my jaw dropped. It was an older home, about 30+ years old or so. The home had not been updated, so walking into the house it was a mix of 70s and 80s style. Not to mention it was so old and worn.

The kitchen was covered with this old, dull, dark flower wallpaper. The dark wooden cabinets made it look very dreary and closed-in. The odor the home gave off was a stench that to this day I can't get out of my memory. There were mirrors hanging from all walls in the living room and huge chandeliers that swung from one side of the bathroom wall to the other. Paint was chipping from the walls, and the ceiling was this popcorn ceiling, very old-fashioned looking. The windows creaked and the doors were layered in dust. Oh, and the flooring, oh dear! It was so old and gross looking, who knows how long that had been there. Yuck! It was hideous and I did not want to step one foot into it, let alone live there.

I remember smiling gracefully, trying my hardest not to complain and not say anything. But, well, my tongue couldn't contain it any longer and the first words that rolled out were, "Out of all the houses, you chose this one?" I didn't stop there; I continued to show my discontent and disapproval of the house, how there was so much work to do on it, and how it was near a major highway, not practical for us to raise children in. I went on and on and on. I gave him an earfull and more.

My sweet husband did his best to reassure me that it would be okay and that it was only temporary, and that the cosmetics could be replaced and worked on. Like always, he pointed out everything good about the house—the large yard, the extra space, the huge schoolroom we would have, and how we were right across the street from the gas station, Target, and grocery store (which, by the way, have become quite convenient). Nevertheless nothing he said comforted me. Unfortunately, it was too late, as the papers had already been signed.

Every wall was infested with termites. The damage was so bad my husband had to replace all five walls in the kitchen, the cabinetry, and boards. When we thought that was the only place he pulled off the mirrors in the living room and bedrooms and they were in there, too. Termites everywhere. We called and had the inspector come back and he apologized and paid for treatment of the home. In total my husband replaced all the walls and boards. It was so gross. This wasn't all; he would later be ripping out walls in our bathroom due to black mold that was lurking behind our shower.

During this time the Lord was using all this to show and reveal my heart to me. This whole time I felt justified in my anger towards my husband. Yet the Lord was about to give me a wake-up call. I complained and nagged my husband for choosing such a rotten home and I'd pitch a fit when he worked long hours and spent every weekend away from us to fix it up and make it livable. Then, to make matters worse, I'd pick a fight when he got home and argue over his dirty socks left for me to pick up. I really let him have it. I reminded him of his poor decision every time I got the chance.

One day he brought me over to the house so I could see the nasty termite damage. When I walked in I saw how destructive these little critters were. It was so disgusting to see. I was appalled at the damage they did. That is when God used it as a visual to me of what I was doing to my home. The way I was treating my husband was similar to the termites eating away the foundation of the home; I was rotting away the bones of my husband, as Proverbs says. I was damaging the foundation we had. I was like black mold, plaguing my husbands spirit.

Oh, gosh, my heart sank; even still just the thought has me shaking my head. My heart was just like this home he had chosen. While I was aged in the Lord, I was in dire need of a remodel, for termites and mold had invaded my heart. From that moment on, I was committed to helping him. I went every night with him to help him paint as the children ran around. We laughed and played, enjoying our new home.

Each coat of paint was so symbolic to me. It was as if the Lord was showing me that my husband chose this home because he saw something of value in it. While it was flawed and while the walls were pulled back and gutted, and as new walls took their place, the Lord showed me that this is what Christ has done with me.

While I was wretched and rotten to the core, Jesus chose me, he hand-picked me to be his; then he took me, gutted me out, and gave to me a New Life and a New Heart. He showed me that I am no longer this old house, infested with termites and mold, but rather I am new, created in his image; I am his masterpiece. I am of worth and value to him.

And while this old house we bought four years ago still has work that needs to be done often on it, it serves as a reminder that Jesus isn't done with me yet and that he will complete the work he began in me.

~ Darlene Lopez, from New Mexico

Letters from my Readers

Dear Erin,

Erin, I just finished reading your article "The ME Monster." I am so thankful for your boldness in writing that article. I've struggled off-and-on with depression and thoughts of having my life end, and I always feel overwhelmed and exhausted, but I'm always too scared to say anything to anyone because "I'm a Christian" and my pride gets the best of me.

My husband and I have been married for almost nine years and we have four children. My husband has struggled with lust and pornography since before we were married; both of us were virgins before marriage so we thought that marriage would resolve his struggles, but it didn't. Because of this, he is an easy target for me to place blame on when I'm having my "down days," when in reality, it's my self-centeredness and ME focus which causes my depression.

I really like your journaling recommendation because it's all-too-easy to listen to Satan's lies and believe them. Now I can write down what I am feeling and look to the Words of Christ and be comforted by the truth. Thanks again, Erin!

~ A thankful wife

Being unselfish in our marriage

The key to a happy marriage is to think about your spouse first. Christ thought about you first. When He was reviled and spit on, He did not open His mouth in retaliation. While you were yet a sinner, He died for you. If He was able to lay down His own selfish desires to save your soul, you can also do good to your beloved husband:

- **Have fun thinking of ways to meet his needs instead of constantly worrying about him meeting yours.**
- **Find out what pleases him and seek to be a blessing.**
- **Give him a reason to want to hold you in his arms.**
- **Have a merry heart. Don't get upset over the little things.**
- **Look past his faults and enjoy all the wonderful things he does for you.**
- **Spend time each day praying for your husband.**
- **Give him lots of smiles, hugs, and kisses!**

Recipe to be a GOOD WOMAN

Proverbs 31:12—A good woman is trustworthy, genuine, and wise. She does not explode one day and apologize the next. She is good to him every day.

"She will do him good and not evil all the days of her life."

Key words: *will do*

Constant in her love, unshaken, unmoved, faithful, ceaseless, enduring, unchanging, loyal, permanent.

~Debi Pearl

Time-Tested Wisdom...

Taken from Created To Be His Help Meet by Debi Pearl

The Help Meet

If you are a wife, you were created to fill a need, and in that capacity you are a "good thing," a helper suited to the needs of a man. This is how God created you and it is your purpose for existing. You are by nature equipped in every way to be your man's helper. You are inferior to none as long as you function within your created nature, for no man can do your job, and no man is complete without his wife. You were created to make him complete, not to seek personal fulfillment parallel to him. A woman trying to function like a man is as ridiculous as a man trying to be like a woman. A unisex society is a senseless society—a society dangerously out of order.

When you are a help meet to your husband, you are a helper to Christ, for God commissioned man for a purpose and gave him a woman to assist in fulfilling that divine calling. When you honor your husband, you honor God. When you obey your husband, you obey God. The degree to which you reverence your husband is the degree to which you reverence your Creator. As we serve our husbands, we serve God. But in the same way, when you dishonor your husband, you dishonor God.

The role of being a perfectly fit helper does not make one inferior to the leader. In our office there is an entire staff of workers. Every person in the office spells better than I do; most know the computer better, and they certainly know finances better. Yet, when I walk into the office, I can tell any one of them what to do and how I want it done, and they all are glad to do my bidding—including the men. My place of authority does not mean I am better, it only means that they are there to help me do my job—better!

Men are created to be helpers of God. Jesus willingly became a helper to the Father. The Holy Spirit became a helper to the Son. Society is structured so that men and women must submit to authorities like government, employers, police, the Internal Revenue Service, child protection agencies, the courts, etc. There is no loss of dignity in subordination when it serves a higher purpose. God made you to be a help meet to your husband so you can bolster him, making him more productive and efficient at whatever he chooses to do. You are not on the board of directors with an equal vote. You have no authority to set the agenda. But if he can trust you, he will make you his closest advisor, his confidante, his press secretary, his head of state, his vice-president, his ambassador, his public relations expert, maybe even his speech writer—all at his discretion.

A perfect help meet is one who does not require a list of chores, as would a child. Her readiness to please motivates her to look around and see the things she knows her husband would like to see done. She would not use lame excuses to avoid these jobs. A man would know he had a fine woman if she were this kind of helper. Such a blessed husband would receive honor from other men as they admire and praise his handy wife. "A virtuous woman is a crown to her husband" (Proverbs 12:4). It is our job to learn how we can help our husbands in every way possible. The very fact that you are reading this book indicates that your heart's desire is to honor God by becoming a real help meet to your man.

~Debi Pearl

Chapter Six
The Virtuous Helper

"And the LORD God said, It is not good that the man should be alone; I will make him an <u>help meet</u> for him… And the LORD God caused a deep sleep to fall upon Adam… and he took one of his ribs…And the rib, which the LORD God had taken from man, made he a woman, and brought her unto the man."
Genesis 2:18, 21-22

What does this mean for me?

If you are woman, you are made for man. God made everything good. He made you to be good for your man. I am not afraid to say that I agree with what the Bible says.

It seems special to have been taken out of a place that is close to his heart. But just because you are near to his heart does not mean you are dear to his heart. Some men are just mean and no matter how much you try, they cannot help from being controlling and selfish. God gave man a drive to conquer and a drive to procreate. It is God's design. If I had the blueprints for man, I probably would have made men to have more feelings and more sensitivity towards women. Since I am unable to change the design, I like to understand the design so that I can accept the differences, embracing them as something wonderfully created. I know that I was made to complete the man, not to compete with the man. I have come to learn that I can be his most-prized gift or his greatest curse. My husband was not perfect, and I know your husband is not either.

What kind of helper should I be?

When I married my man, I think we were both unsuited for the married life. He was bashful, and I was a fool. He could not lead because I dominated him and manipulated him. He was a middle child from a divorced home. His mother was hurting and bitter from the divorce and could not build him up in the role of a man. She did not encourage him in having a relationship with his father, so he did not have that manly example. I guess she determined in her heart that his father was not suited to be that example.

Used to being shaped by the commands and guides of a woman, he did not know how to lead.

I have a little love story to share with you

I remember the first time I met him. We were at a Bible camp for kids. Because I was a big showoff, I introduced myself as a **black belt** in Tae Kwon Do. He started to laugh at me and made little karate chops in my direction along with a few mock karate battle cries. I was used to the likes of him. I knew how to handle him. I told the leaders of the camp that since I was teaching a self-defense class to the kids, I needed a proper *dummy*. I figured it would serve a two-fold purpose: To flip that jerk around while entertaining the kids. You must know, Mark is 6'5" and I am 5'1". This was to be no small show. The very first class, I flipped that big boy right off his feet. I guess I swept him off his feet, literally! He will tell everyone that he let me.

He and I were in charge of a cabin of ten-year-old kids. I had the girls and he had the boys. In the afternoons I worked with a friend in a nature center teaching kids about God's creation. Of course I told her my whole life story. I told her about my abusive past and how I just would *never* marry. To me men were perverts. They were there to use women. I had HAD it with men. I told her how all I wanted was to be in a foreign country serving in an orphanage. I just loved children. She looked at me and said, "No. You were created to be a help meet to a man. You need to pray specific things about what you want in a man."

I went on a walk that afternoon, and looked up to the sky, crying out to God, "Well, God, if I have to get married, I want a man who wants to have a family, a bunch of kids, some farm animals, and wants to live out in the country."

I had no idea God was listening. The very next day Mark and I had to take the campers on a long canoe ride. I watched as the canoes started to fill up one by one until we were the only ones left. I sighed as I looked at him. We walked over to that lone canoe and started paddling in the lake. I was not at all interested in him, and was kind of irritated that I was stuck in a canoe with him. After a long silence and the sound of water being pushed over the paddles, I thought I would try to talk with this guy.

I asked him a typical Erin question. "What do you want to do with your life?"

He responded, "Well, I would love to settle down, get married, start a family, have a bunch of kids, and live out in the country. Maybe I would get some farm animals…"

I jumped to my feet that instant, before he could even finish his sentence, nearly dumping the canoe over, "We're getting married!" He steadied the canoe and said in a gentle voice, "Okay."

I ran back to the old Creation shack to tell my friend that God had answered my prayers. She was horrified and said, "No, that is my brother!" She went on to tell her mother about me and all my baggage. I was not received well. I was not pure enough for him, but he stuck by me. Because I had been so abused and in abusive relationships with guys who would hurt me and use me, I saw Mark as a man who would never hurt me.

A few months later I asked him, "How can I ever thank you for being so good to me?" He smiled and answered, "I will tell you later." That very night he took me to a beautiful bluff overlooking Lake Michigan with the moon cascading over the ripples of water lapping into the shore. He looked at me and asked, "Do you remember when you asked me how you could thank me?" I replied, "Yes." Then he grabbed my hand and said, "You can thank me by spending the rest of your life with me. Will you marry me, Erin?" With tears in my eyes, I said, "Yes!"

Two years passed until our wedding day. The blessing from his mother never came but we planned our day anyhow. The beginning of our marriage was filled with a lot of woe. If I yelled at him or hit him with wooden spoons, he would just ignore me and go for a drive. I fussed at him for him making me his maid. I would snarl at him for leaving his beard hair all over the sink and water drops on the bathroom mirror. Not to mention all the piles of dirty clothes laying everywhere for me to pick up. What was his problem?

Thankfully, I later read a book about being a good wife. In that book, a woman shared a story about how she fussed at her husband for leaving hair and water spots all over the bathroom. He left piles of dirty laundry and she, too, felt like a maid. One day he did not return. Instead she got the call we all dread, the call from the police informing her of his sudden death. The regret which this young widow felt reached down and touched my soul. She yearned for another spot, another hair, and the piles of dirty, smelly laundry sitting on her bedroom floor, because it meant that he was home. Now her bed was forever cold. The kids knew they were waiting in vain when they looked out the window for Daddy's truck which would never return. I bawled as I read those words. I thought to myself, from that day forward, his mess was my special gift. It meant that he was home with me. Even to this day, he still leaves the same piles, the same beard hairs, and the same water spots. Every time I clean up after him, I smile and thank God that I have a husband to clean up after when there are others who do not. It is all a matter of perspective!

My husband was not the type to lead. He was very passive by nature. Not a fighter. Not a commander. Nor a pot-stirrer. He was just **steady.**

Keeper Tip...

Ask Him. Adore Him. Smile.
1. Give him a chance to lead.
2. Be his biggest fan.
3. Give him lots of smiles.

A woman can make or break a man

He was incapable of feeling confident because he was beaten down for so many years by a woman. **How do you get a downcast man to feel important, to have authority?**

Step One: I found it helpful to ask him first before I did anything. "Can I go to the grocery store?" "Can I paint the room?" At first he did not know what to say. Eventually he discovered his new favorite word—"NO." His "no" was just what I needed to keep me from going too far one way or the other. It was my protection.

Step Two: I found it a real ego-booster for my not-so-confident man to become his greatest fan. I started telling him what a good provider he was to our family, what an amazing husband he was. I told him that he was such a good daddy. He was good at handling our finances. That I trust him. He was the best builder, the best-looking guy I knew, etc. Soon he was feeling like he mattered. He felt loved, appreciated, and needed instead of scolded, belittled, and ignored.

Step Three: Smiling and being cheerful did a lot to make my husband enjoy my company and be my buddy. Who likes a frowning old frump? I sure would not like being around me when I was like that. No way. Little crabby frown and scowling eyes. Not very inviting, I must say. A smile goes a long way.

Soon my husband turned into Mr. King. He started to become the leader. When I would tell him what to do, he would say, "Ah, I am in charge. Don't forget it," all with a big smile on his face. It was such a joy to have him tell me what to do. I was called to be his helper. I thank God that I could be used to help him be all he was created to be. It was simple and fun to be his cheerleader and buddy.

It is God's will that we balance each other out

I believe God's intent is not for us to stay where we are at. He gives us the grace to improve our weaknesses, make the most of our circumstances, and grow into His precious image. Little by little, as we learn what our strengths and weaknesses are, we can learn how to build on what is wonderful and work past the areas of difficulty. Just as we appreciate others noticing our strengths and glossing over our weaknesses, we can do the same with how we respond to our husbands. If we recognize what our husband's personality is, we can learn to be a better help meet to him. There are three kinds of men (detailed descriptions can be found on page 91):

- **Command**
- **Visionary**
- **Steady**

The Balancing Act

Women have different personality types as well with various strengths and weaknesses.

The Go-to Girl

STRENGTHS:

- Dependable
- Confident
- Loyal
- Independent
- Organized
- Detailed

WEAKNESSES:

- Impatient
- Selfish
- Dominating
- Apathetic
- Controlling
- Obsessive/Compulsive

The Dreamer

STRENGTHS:

- Creative
- Loving
- Flexible
- Passionate
- Intuitive
- Lively/Exciting

WEAKNESSES:

- Impulsive
- Judgmental
- Easily Distracted
- Lazy
- Pot-Stirrers
- Unorganized/Messy

The Servant

STRENGTHS:

- Forgiving
- Unselfish
- Thoughtful
- Compassionate
- Sensitive
- Content

WEAKNESSES:

- Inflexible
- Unconfident
- Wallflower/Shy
- Indecisive
- Can't Say No
- Easily Embarrassed

All people have the propensity to overcome and gain victory in their lives, equally. You can actually be trained to be more dominant in one

Different Kinds of Men:

God is **dominant**—a sovereign and all-powerful God. He is also **visionary**—omniscient and desirous of carrying out his plans. And, God is **steady**—the same yesterday, and today, and forever—our faithful High Priest. Most men epitomize one of these three aspects of God.

> ## Command Man *A few men are born with more than their share of dominance and, on the surface, a deficit in gentleness. They often end up in a position to command other men. We will call them Command Men. They are born leaders. A King wants a Queen, which is why a man in command wants a faithful wife to share his fame and glory. Without a woman's admiration, his victories are muted. If a wife learns early to enjoy the benefits of taking the second seat, and if she does not take offense to his headstrong aggressiveness, she will be the one sitting at his right side being adored, because this kind of man will totally adore his woman and exalt her. She will be his closest, and sometimes his only, confidante. When a woman is married to a bossy, dominant man, people marvel that she is willing to serve him without complaint, so she comes out looking like a wonderful woman of great patience and sacrifice.*

> ## Visionary Man *Visionary men are street preachers, political activists, organizers and instigators of any front-line social issue. They love confrontation, and hate the status quo. The Visionary is consumed with a need to communicate with his words, music, writing, voice, art, or actions. He is the "voice crying out in the wilderness" striving to change the way humanity is behaving or thinking. Every Mr. Visionary needs a good, wise, prudent, stable wife who has a positive outlook on life. A woman married to the impulsive Visionary Man, who puts the family through hardships, will stir amazement in everyone. "How can she tolerate his weird ideas with such peace and joy?" She comes out being a real saint, maybe even a martyr.*

> ## Steady Man *God is as steady as an eternal rock, caring, providing, and faithful, like a priest—like Jesus Christ. He created many men in that image. We will call him Mr. Steady—"in the middle, not given to extremes." The Steady Man does not make snap decisions or spend his last dime on a new idea, and he doesn't try to tell other people what to do. He avoids controversy. He doesn't invent the light bulb like Mr. Visionary, but he will be the one to build the factory and manage the assembly line that produces the light bulb and the airplane. Being married to a Steady Man has its rewards and its trials. On the good side, your husband never puts undue pressure on you to perform miracles. He doesn't expect you to be his servant. You do not spend your days putting out emotional fires, because he doesn't create tension in the family. You rarely feel hurried, pushed, pressured, or forced. If you are married to a wonderful, kind, loving, serving man, and you are just a little bit selfish, then you are likely to end up looking like an unthankful shrew. He helps you, adores you, protects you, and is careful to provide for you, and you are still not satisfied. Shame on you!*

~Debi Pearl

personality type than another just based on life experiences. For instance, I believe I am mostly the Dreamer type. I was wildly creative, easily distracted, and full of energy. Because I was abused, I took on the characteristics of the Servant type. When you have been subdued, controlled, and misused, you become something you were not meant to be initially. My mother was a nurse and it was within her character to serve. Some things are learned by example such as this. I learned to serve others, which was not within my God-given personality. What Satan meant for destruction, God used for my benefit.

Even though it was a terrible thing to be abused as a small child, I am thankful that I learned to be more careful. It taught me to watch my back and listen to sound instruction. As a parent, it made me very protective of my own children. When you go through something traumatic, it gives you a level of understanding and compassion. I learned to be compassionate, protective, giving, and unselfish through my trials.

My dad is more of a Visionary man. He is passionate, creative and full of vision, desiring to make a difference in the world. Yet, he was also a leader. He directed a high school band for many years. Being a teacher made a leader out of him. Later, he started a business and put me in charge of the dog kennel. That forced me to stay focused and be responsible. I had to juggle a lot of things so I had to learn to be more organized, thus training me to be a Go-to Girl.

In marriage I have found that you become most happy when you try to encourage each other in your strengths and work with each other's weaknesses. You become a good helper to your man when you recognize how to help him become more balanced.

Mark and I had a lot of bad years where we clashed and collided with our many differences. Instead of embracing those differences, we constantly butted heads. Learning to compliment each other's differences is the first step to a good relationship. We help each other…

- **When I freak out because there was a big spill on the floor I had just mopped, Mark tells me it will be okay and helps me clean it up. He calms me down.**
- **When he becomes impatient or upset because he can't find something, I tell him that I'll help him look for it. Later, I find a spot for him to put that item so he'll know where to find it.**

- When I devise a crazy, industrious plan that requires a measure of risk, Mark will weigh the risks and proceed with caution. Most times he likes my crazy ideas, but there are times his "NO" was divine intervention, and it prevented us from ruin.
- When he is shy around others, I introduce him. I break the ice.
- He helps me temper the amount of information I give out to others and I help draw more information out of him.
- If either one of us is acting like a jerk, we have enough sense to help correct each other. We have made an agreement that we would help each other be sweet.

What happens when you cannot find balance?

Disaster! There was a couple I met that seemed happy from the outside. When they came to me with a matter they had between them, I quickly recognized the fact that they were not balancing each other out. The husband was too forceful with his grand ideas. The wife did not trust him. He accused her of not listening and appreciating his sacrifice to his family. She accused him of being harsh with his words. The more he spoke, the less she listened. The less she listened, the more frustrated and louder he became. When she pointed out his faults, he stood his ground and tried to defend himself. The more he defended himself, the more she would hold up her finger and try to shut him down with her quiet disrespect.

After I tried to get her to see her own pride and selfishness, I could clearly see she was not interested in listening. Her mind was made up. I could see why her husband was so frustrated because, by that time, I was feeling the same frustration. I concluded that their marriage was bound to fail if nothing changed. If she continues to see his weaknesses as her burdens to carry, she will eventually be crushed by the weight of them. His dreams will go unexperienced because she will make sure to tell him how tired she is of following them. His ideas will grow dim without the power to fuel them. She holds the key to that power.

When she was tired, how precious it would have been if he could have given her space. When he was excited about his visions, how precious it would have been if she could have been enthusiastic. If they could help balance each other out, what joy and love they could experience together—being co-heirs in God's infinite grace and mercy.

Tales of Victory...
Becoming His Kind of Woman

My Dad was not the type of guy to check with you before he made a decision. We would be driving down the road when all of a sudden he would pull in to a restaurant and say, "Let's eat!" as he was getting out of the car. Everything was at full speed; there never seemed to be any hesitation in his decision-making process, and it never occurred to him to ask your opinion when he had already deduced in his mind that this was the best choice. When I think about my parents during my childhood, I laugh. I see Mom bouncing around Dad as this feisty bulldog personality, always full of heart and ready to start dancing. Dad, on the other hand, was cool, logical, and unmoved by others. She always had him listening to her and smiling at her, but in the end, his decision was made with biblical backing and fact-deducing logic. People would look at Dad and think, "How does his poor wife put up with him?" He did not ask; he told. He liked things one way and was not open to changing them. Mom knew that Dad's unchanging decisions were not to lord over her; they were just a part of who he was.

When I got married, I expected my husband to be that alpha male that my dad was; but he was not. We would be driving down the road and he would say, "Where do you want to eat?" I would smile and say, "Wherever you want to eat," expecting him to quickly turn in to this or that place without hesitation. Instead, he would smile and say, "I don't care. I want to take you where you want to go. Where would you like to go?" I wanted to be his Help Meet, I did not want him to be mine, so I would say, "I would like to go where you want to go. Where would you like to go? I am good with anything." Whether I made the choice or he made the choice at that point, both of us were feeling a little unsatisfied.

My husband James is an idea man—what many call a "visionary." He comes up with all kinds of "wild" ideas. They are only "wild" because 99.9% of the population don't think about what makes a car fly or where The Cheesecake Factory gets their stainless steel countertops. He is a thinker, but usually about things unrelated to personal things.

I am very much like my dad in personality and I was used to submitting under a strong personality like my own. I was ready to obey my husband and I tried to tell him. I did not understand why he wouldn't just boss me. I was frustrated that he did not lead me. Every time he asked my opinion, I would work to help him figure out what his was. I didn't want to give him my opinion because I wanted to help him realize he was the leader of this home. Both of us felt frustrated. I felt like I was trying so hard to submit, but he would not let me. That's when I really thought about what I was actually doing; it was the opposite of what God designed me to be—my husband's Help Meet. What did James need? What did James want? What did James appreciate? What was James' will? Well, he kept asking for my opinion. He seemed pleased when I worked with him. He liked me looking tailored and well put-together. Those were easy to do and see when I was just paying attention, but what else? How could I help him? How could I make his life better? What exactly did he need? I knew he had a hard time seeing what was in front of him. He struggled with simple decisions because his brain was so busy with complicated ones.

So I began to help him see what did not come natural to him. Instead of trying to make him lead, I stopped my control issues and helped him. If he asked where I wanted to eat, I told him. If he asked my opinion, I gave it. In fact, I started telling him where I wanted to go, what I wanted to do, what my opinion was on this or that. He loved it! We became best friends. He needed me to be strong. He needed me to help him balance life. I found that it was a blast living as his Help Meet. He likes it when I am creative, working with him, and strong enough to stand on my own when he needs me to do so. We both found that we were two halves, but together we were whole.

~ Shoshanna Easling

Letters from my Readers

Dear Erin,

Amen! What a blessing it is to read what you have to say. I have been trying to get my head around a few things lately. I have just finished reading Created to Be His Help Meet; thanks to you and your blog, I discovered this book. I feel like I have been given this whole new way of looking at things. This offense thing plays a big part in marriage, doesn't it? Most of my day-to-day offenses would have to come from my husband—all those little things. I think it takes a lot of strength of character to choose not to be offended. I used to think it felt weak to let my husband "get away with things" and that it was up to me to correct him or show him where he was wrong. Do you think it is like most things—the more you do it the easier it becomes, like a good habit? I know the woman and wife I want to be and God wants me to be. It is up to me to make that vision a reality, by choosing God's way and praying a lot!

Blessings,

Jo

Dear Jo,

Yes! It truly takes practice to retrain yourself to not be easily offended. I have to continue practicing because, as a woman, I have sensitive feelings myself and I do have the temptation to get stirred up. God created us with emotions. We have to learn to control them. It takes practice!

In Christ,
Erin Harrison

Chapter Seven
Virtuous Marriage

Being virtuous in marriage

If you want to have a good marriage, a virtuous marriage, you cannot be lazy. It takes dedication and work to achieve. To be virtuous in marriage, you must be willing to accept your spouse for who God created them to be, but also be willing to help them grow. No person can grow under condemnation or humiliation. It is just as unlikely for you or your spouse to have any sort of real victory and joy in your marriage if you get easily offended by things. I have met my fair share of woman who are endlessly miserable in their marriages. I have been there many different times in my marriage, so I understand the hopelessness they feel. There are times I write about things that people perceive as an open door for an abuser to attack—that the act of loving and doing good should put another person in a situation where they are being misused or abused. Oftentimes this is not the case; but what happens when that line is crossed? Sometimes it helps to recognize what constitutes real abuse versus being easily offended.

Have you ever heard the phrase, "Walking on Eggshells?"

Have you ever tried walking on eggshells? Real eggshells? If you lay egg shells out on the floor and try to walk on them, they cut into the bottom of your feet and it makes you pull back. They break under your feet because they are so fragile. You must walk carefully in order not to destroy them completely as well as being careful of hurting yourself in the process.

In the same way, some people are so sensitive and so easily offended that you feel you have to tiptoe around them just to make sure you do not accidentally hit a nerve. You have to withdraw yourself invariably to protect yourself from getting hurt as well. You have to "walk on eggshells" when you are around them.

I have to throw this out there because when you start getting to the heart of Proverbs 31, you will hit some nerves. God's Word will hit people's nerves. God decides to write a chapter about this woman whom he praises. In turn, I decide to write about how it impresses upon my life. Subsequently, people read what I write and they think that somehow I know them personally, and have somehow made a personal assault on them. Everyone has their own level of sensitivity.

We all have buttons. If people push a certain button, we get our feelings hurt. We are touchy.

Touchy, touchy

I know we all have sensitivities. Some people have had certain situations happen in their lives which makes them sensitive. Circumstances can shape us. They can make us react in many ways that we ourselves cannot comprehend. If we have lost everything, it is hard to rejoice with someone who is having a season of abundance. If we are talented and capable, but have a husband who is controlling, we have a hard time when another lady has more freedom.

If we are lazy and we do not feel motivated to get up and clean our home each day, our first reaction is to lash out and say that other people who clean their homes do not spend time with their kids or put faith as an importance in their home. The hypocrites of this world love to throw stones at people who are working hard at something because it makes them feel better about their unproductive life.

Another person might have a lousy relationship with their husband and children. They nag and rag and live in constant stress. When they see someone who actually has a *happy* family life, they automatically assume it is dysfunctional and that the person enjoying the bliss of it all must be delusional, or they have done sick and twisted things to produce it. Wicked imaginations. Well, newsflash—sometimes people choose to be obedient to God's word, love their neighbor as themselves, joyfully submit to their amazing husband, and teach their children by example; it takes effort and—tadah!—enjoy the blessings that follow.

Jealousy can cause us to behave beneath our dignity. We are upset with our lot, so we get nasty when others succeed. People have to be so careful around us because if they say the wrong thing, we may get our undies in a bundle.

If someone is telling you they feel they have to "walk on eggshells" around you, what is that telling you?

- **They cannot be themselves around you.**
- **They feel trapped. There is no pleasing you; everything upsets you.**
- **They have to be careful what they say to you because they fear your reaction.**

I have put people in prison like this before. I have had people tell me this in the past and I took it to heart. I saw the ugliness of this and strived to overcome my sensitivities. I was very fragile, easily broken. I was easily offended and hurt.

What are offenses?

By definition…a breach of a law or rule; an illegal act, annoyance or resentment brought about by a perceived insult to or disregard for oneself or one's standards or principles.

Stumblingblocks

You can offend people who are weaker in the faith, causing them to stumble. We have to be mindful not to do things to cause this type of offense.

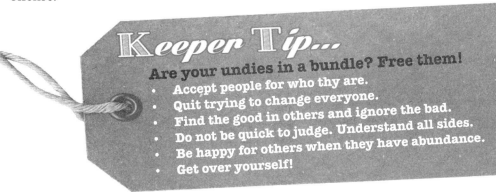

Keeper Tip…
Are your undies in a bundle? Free them!
- Accept people for who thy are.
- Quit trying to change everyone.
- Find the good in others and ignore the bad.
- Do not be quick to judge. Understand all sides.
- Be happy for others when they have abundance.
- Get over yourself!

"Let us therefore follow after the things which make for peace, and things wherewith one may edify another.
For meat destroy not the work of God. All things indeed [are] pure; but [it is] evil for that man who eateth with offence.
[It is] good neither to eat flesh, nor to drink wine, nor [any thing] whereby thy brother stumbleth, or is offended, or is made weak."
Romans 14:19-21

Persecution

Some speak truth or follow truth and when persecution comes they get offended because it hurts when people accuse you or judge you for choosing the right path. I have been spit on for the gospel, ridiculed, and even told I will be all alone with my Bible, but I had to keep pressing forward through those fiery darts. It is easy to become weary and stop the good fight of faith.

"When any one heareth the word of the kingdom, and understandeth [it] not, then cometh the wicked [one], and catcheth away that which was sown in his heart. This is he which received seed by the way side.
But he that received the seed into stony places, the same is he that heareth the word, and anon with joy receiveth it;
Yet hath he not root in himself, but dureth for a while: for when tribulation or persecution ariseth because of the word, by and by he is offended."
Matthew 13:19-21

Abuse

There are offenses that are vile. If a child is abused, it is considered an offense, and Christ tells us how much he detests the perpetrator. Woe to the person who defiles an innocent child…

"But whoso shall offend one of these little ones which believe in me, it were better for him that a millstone were hanged about his neck, and [that] he were drowned in the depth of the sea.
Woe unto the world because of offences! for it must needs be that offences come; but woe to that man by whom the offence cometh!

Wherefore if thy hand or thy foot offend thee, cut them off, and cast [them] from thee: it is better for thee to enter into life halt or maimed, rather than having two hands or two feet to be cast into everlasting fire.
And if thine eye offend thee, pluck it out, and cast [it] from thee: it is better for thee to enter into life with one eye, rather than having two eyes to be cast into hell fire."
Matthew 18:6-9
How desperate is a person to follow righteousness these days?

Conviction

Some people hear the truth and know they are guilty. They get offended because they do not want to deal with their own sinfulness. Their heart races and their face snarls. They fight back the Holy Spirit who is convicting them. The first instinct is to blame the deliverer of the truth, to find fault with the messenger. They may get out their ugly claws for a time, but if they love the Lord, He will begin to show them truth in time.

I have seen people come around on things which at first set them off, because in the end they want to follow what is true and right. The beauty is this: If a person has been offended by truth but later decides to accept it, they become more steadfast than the person who passively agrees to start with. Paul is a grand example of this in the Bible. He was the vilest offender to the work of Christ, actively persecuting its followers. When he finally came to the knowledge of the truth in his heart, he became its greatest defender.

What if you have offended someone?

I have offended people. I stick my foot in my mouth and then have to eat my words. It is such a horrible feeling. I have done things which I should not have done and it took me years to mend those relationships and build their trust in me again. We reap what we sow.

"A brother offended [is harder to be won] than a strong city: and [their] contentions [are] like the bars of a castle.
A man's belly shall be satisfied with the fruit of his mouth; [and] with the increase of his lips shall he be filled."
Proverbs 18:19-21

If you have offended someone and they are not willing to work with you towards reconciliation, the only thing you can do is to pray for them. It may take time for them to see the repentance you have made in that area and to realize you mean business. If you have done all you can and they still remain bitter, they are only hurting themselves.

People have a choice as to whether they will take offense—especially whether they will choose to take offense easily. When you stop allowing other people to control your feelings, you will start having more peace and joy in your life. Here are a few realizations I have made that helped me overcome in this area.

- **God created each person as unique; they do not have to be just like me. I cannot expect others to see things just as I see them.**
- **God gave us all a free will; therefore, they have a right to be who they want to be. I do not have to answer for them.**
- **I do not have to let things bother me. When I get hurt, it is my own fault.**
- **If someone does not agree with me, it is okay. They have a right to their own perspective.**
- **I can't control others. They have to make their own decisions and make their own mistakes just as I have.**
- **I need to love my neighbor as myself.**
- **I cannot please everyone. It is an unrealistic goal.**
- **When I get easily offended, I am really just feeling sorry for myself.**

What about those who love to offend other people?

Whoa, Nelly! Do you mean that there are actually people out there who LOVE to offend people—on purpose?

Just for kicks

There are people out there who thrive on pushing buttons. They like the feeling of power they get when they set off a bomb. It is a cheap thrill for them. In fact, there are people who incite riots just to sit back and laugh at how crazy people can get. Now more than ever there are insecure people who get a rush out of being a bully. It is more convenient than ever because now you can bully people around on the internet. No one knows what you

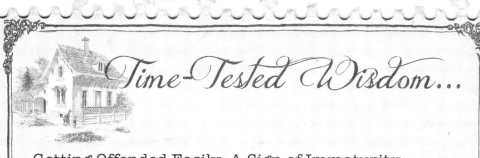

Getting Offended Easily: A Sign of Immaturity

As I have gotten older, I've realized this truth: The wiser you become, the less offended you get at things. I used to get offended all the time by my husband Ken. If he said something or did something I didn't like, I would get all offended and pout, get angry, and give him the silent treatment. Looking back on that behavior now, I realize that was ugly behavior. When we get older, we are told to put away childish things, and pouting and stewing are childish.

People have a right to their opinions—they can act stupid if they want. If we get offended by that, we are only thinking about ourselves and our feelings. Let people be who they are, think what they want, say what they want, and act how they want. You are not responsible for them.

You are only responsible for your actions, and responding in anger, pouting, and giving the "silent treatment" isn't a mature way to act. If people disagree with you in your faith, politics, beliefs, or your convictions, give them grace to believe as they want and love them anyway.

That is what life is about, remember—loving God and loving others. Learn to dialogue with them in a loving way, realizing that the relationship is way more important than being right.

"With all lowliness and meekness, with longsuffering, forbearing one another in love;"
Ephesians 4:2

~Lori Alexander
From Blog: Always Learning

look like, who you are, or what kind of life you live. They do this just for kicks.

You can pretend to be someone else, empower yourself to cause division, dissension, and mock people without ever having to face them in person. These people are not truly offended—they just love to stir the pot. When there is a good preacher or teacher of God's word who is speaking truth, these cyber bullies will come out of the woodwork and try to shed doubt in the heart of the hearers. They put up a hateful comment and usually try to trick people. Their purpose is not to share their heart; they do this solely to get the readers to see that comment and reread what was taught, second-guessing everything—mainly to get them to jump into the trap they have set. It is all a game for these types of people. They have feet that are swift in running to mischief, sowing discord among the believers.

If you go head-to-head with them, they actually get a kick out of it. Know that you are not talking to a normal human nor to a true believer—do not feed into them. They are there for the purpose of bringing others down. They love the control they have over others. What a waste to spend your days trashing other people just for the fun of it!

According to God's word, there are six things the Lord HATES…
"These six [things] doth the LORD hate: yea, seven [are]
an abomination unto him:
A proud look, a lying tongue, and hands that shed innocent blood,
An heart that deviseth wicked imaginations, feet that be
swift in running to mischief,
A false witness [that] speaketh lies, and he that
soweth discord among brethren."
Proverbs 6:16-19

The moral of the story

You get what you put into life. If you are constantly getting offended and hurt, your life will be full of hurt and bitterness. If you let things roll off your shoulder, and choose joy no matter what the circumstance, your life will be full of gladness. Joy is a choice. Being offended is also a choice. You are in control of your mind. God cannot make you feel happy.

If you are a person who has been told others have to walk on eggshells to be around you, examine your heart today. Figure out why you are so touchy. Remember, it is hard to be around you when you are so fragile. Try to put yourself in the other person's shoes. Would you want to be careful about everything you say? Probably not. Why place that burden on others if you would not like it yourself?

If you are offending others on purpose, ask yourself what this nasty behavior proves. Are you a part of the world's problem, or are you a part of the solution? There are plenty of people out there swift to cause mischief and dissension, and you are just playing right into the devil's hands. I speak from experience when I say that serving Christ is way more fulfilling than your greatest thrill of self-gratification. It is much more rewarding to love than to hate.

Now that we have dealt with offenses, it is time to examine abuse and what that means.

There are several types of abuse

- PHYSICAL ABUSE **is an act of another party involving contact intended to cause feelings of physical pain, injury, or other physical suffering or bodily harm.**
- SEXUAL ABUSE **is forcing undesired sexual behavior by one person upon another.**
- VERBAL ABUSE **is the most common way to attempt to control the behavior, thoughts, and feelings of another human being. This can be comments made to harm another person or degrade them. The comments are mean-spirited.**
- EMOTIONAL ABUSE **is the result of all three. When someone is abused, it affects them emotionally.**

I want to reiterate that I do not advocate abuse in any form. I do not believe women are designed to be abused and just endure that abuse for their entire lives. It is not good for her, her children, or her husband in any way.

Men can misuse the authority and position they have been given by God. A woman who truly loves her husband does not wish for him to spend his days being abusive and unloving toward her, knowing that he will receive his just reward for how he handled the position he was given.

Servitude or Service

When a woman has been truly abused, her broken emotional state renders her incapable of understanding the difference between service and servitude, and between humility and self-degradation. Gracious, joyous service is healing to any relationship; but broken, sad surrender to a narcissistic tyrant or an addict elicits only disgust and further abusive behavior.

You may have heard the term "enabler." In the process of treating alcoholics, Alcoholics Anonymous (AA) discovered that the addiction was often dependent upon the alcoholic's support group—spouse, family and friends. The very people closest to the alcoholic, the ones hurt the worst by the self-destructive behavior, actually provide a sympathetic network to carry out damage control. Drunks, drug addicts, violent abusers, pedophiles, and porno freaks are notorious liars. They will deny they have a problem until they are ready to go into treatment. The support group develops habits of excusing the negative behavior and hiding the consequences, thus enabling the negative behavior to continue.

Don't be an enabler. When he is hurtful to the children, acting like a fool, you can respond in one of three ways—two of which will compound the problem. You can become the protector of the kids, screaming back at him, huddling the children around you, calling him names, threatening to leave him—in short, ditching your faith and dignity. Or you can cower with the children, urging them to act in ways that will not provoke him, making them responsible to prevent his outbursts, remaining silent, offering no explanation as to his foul behavior because you do not want to dishonor him, and possibly offering excuses for his devilish displays. The children will be hurt and your husband will not know that the great pain he is causing is unacceptable—even abnormal. He will think he is normal and you are a wimp with no backbone who must be managed, for your own good. These two responses are both enabling him to continue in his inappropriate behavior. In the first response he feels superior because you are emotional and unreasonable. In the second response he feels he is the only adult in the room.

The third response is the road to healing; your healing first, and then the kids and possibly your husband's. This is the hard part. It will take a woman filled with the Holy Spirit and the grace of God. You will have to endure abusive words without feeling abused. You will have to live in the love of God when you are not getting love from your husband. You will have to gain your self-image from what God thinks of you instead of what your husband says in his selfishness and anger. You will need to put on the whole armor of God to stand against the fiery darts of the wicked one—yes, the devil in your husband.

A man is given a responsibility to love his wife as himself, to cherish and protect her. He was not given a wife to browbeat and treat worse than an animal.

I have seen this happen and it is very sad. The wife enables this behavior because she feels afraid. This is especially true with Christian women. They feel they are meant to submit to the abuse as if it is a calling by God to do so. Submission is a beautiful thing in the context of a healthy relationship. The submission can be used to win a husband to the Lord in some cases. When I try to help women in abusive situations, it can be very tricky. It is tricky to know if she is just frustrated with the relationship or if she is truly being abused. When I find out that she is being verbally abused, she is usually unwilling to do anything about it and that becomes a difficult situation for me. I can comfort her, but unless she is willing to help fix the situation, the comfort will not be a lasting fix. Instead, I first ask if she is provoking her husband to wrath in some way. A woman can frustrate a husband by her disrespect or nagging and complaining. When a husband feels like he is stuffed into a corner, he can get mean and react out of frustration—which is not always considered abuse but rather a negative response.

How can a woman frustrate her husband?

- **She can complain about how long he is working and that he "NEVER" has time for her. This frustrates a man because he feels he is working so hard "FOR HER" and providing the family with a living. He does not feel like he is doing anything wrong, and can get mad because he feels he cannot win.**
- **She can criticize her husband for how he spends money or how well he completes a job. It can be frustrating when a husband feels he is doing his best and he is not appreciated.**
- **A woman can frustrate a man if she is neglecting his intimate needs as she shoves him aside.**

There are many more ways a woman can frustrate her husband and provoke him into being grumpy and less loving towards her. She can help the situation by being a good helper and an encourager. Some men are just plain mean no matter what. If she does all that he asks—is submissive, warm, joyful, and looking to please him—and he still treats her like garbage, I would venture to say that he is crossing the line into becoming verbally abusive.

Of course, men can frustrate women by how they neglect attending to their needs or noticing the things they do for them and showing appreciation. Men can often frustrate their wives by overlooking their sacrifices and devotion. It is truly a vicious cycle to which the end is always disappointing, but not usually a case of TRUE verbal abuse.

Here are a few examples of verbal abuse from a spouse...

- **Name calling… "you are lazy, fat, ugly, pathetic, a loser, a pig," etc.**
- **Degradation… "I made a mistake to marry you. You are a lousy spouse. You cannot do anything right. You are not worth anything. You make me sick. You are worthless and do not deserve anything."**

This abuse can be on the part of the wife or on the part of the husband. Some women are notoriously mean-spirited and verbally abusive to their husbands but husbands usually do not seek help for this. They just get frustrated. Both parties feel beat down and the marriage suffers greatly.

Some men have a personality that can come across as gruff or unthankful. My husband can come across that way because he is very quiet and does not smile very often. I used to think he was mad at me all the time when we were first married. He would seem cold and uncaring because he never told me that I was pretty, or special, or that I did a good job with anything. I figured out soon enough that he was and is very happy in our relationship, and he is very much in love with me. I have to ask him if he likes the meal I made and he will say that he loves it. He does not often offer compliments. I usually ask him if he is happy and he always says yes. When I ask him if he loves me, he says, "Of course I do."

Verbal abuse is the most prevalent abuse that gets swept under the rug. Physical and sexual abuse are more cut-and-dry. You know and understand that steps need to be taken in order to protect yourself or any other victims. Verbal abuse can be overlooked because it does not leave physical scars or evidence, but it can be very destructive in an emotional/spiritual way. In fact, I was abused in all three manners, and I would venture to say that verbal abuse was equally as hard to deal with. It was hard because when you are told what an ugly, stupid piece of trash you are over and over and over, you start to believe it. The Bible tells us that life and death are in the power of the tongue. You can build up or tear down. If it was important enough for God to mention this in his Holy Word, why can't people see the importance of their words towards others?

> *"Death and life are in the power of the tongue:*
> *and they that love it shall eat the fruit thereof."*
> **Proverbs 18:21**

> *"But the tongue can no man tame; it is an unruly evil,*
> *full of deadly poison. Therewith bless we God, even the Father;*
> *and therewith curse we men, which are made after the similitude of God. Out*
> *of the same mouth proceedeth blessing and cursing.*
> *My brethren, these things ought not so to be."*
> **James 3:8-10**

Men and women can be guilty of sinning with their mouths. It goes both ways. The sad part is that the children oftentimes see this ugliness and learn from it. More is caught than taught. You can have a perfect little Christian home, but if Daddy is nasty and mean to Mommy, the boys will learn how to be nasty husbands from his horrible example. The girls will think it is normal to have a husband who treats them like trash as well. Does Daddy want his little girls to have a husband like him? Or does Mommy want a nagging, nasty wife for their sons just like she has been to her husband? No! Yet, we have a lot of lousy relationships flourishing in the Christian churches.

As a wife, I would like to offer some advice to women who are in a situation of being abused:

- **If you are being physically abused you need to call the police or get help immediately if you feel threatened or if your children are in danger.**
- **If your husband is sexually abusing you or your children you need to call the authorities for that as well. It would be a sin for you**

to allow this to go on.

- If you feel your husband is actually crossing the line and being mean-spirited as a default and it seems like he wants to hurt you with his words you need to first examine your own conduct and words. Have you done anything to frustrate him? Have you been pure in all your ways?
- Verbal abuse is a very touchy subject because it can be a term used loosely to define discontentment in a relationship. Negative words get tossed across an endless sea of selfishness. I hesitate because people could jump the gun on this one, completely ignoring their own involvement.

First, try to win him with kindness. Do all you can to make your relationship joyful, peaceful, and loving. If this fails after a time, I suggest talking with your husband about how he is treating you. It would go something like this: "Husband, I need to talk with you about something. Have I been frustrating you in any way? Are you happy with me? I noticed that you talk to me this way and that way and I feel like you really do not love me the way you used to." You can say it in many different ways; this was just an example to illustrate my point.

If he gets worse and even more mean-spirited, you need to find an older woman in the church whom you know to have integrity in her conversation. She should not be given to gossip or backbiting and she should be in a healthy relationship with her husband. Go to her and tell her what is going on. Seek her counsel diligently. Pray and ask the Lord to soften his heart and to give you the grace you need.

Have a meeting with a couple who has been married a good amount of years and is known to have a good relationship. If you can get your husband to agree to a meeting with this couple in order to talk things out and find a solution, that would also be a good step to take. This could be with a pastor and his wife or marriage counselor as well.

My husband's two cents:

"Now, if he should continue in this manner, not seeking counsel or direction from other men in the church, it may be time to get drastic to get his attention. It may be necessary to separate for a time in some extreme situations until healing can take place in the relationship. Listen, a man has an even greater responsibility from the Lord to love his wife as his own flesh. If he is treating her like trash and throwing away the precious gift he has been entrusted to cherish and love, there will come a time where he will have to give an account. A wife who truly loves her husband would wish for him to finish well. If she hates him, she will endure, enable, and essentially heap coals upon his head on the day of judgment by her downcast and browbeaten kindness. She can be the martyr and get a grand reward for all her wonderful mothering and submissiveness but her husband whom she honored and obeyed will have to answer to God for how he ruled while here on this Earth." ~ Mark Harrison

What I do know is that a marriage is meant to be glorious and wonderful. It should be a sanctuary of acceptance, peace, and love. My husband and I had to work very hard to get where we are today by the grace of God. All relationships take time to develop into something sweet. We are in this 100%/100%. Not 50%/50% or 30%/70%. We both give each other all we have. Mark and I are the best of friends and the biggest sweethearts. God has truly given us such a special vision in our home to love one another as He teaches us to love one another. We esteem each other above ourselves and treat each other the way we would want to be treated. It works. **God's plan works for everyone.**

"Thou shalt love thy neighbour as thyself. There is none other commandment greater than these."
Mark 12:31

"Let nothing be done through strife or vainglory; but in lowliness of mind let each esteem other better than themselves."
Philippians 2:3

"Therefore as the church is subject unto Christ, so let the wives be to their own husbands in everything. Husbands, love your wives, even as Christ also loved the church, and gave himself for it;"
Ephesians 5:24-25

"If thine enemy be hungry, give him bread to eat; and if he be thirsty, give him water to drink: For thou shalt heap coals of fire upon his head, and the Lord

shall reward thee. The north wind driveth away rain: so doth an angry coun-
tenance a backbiting tongue. It is better to dwell in the corner of the housetop,
than with a brawling woman and in a wide house."
Proverbs 25:21-24

Virtuous Charity
ANGER MANAGEMENT 101

Charity "is not easily provoked"
I Corinthians 13:5

The word *provoked* means to give rise to, stir up the emotions, or incite anger. When you are provoked you are allowing things to incite extreme emotion or anger. To be easily provoked would mean that things incite anger or emotion quickly in your spirit. It is a feeling of frustration that comes over you in a sudden wave.

The result is a quick reaction..

- **A quick sharp stare (the EVIL eye).**
- **A cold front (the COLD shoulder).**
- **An outburst (yelling).**
- **A clench of the fist.**
- **A slam of the door.**
- **A hanging up of the phone.**
- **A stomp of the foot.**
- **A pound of the hand on a table.**
- **A striking hand.**
- **A crying fit.**
- **A nasty comeback.**
- **A rolling of the eyes.**

Some of these reactions are subtle and can go unnoticed. Some of you reading this are "Silent Seethers" who seethe with anger quietly (mind games!). You are the type that, when your husband or friend does something you do not like, or gives you an answer that rubs you the wrong way, you repay them with a nice old COLD shoulder and ignore them for awhile.

I know a few ladies who are like this and it is so silly. One day they are your friend, the next day they act like they never met you in their life. (AKA, Jekyl and Hyde, moody, or bi-polar). Or you may have a friend say something that quickly offends you and so you unfriend her on Facebook. A really easily-provokable thing to do at just the click of a button. "There, see how you like that!"

Some of you get mad at your children and give "the old EVIL eye" or the sourpuss face. If you are doing this, you are guilty of being easily provoked. Okay, others of you ladies will hear something and you will get your feelings hurt. That is being easily provoked in your emotions. You are allowing a word or action to alter your mood. You cry, or whine about so-and-so saying this or doing that. How dare they! Oh, and what about if someone does not respond to your text, or your email? They must be mad at you, right?

Patience, dear sisters, patience

Do not think your silence goes unnoticed by the one who knows your heart. On the other hand, my reactions are very noticeable. I yell. I stomp. I am loud, but once I have blown my top, I am again smiling and joyous. In fact, most times I will bust out laughing at myself for how silly I was acting. I get this wave that comes over me, like my blood is boiling. Usually it is due to many factors pressing me at one particular moment:

> The pot is boiling over on the stove, while the phone is ringing, while the dog is peeing on the floor, while the kids are walking through it, while they are dumping the airsoft bbs all over the kitchen, after they wasted their dinner, when the dinner I made was left out all night to spoil, the garbage can is over-flowing, and the neighbor is on the phone complaining about something my child said to her child that was not acceptable. Ugh!

I politely end the conversation on the phone, and then I yell!

Call me OLD YELLER!

I yell. One morning I asked my husband, "Why do our kids yell so much? Why is it so loud here?" He said, "Because you yell."

Simple. To-the-point. That is my husband's style.

"Okay, I suppose you are right. So do I stop yelling?" I asked in an annoyed tone as if I did not want to face my own shortcomings again.

"YES. If you want them to be more peaceful, you must exemplify peace." He explained it with such ease, as though this would be an easy fix or something!

I get this feeling that comes, almost like I will POP! It is a very bad habit. I started in on this habit when I was bedridden. I would be looking out the front window from my hospital bed and see one of the kids chasing another with a shovel and I would pound on the window and yell so loud they could hear me from in the house. Since I could not get up and run outside to scold them, I got in the habit of just screaming as loud as I could so they could hear me from the other side of the house. I am sure I sounded very loud and horrible to my family.

Habits are hard to break

There is an old saying: "It is hard to teach an old dog NEW tricks."

I believe, RATHER, this is something I can overcome through Christ. He died to set us free from the vices of our flesh. We have the power to walk after the spirit. We just choose to walk after the flesh when we react in our emotions.

Here is what the Bible teaches us about walking after the flesh and the fruit of the Spirit:

"Now the works of the flesh are manifest, which are these;
Adultery, fornication, uncleanness,
lasciviousness, Idolatry,
witchcraft, hatred, variance, emulations,
wrath, strife, seditions,
heresies, Envyings, murders,
drunkenness, revellings,
and such like:

114

of the which I tell you before,
as I have also told you in time past,
that they which do such things shall not
inherit the kingdom of God.
But the fruit of the Spirit is love, joy, peace,
longsuffering, gentleness,
goodness, faith, Meekness,
temperance: against such there is no law.
And they that are Christ's have crucified the flesh
with the affections and lusts. If we live in the Spirit,
let us also walk in the Spirit.
Let us not be desirous of vain glory, provoking one another,
envying one another."
Galatians 5:19-26

I believe the Word of God with my whole heart. I know that if it says something, **that means it is doable.** It may take time to form a new habit, but it is doable.

"I can do all things through Christ which strengtheneth me."
Philippians 4:13

Keeper **T**ip...
Start a habit of exemplifying peace.
When a sudden emotion comes over you, REJECT it, take a deep breath, pray and focus on the fact that Christ overcame in all things.
That means you can overcome, too!
You have the power to make some better choices TODAY! Don't get angry, choose peace!

Chapter Eight
Virtuous Work Ethic

"She seeketh wool, and flax, and worketh willingly with her hands."
Proverbs 31:13

A virtuous woman is a woman who works willingly with her hands.

- **She seeks how she can find things that will help her complete her task.**
- **She would rather not wait for things to fall into her lap.**
- **She is an "A" worker.**
- **This woman is not lazy.**
- **She does not need everything done for her.**
- **This virtuous woman does not look for a life of leisure or entertainment.**
- **This willing worker is content to be busy serving her family in her home and helping fill needs beyond this if time allows.**
- **She never needs encouragement to stick with her work.**

Women of steel

Women of early history HAD to work hard because times were difficult. You see this in primitive cultures around the world today who lead lives that are unchanged from hundreds of years ago. I have heard stories of native women, working willingly with their hands in the heat of the day, who give birth in a bush and then return to their work minutes later. As the baby cuddles close within her sling wrapped around her shoulders, she is able to care for her new baby and continue on with her duties.

I cannot even imagine how that would be, nor do I recommend it, but this letter to King Lemuel was written in such a time. It is interesting to see the vast differences in the amount of work we do today versus the load of work that women of long ago and in primitive cultures today still produce. I think these women have built up a threshold of pain and endurance which cannot be matched. I see Amish women who work unceasingly. They will take a break after having their babies, though, which I think is really great for them. They hire a maid for two weeks who takes over all her duties on the farm and in the home so she can recuperate. It seems to be the only vacation she gets all year. I would take it, too!

Women "working bees"

I have done *working bees* with a group of Amish women. You blink and a chicken is ready to go into the freezer. These women, without a thought, will walk over to grab a live chicken and the next thing you know, it is in a pretty package. What I have noticed, in our culture, is that women sometimes shy away from "dirty jobs" and strenuous tasks. To get a group of ladies together to slaughter 100 chickens before lunch is served is out of the question, unless they were raised on a farm and know how it is done. It is not a nice job; it stinks. It is disgusting work. I can assure you, it is not the life for everyone.

I had to train myself to work alongside the Amish. I remember times when I thought I would faint and die from standing there all day working until sweat drenched my entire dress. I mean, they WORK. And you do not just stand around waiting for them to tell you what to do, you just get in there and figure out what you can do to help. It made a worker out of me. I was a pampered city girl with all my pampered ways. I had to lay that aside when I was seeking to learn how to do various homesteading-type jobs. Seeking out the teachers, the dirty work, and finding joy in the fellowship was something I will always carry with me throughout life.

I am not saying these things to hail the homestead life nor am I trying to say the Amish are the only ones who work hard. We all work hard in our own way with the time we have been given. Whether you are a city girl or a country girl, it makes no difference as long as you have the right heart in your willingness to work with your hands and serve your family as unto the Lord.

Working willingly

Attending working bees regularly trained me to work willingly with my hands. I seek to find more things to learn and accomplish. If I have an opportunity to learn from a quilter I will come ready to thread my needle. I do not like to visit just to sit and talk. I want to be diligent because my time here is short and my days are numbered. I want to do something that is meaningful and worth something. Investing in purpose and in things of eternal value. I want to work and learn.

Recently, an older woman spoke to me. I tasted her pretzels, and I asked her if I could find out how she made them. She told me it would be such a joy to spend an afternoon teaching me.

I do not like to sit around and chat on the phone or watch Facebook feeds when there are things to be done. I know there is laundry to fold, meals to prepare, more I can improve on, more to learn, children to care for, and people from whom to pray. There is no end to the possibilities of things I could do or seek out. You never know what your life could be if you never try—if you never seek things out and work willingly to their end. Sometimes when you try, you'll make mistakes. I see every mistake as an essential part of life. It is those mistakes which teach us the most.

On the flip side: The life of leisure

After many centuries, and also the Dark Ages, there came a new concept to women (mainly for the women of wealth or power). It was the concept of leisure. Leisure is the use of *free time* to do things of enjoyment. They had servants to do any hard labor, and they could afford the leisure of sitting in the parlor to read a good book, or play the piano, or paint a picture. It was a disgrace to see a woman of high rank dirty the hem of her dress doing a job outdoors. Some women in history actually hated the life of leisure because there was no balance at all. If she had a certain social status, she was not allowed the luxury of cooking or cleaning or even rearing her own children. She had nursemaids, servants, and nannies for this. I would have hated it.

We now live in a society which has a bit more balance. People do work but they also have time to relax. We are not bush people that hunt for our food. We have luxuries and conveniences to aid in our work which streamlines things to the point where we have time to hop on computers or devices to relax. We can sit in the recliner and watch movies. Times have changed. I do see a trend of young people playing video games and entertaining themselves for hours at a time. Hours that may have been better spent in doing something productive. It pains me to see the newer generations of girls without work. Young ladies who stare at their phones, smiling because they see what their friend posted. It is a vortex, distracting and taking into its pull all their precious minutes/hours that they have to make a difference in the world. Instead, they could be learning from our example to SEEK out things to do, if only we would teach them.

Today, many women are feeling overworked and unappreciated. The thankless job of the wife and mother really is daunting. There is so much to be done, work that never seems to end—but it takes doing. The children are observing us and what we do with our time. It is easier to let them go off into the silent mode of a virtual escape, but it will not teach them how to be a diligent worker in the long run. What is our overall attitude about the work? Are we huffing and puffing and nagging and ragging? Or are we willingly working with our hands in a joyful way?

I consider working with my hands the will of God for my life—being a Keeper of the Home. I feel best when I am doing a job with my children, knowing it is a good thing. Yes, we do have leisure as well. There has to be a balance. You have to enjoy working and playing together. It is not bad to have times of rest in-between our work, or days of respite. God gives us all good things to enjoy. Somehow God saw fit to give us a picture of a virtuous woman in Proverbs. Proverbs is a book of good wisdom which contrasts foolishness and idleness with the upright ways of the diligent. The icing on the cake, the final admonition, is to praise this woman who can do it all.

We can do all things through Christ who strengthens us. We need not beat ourselves down for all the years we may have failed. I have failed much, but I have also learned much. Find a balance—don't be a workaholic, but then don't be a lazy person either. Work and play in the time you are given. Enjoy the journey, whether you are working willingly or whether you are taking time to smell the roses with your little ones. The beautiful thing about God is that his mercies are new each morning. We can get up each morning and choose whom we will serve. Is it ourselves? Is it our flesh? Or will we rise up and seek out the things that need doing? Let us find joy and contentment in what the Lord has for us today. Lord, give us a measure of grace to face our mountains and climb them one step at a time, yet take the time to enjoy the view. Let us not grow weary in well-doing, for in due season we shall reap if we faint not.

Four Types of Work Ethic

"He becometh poor that dealeth [with] a slack hand: but the hand of the diligent maketh rich."
Proverbs 10:4
"The soul of the sluggard desireth, and [hath] nothing: but the soul of the diligent shall be made fat."
Proverbs 13:4

Work is a big part of life
Definition: WORK

- Activity involving mental or physical effort done in order to achieve a purpose or result.
- Physical activity as a means of earning income; employment.
- A task or tasks to be undertaken; something a person or thing has to do.

There are four different types of workers:
1. "A" worker—sees what needs to be done and does it.
2. "B" worker—asks for work: "What can I do next?"
3. "C" worker—has to be told to work.
4. "D" worker—avoids work.

THE "A" WORKER...
I like to use "A" because "A" is the first-place winner, the highest grade, the first letter in the alphabet.

- **The "A" worker does not have to be told what to do. They have the ability to see what needs to be done and they take the initiative to get the job done. They work on every task until it is complete. If an "A" worker is walking in a parking lot, you will see them reach down to pick up a piece of trash they find on the** ground. This type of person is not put off by the fact that someone else was lazy enough to leave it there, they just see that it needs to be picked up.

- The "A" worker will look around a room and see things out of place and they will take the few seconds to set things right. Whether it be a decorative pillow laying on the floor, or a pencil sitting on the table, the "A" worker will see to it that things are put where they belong.

- "A" workers do not leave a trail behind them. After they are finished eating, they will make sure to pick up their plate and fork, rinse them off, and clean up any mess that was made by them. They would be horrified to have someone else clean up after them. What an embarrassment.

- This inventive "A" worker does not need to be told to work. They find work. They would sooner die than have someone ever tell them what they should have done or how to do the work better. These are your CEOs of companies, your entrepreneurs, and inventors. They make things better. If there is a problem, they will figure out a way to fix the problem.

- All the other types of workers pay the "A" worker. They never lack for work because they see the needs of others. They make a difference in society by taking action. They are not benchwarmers in church; they are actively helping minister to others with the gospel, cleaning the church, or doing whatever needs doing. The "A" worker usually makes enough money to be more giving in the ministry.

- Being an "A" worker can be built into certain personalities but it can also be a learned behavior.

- The "A" worker is the most desired class of worker. It is also the most rare.

How do you train yourself to be an "A" worker?

If you desire to be an "A" worker, you must learn the art of noticing. You must notice things that are out of place, things that are left undone, or seeing a need in every situation because you are seeking it out. We do not see what needs to be done when we are not looking for it. Have you ever

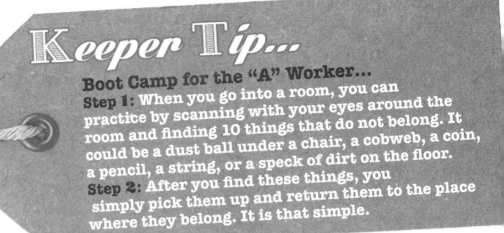

Keeper Tip...

Boot Camp for the "A" Worker...
Step 1: When you go into a room, you can practice by scanning with your eyes around the room and finding 10 things that do not belong. It could be a dust ball under a chair, a cobweb, a coin, a pencil, a string, or a speck of dirt on the floor.
Step 2: After you find these things, you simply pick them up and return them to the place where they belong. It is that simple.

seen a "Seek-and-Find" picture? It is a picture where you have to find the things that do not belong. You stare at the picture and look for things. This is a way to train you to notice the things that are out of place. If you did not have the instruction to look for things, you would just see a pretty picture and miss all the many things that were not right.

- **If you see a sink full of dishes, go to the sink and begin washing them!**
- **If the trash is overflowing, take the trash out!**
- **If there is an elderly lady struggling to put her groceries into her car, go there and lend her a hand!**

How do you make money being an "A" worker?

Figure out a service that every person needs, such as house cleaning, washing cars, picking up dog poop, washing windows, cleaning out gutters, mowing grass, pulling weeds, walking dogs, or watching other people's children. If an "A" worker wants a job bad enough, they will actually approach the head of a company who already refused them and say, "Can I work for you for free as an intern, to prove to you that I am worthy of your hire?"

How can an employer resist that type of offer? They see initiative and drive. If that person works their tail off and never arrives for work late, the employer will see their value and hire that person after a short time. They would be a fool not to do so. If the worker continues to work hard, if they go above and beyond the call of duty, doing things that help the company, they will be valued even more. In no time, that person will be helping run the company.

My parents owned and operated a dog kennel. When I was ten years old I began learning the trade. My dad would wake me around five o'clock each morning to help him let all the dogs out. We would have a kennel full of other people's dogs. They would drop off their dogs and give us instruction as to how we should care for them. I loved dogs so much that I would spend time walking the dog, playing with the dog, and sometimes I would take the dogs into my home if they seemed calm enough. I went way beyond the call of duty.

If my dad would wake before me, he would come into my room and sigh, "I guess I will run the dogs by myself." Oh, how I hated for my dad to have to run the dogs by himself! It wasn't long before I would hear the creak of his footsteps up the stairs to wake me, and I would pop out of bed to meet him at my door telling him that I would be right down. The smile on my dad's face was precious to me.

When I was at the kennel I would not only feed and water the dogs, but I would vacuum and mop the floor each time so it looked perfectly clean. If one of our customers came, I could give them a tour and not ever be embarrassed! My dad would smell the kennel and say, "It smells like a hospital down here." I loved those words. It made me feel valued as a helper. After the dogs were in, I would scoop up all the poop in the runs outside, and spray down the floors with the hose so our kennel did not stink.

I made 25¢ per dog for each running and I ran the dogs four times a day. If there were thirty dogs in one day, I would make $7.50 per running, which equaled $30 a day. That was a lot of money for a 10 to 12-year-old! When the customers would pick up their dogs, I would tell them how much fun I had with their dog, walking it and playing with it. They would give me a tip! I would hate taking the tip, so I would put it in the till for my dad. That is just how I was. To this day, I have a hard time taking money from people. I just love helping out!

Homesteading, gardening, having a hobby, playing an instrument, or simply having a house pet are great ways to train "A" workers. Not everyone can grow up at a dog kennel like I did. Having a garden or a pet will give an extra set of chores. Having to practice an instrument each day teaches good work ethic. Watching my dad work with dogs and being a businessman prepared me for success all throughout my life. I ran several of my own businesses and did very well.

Poop Patrol

Poop Patrol was the name of a business in the town where I grew up. This young guy figured people did not take the time to clean up outside after their dogs. Maybe he saw the need when he visited someone and stepped in one of these land mines. He would go door-to-door and ask people if they would pay him $10 to clean up all the dog poop in their yard. I had enough experience scooping up dog poop to know that it is not a hard job and it takes only a few minutes to do. After the first year, this guy had a whole crew working for him with trucks passing by in the neighborhood. All the trucks had signs on them. What a great idea and an easy way to make money. If a person has a crew and can afford a company truck, you know they are literally scooping in the money! Soon, other companies were putting up signs, offering same service. Other people in Wisconsin wanted a "pile" of that success.

The reason for his success was because he was an "A" worker. He saw a need and created a business to fulfill that need. There are plenty of needs out there, you just need to find them.

How do you train a two-year-old to be an "A" worker?

You start by training them to pick up after themselves as early as they can pick up things in their little hands. If they drop a toy on the ground, you should show them the toy and make a game of picking it back up. I used to create work for my little ones. I would spend hours playing "the work game." We would sprinkle "critters" (little pieces of dirt and garbage) onto the floor and I would have the kids sweep them into a little dust pan. I would say, "Oops, you missed that little critter over there. He is going to be lonesome over there all by himself, so we'd better sweep him up." This was great fun for them as toddlers. They would find each little critter, and it was training them for the rest of their lives to notice the little things. If they could finish getting every little speck, they will transfer that technique to every area of their lives. When they start a job, they will finish it. They will do a thorough job every time. If you are consistent in your training, your child will be an "A" worker.

- **Let the child help with all of your work. It may take longer, but they need to learn from you!**
- **Let them help wash dishes. Give them a rag to fold. Let them wash the wall with a baby wipe. Give them stuff to do that is productive yet playful. Work will be a part of their normal everyday life. They will not think it strange when you ask them to help you later in life. They will be geared for helping.**

My husband said he was not an "A" worker at all when he was growing up. He said he was lazy when we first got married. It wasn't until he had to provide for our family and take on that responsibility that he started training himself to be a better worker. Sometimes people learn out of necessity. If they do not work, they will not have money to pay for the needs that come with living expenses.

THE "B" WORKER:

- **I like to think of "B" as the first runner-up.**
- **The "B" worker is always on time and ready to work. They do not like to stand by idle.**
- **The "B" workers are eager for the task. So eager they will ask "What can I do next?"**
- **"B" workers are valuable members of any workplace because they both work hard and they have a good attitude.**
- **"B" workers never lack for work.**
- **They have a desire to do things the employer's way.**
- **"B" workers like to be useful and needed at all times.**
- **They like to finish a task in a timely manner.**

One of the greatest qualities of a "B" worker is that they ask you, "What is next?" What employer could complain about a worker who completes a task and asks for more work? What parent could complain when their child asks them what job they can do next? None, I can assure you! I would rather have a person ask me, "Is there anything else I can do for you?" than for me to have to see them sitting there doing nothing after they finish a task.

While the "A" worker has the confidence to jump into a job doing it their way, the "B" worker does not want to step on anyone's toes. They have the sense to ask first so as not to overstep their bounds. When you are a "B" worker you see an "A" worker working their tail off and you want to assist in some way. You notice they could use some help, but you do not want to take the lead so you ask them if they need help.

How do you train yourself to be a "B" worker?

My biggest word of advice for learning how to be a "B" worker is "B" willing to help. "B" flexible; "B" a blessing:

I can be an "A" worker, but I would say I am also a "B" worker. When I am home or running a business with our family, I am an "A" worker. I am working hard to find jobs for the children, planning meals, cleaning, doing whatever needs to be done around the house. Being a wife, you can sometimes take on the "A" role, and other times the "B" role because you ask your husband what you can do to help him.

When I work for someone else, I try to be as inventive and creative as possible. I prefer not being told what to do. I love doing a really good job and making it so my employer does not have to work as hard to come up with all the ideas, but sometimes people do not like my ideas. I have to submit to their way. If my first attempt is not well-received, I become the "B" worker blessing. I ask how they would like it to be done, and I make it happen. If I am flexible to meet whatever the need is, I become even more valuable as a worker. My employers are glad that I am willing to run with their visions. **The "B" worker is an asset to any home or workplace.**

How to train a child to be a "B" worker blessing:

Every time you are working, keep your child working by your side. Talk with them while you are working and invite the questions that the work may bring. If they feel comfortable asking questions and working with you, they are learning to be helpful in so many ways. When my children were little, I had them sitting with me at the table cutting up salad. They would ask, "Why do you cut it like that?" or, "Why do we need to eat salad?" I would answer their many questions by saying, "Look at this pretty green lettuce! It is so bright. The brighter our food is, the more alive it is and the healthier it is for our bodies. When we cut it up, it makes a nice salad for us to eat." If I give a two-year-old a butter knife, some fresh lettuce, and their very own cutting board while I am working on my own cutting board, they are learning to help. Learning to help is the essence of the "B" worker blessing!

Whether it is baking, cleaning, folding the wash, planting a garden, pouring in an ingredient, or stirring the soup, children enjoy the fellowship of working with their parents and in so doing they are learning to "B" useful and productive.

THE "C" WORKER:

I like to think of "C" as common and consistent…

- **The "C" worker has to be told to do work because they have a hard time thinking of doing work on their own.**
- **The "C" workers do well in factory work where they punch a clock and know what is expected of them.**
- **"C" workers are hardworking, dependable people who will be satisfied with mundane tasks.**
- **"C" workers are content working for others their entire life.**
- **The "A" workers need "C" workers to assist in building their masterpieces, and completing all the background tasks without complaining.**
- **While the "B" worker is constantly competing to be as useful as possible and asking for more things to do, the "C" worker will gladly just keep peddling at the same thing without questioning.**

Pros of the "C" worker

One of the greatest qualities of the "C" worker is their consistency.

They just work at whatever job they are told without complaint. They also have the ability to work at the same job for their entire lives and never wish for something else to do like an "A" or a "B" worker will. This "C" worker can fit one part on a machine that the "A" worker invented for 8 hours, 5 days a week! They do not care about the person who invented it nor do they understand why the part was needed. They just systematically fit the part in place because that was what they were told to do. "C" workers are happiest when they can drive into a parking lot, punch in, and work all day until they get their paycheck. They are doers. The "C" worker is faithful and good to have on the work force. It is nice for the "A" workers to have their "C" workers that do not question the work they are given no matter what the conditions may be.

Cons of the "C" worker

The "C" worker will only do what is required of them. They will not look for more to do like the "A" worker and they will not ask for more to do like the "B" worker. They will just do what is expected and then they are done as far as they are concerned. The "C" worker will work hard as long as they have something they are told to do, but you can find them sitting around until you give them more work. They will not be eager to go above and beyond the call of duty. "C" workers will usually never be wealthy. They will always just have enough or feel strapped. They go from paycheck to paycheck. The "C" worker does not have the confidence to jump into advancements or take risks to start their own business. They tend to stay working a 9-to-5 job and make a steady income even if it keeps them in a low-income bracket. "C" workers can be more self oriented because they never accept the challenge of thinking about others or making the world a better place. They work all day long and come home beat.

How do you train someone to be a "C" worker?

Anyone can be trained to be a "C" worker very early in life.

"C" worker lists are the perfect place to start when training a child to be productive

I love lists. I create a list for myself and my children every day. A

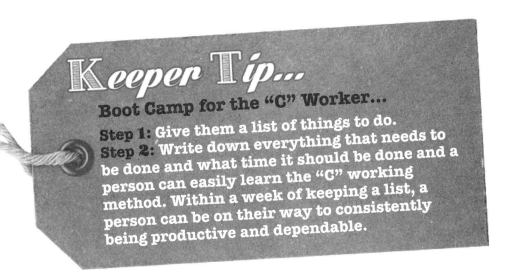

child is given to us to lead and guide. They do not automatically work and find ways to be productive. It is a parent's duty to lead them into a life of good work ethics. Starting when they are very small, a parent needs to tell the child what to do and what they need to take responsibility for. A two-year-old can be given a list. They may not be able to read that list, but it will keep a parent in the mode of training.

Many parents in today's culture like to ask their child what they want for each and everything in their lives. For breakfast, the parent will ask the toddler, "What would you like for breakfast?" The child will sit there and think. They may change their mind, but that is no bother. Mother will make them a few different things. As the toddler shoves one plate away and snarls and whines, they beg for something else. They say, "I don't want cheese, I want a donut! Give me a donut now!" Mom becomes the child's servant and the roles are sadly switched. The child was not given to a parent so the child could tell the parent what to do, the child was given to the parent so the parent could teach the child how to become a functioning member in society, and more importantly, how to become a parent themselves one day.

Instead, the parent should tell the child, "It is time for breakfast. We are having scrambled eggs. It is time to get dressed and pick up your toys." Period. End of discussion. After they are finished eating, a little child can be told, "Now it is time to clean up our dishes." A two-year-old can carry their bowl to the sink, pull up a chair, and stand on the chair to rinse their bowl out. When you ask a child if they want to do a task, the child is intelligent enough to realize that when given the choice to do work, they can easily say "no," thus avoiding the work altogether. A child who is used to having their way and getting what they want will be handicapped for their entire lives. They will learn to be self-serving, lazy, and ungrateful for what they have and will not be a productive member of society. They will learn to take handouts and they will never want to work for anything. They need structure to learn how to work from an early age. This structure will give them a feeling of being needed and being a part of something important which will give them the self-worth they need as they mature.

Making a list for your "C" workers

For example, here are some age-appropriate chores that can be added to a To-Do List for any age of child:

Having "C" workers is nothing to feel bad about. They are hard-working and dependable.

Age-Appropriate Chores for 2 to 6-year-olds...
- Put shoes away.
- Put dirty clothes in a hamper.
- Put dirty dishes in the sink.
- Pick up toys.
- Fold dish towels or rags, with assistance.
- Wash or rinse dishes, with assistance.
- Sweep floors, with assistance.
- Make beds, with assistance.
- Help cook a meal.

Age-Appropriate Chores for 7 to 12-year-olds...

- Wash, rinse, and dry dishes.
- Wash loads of laundry.
- Clean bedroom.
- Pick up living room.
- Fold laundry.
- Sweep and mop floors.
- Help bake and cook.
- Feed, water, and care for animals.
- Wash and vaccum car.
- Rake, garden, or help with yard work.
- Help watch younger children (at age 10).

Age-Appropriate Chores for 13 to 18-year-olds...

- Make meals.
- Wash, dry & fold laundry.
- Kitchen duty.
- Pick up & organize room.
- Sewing or building things.
- Sweep and mop floors.
- Start their own business.
- Feed, water, and care for animals.
- Clean and fix cars.
- Rake, garden, or mow lawn.
- Help watch younger children.

THE "D" WORKER:

- **The "D" Worker is unmotivated and lazy.**
- **"D" workers have to be found in order to tell them to work.**
- **A "D" worker is a procrastinator and is always late.**
- **These type of workers are not dependable because they never follow through.**
- **The "D" Worker will start many projects but never finish them.**
- **They think they deserve benefits without working for them.**

Avoiding responsibility

If a "D" worker knows a person expects work out of them, they tend to figure out how to get lost before that person arrives on the scene. They think, "If Dad comes home at 3pm, he will probably have some work for me to do. I will go somewhere else around that time, so when I show up it will be time for dinner, and my parents won't make me starve." The "D" worker thinks this way their entire life. Skirting responsibility is their game. They have a huge list of excuses for why they did not get something done. Something always comes up at the last minute so they do not have to keep any of their commitments.

Medals of disHONOR

IF you can get a "D" worker to actually do a job, they will complain. They have a knack for being so annoying that you get frustrated enough to let them off the hook. It is easier to do the job yourself than to listen to them fuss about it the whole time. If the "D" worker completes a job, they want a reward. They feel they deserve a medal of honor. You know this because they remind you how "hard" they worked and all they did. Even though you may have done about ten times the amount of work that the "D" worker did, they will actually think in their mind that they worked harder than everyone else.

They are quick to notice if anyone else is being lazy. If there are five people in the room and four had worked for eight hours, the "D" worker who watched them work all day will say they are lazy if he/she is asked to do one task while the others are sitting there. The "D" worker will see this as unfair. This person would be so focused on themselves the entire day that they would not even notice how hard the rest of the people were working. If they were the only one working, they would become bitter in their heart toward the other people, thinking they had to work the hardest, even if it was a job that only took ten minutes.

How to make money being a "D" worker

"D" workers love money. They want to have money without working for it. The "D" worker does not feel bad about asking others for money or applying for government aid. They will gladly take food stamps and unemployment. If they are a child, they will be perfectly happy earning an allowance for doing the minimal amount of chores. The sad fact is that the "D" worker will never be able to hold a job. They will always scrape by, shaking their fist at God for not blessing them. They will blame their financial trouble on all the people who "robbed them blind" or who "treated them unfairly." "D" workers always feel they got the short end of the stick and they keep a chip on their shoulder throughout their lives.

"Go to the ant, thou sluggard; consider her ways, and be wise."
Proverbs 6:6

"A Fed Bear is a Dead Bear"

If you visit Yellowstone National Park, you will see signs posted saying, "Do Not Feed the Bears: A Fed Bear is a Dead Bear." The signs are there for good reason. If you start feeding the bears, they will stop hunting for their own food. If they stop hunting for their own food they will starve or become dangerous and have to be put down. The bears will actually see humans as their feeders. They will fight you for your food. Watch out! Trying to hand-feed the Grizzly Bear will not be good for your health!

The same goes for the "D" worker. If you give them too many handouts, you enable them to be lazy and not work for their food. They will never get anywhere. If everyone stopped feeding them, they would either die of starvation, become dangerous and steal to eat, or they would have to get a job. I realize that some people have had situations come up that require assistance to support them for a time. That is entirely different than the "D" worker who has a pattern of leeching, begging, stealing, or trying to get free money. A person who is temporarily in a state of need will actually feel bad about asking for help.

Employers do not like "D" workers. They drag the entire company down with their attitude and poor work ethic. The "D" worker brags about what a good worker they are but they cannot live up to their great, swelling words. They tend to show up late for work, do the bare minimum of work, and sometimes they do not even show up for work at all. For instance, when you tell a "D" worker to sweep the floor, they will never move furniture, they will take the easy route by just gathering up the few crumbs in the middle of the room and will not do a thorough job. The employer generally fires the "D" worker for their lack of consistency and lack of dependability.

Life of leisure

The "D" worker would much rather play video games, watch television, or read a book instead of working. In fact, the "D" workers generally gravitate toward anything that feeds their flesh and makes it so they do not have to think very hard. They could spend nearly all day on an entertainment device and not realize where their time went.

FROM "D" WORKER TO "A" WORKER

All children are born to be some kind of worker. What kind of worker they develop into depends on what they are taught by example. As parents, we teach them to work and encourage them to have a drive to accomplish things each day. This is a small start, but they learn quickly to work their way up the work ethics scale. Working your way up the scale can be learned. We all can be "D" workers in the course of a typical day. There are days when I myself just do not feel like doing anything. I am a solid, unmotivated "D" worker. I have to urge myself to be focused and become a "C" worker by making a little list for myself of things I should accomplish that day. I work my way up to the "B" worker when I ask my husband, "What can I do to help you?" Then I add a few more things to my list. As the day goes on, I start noticing dirty laundry, and things out of place. As I notice things that need doing, I jump up to the "A" spot by returning the things back to their place. I start working myself into a groove, and before I know it, I am a solid "A" working machine!

Becoming a graduate

Anyone can work their way up the work ethic scale when they start out small, taking baby steps toward the goal. Some people can't fathom climbing an entire mountain; but if they take one step at a time, they find out they are getting pretty far along. By the time they reach the top, they can hardly believe it was that easy. For instance, it is hard for my children if I tell them to clean the entire kitchen. They see it as a monumental task. But I know that it only takes about one hour to do a thorough cleaning. Looking at the big picture is hard for most people. But, if you give them a list of small tasks and have them check off each one as they go, they feel it is doable. Try not to beat yourself up if you feel like you are having a "D" day. Get off your seat and make a little list. Graduate yourself immediately to the "C" status. A "D" worker can easily learn to be a "C" worker in a short time with a little list. A "C" worker can easily learn to simply ask what they can do next in order to break past the next barrier to become a "B" worker. That same "B" worker has only but to look around and start noticing what needs to get done to excel to the "A" level. It seems hard but it is really just a few baby steps away!

Keeper Tip:
MOM BUCKS MIRACLE

Winter brings something we all dread… "cabin fever." The kids are full of pent-up energy and have nowhere to go to run it all off. It's cold, damp, and raining most days, so the kids just stay in. They bicker and quarrel. They sit around and do nothing. As a mom, I shake my head and wonder what I did to create these monsters. As I sat in my bed early one morning, talking to my half-asleep husband, I searched my heart to no end. How could my children be so nasty to each other? So contentious? And my home so full of chaos? The laziness creeps its ugly presence around each bend of the home. Nothing seemed to be getting done. Winter brings the cold, and cold for me translates into pain. When I am doing less, maybe it is an example for them to do less. Everyone is eating, slouching across the furniture as the occasional wrestling match breaks out, and it seems like pulling teeth to require any work out of them.

As we moved forward that morning, our weary bodies made the grand exodus from our bed and the warmth of our slumber; we found our owner's manual for parenting—the Bible! God is faithful to give wisdom in times of need and His Word is full of verses that pertain to work ethic…

"And whatsoever ye do, do [it] heartily, as to the Lord, and not unto men;"
Colossians 3:23

"For even when we were with you, this we commanded you, that if any would not work, neither should he eat."
2 Thessalonians 3:10

"In all labour there is profit: but the talk of the lips [tendeth] only to penury."
Proverbs 14:23

"He that tilleth his land shall be satisfied with bread: but he that followeth vain [persons is] void of understanding."
Proverbs 12:11

"He becometh poor that dealeth [with] a slack hand: but the hand of the diligent maketh rich."
Proverbs 10:4

I have learned in life that everything is doable if there is a system in place. All of a sudden, like a flash of light bursting out of a black cloud, an idea came to me—MOM BUCKS! It became the new currency in our home—paper play money. We started out using Monopoly money, until it all wore out. I eventually designed my own MOM BUCKS on the computer. Many people have downloaded them and have enjoyed using them as their training currency.

Keeper Tip…
All printouts from this book including MOM BUCKS are available for downloading at www.KeeperoftheHomestead.com

This is how it works

Think of all the things you need done around the home and put a value on each job…

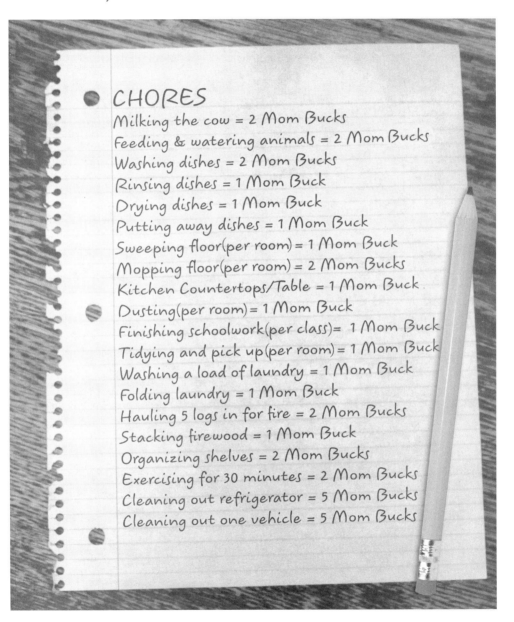

CHORES

Milking the cow = 2 Mom Bucks
Feeding & watering animals = 2 Mom Bucks
Washing dishes = 2 Mom Bucks
Rinsing dishes = 1 Mom Buck
Drying dishes = 1 Mom Buck
Putting away dishes = 1 Mom Buck
Sweeping floor(per room) = 1 Mom Buck
Mopping floor(per room) = 2 Mom Bucks
Kitchen Countertops/Table = 1 Mom Buck.
Dusting(per room) = 1 Mom Buck
Finishing schoolwork(per class) = 1 Mom Buck
Tidying and pick up(per room) = 1 Mom Buck
Washing a load of laundry = 1 Mom Buck
Folding laundry = 1 Mom Buck
Hauling 5 logs in for fire = 2 Mom Bucks
Stacking firewood = 1 Mom Buck
Organizing shelves = 2 Mom Bucks
Exercising for 30 minutes = 2 Mom Bucks
Cleaning out refrigerator = 5 Mom Bucks
Cleaning out one vehicle = 5 Mom Bucks

Next, come up with the value of privileges. I was first met with opposition when one of my older children wondered if it was normal to pay for meals. I replied, "Well, we work for money and we have to pay for food. Who else pays the food bill? You can just come in and sit down, you eat the food that we work hard to pay for and then you walk away. You do not have to worry about money. This is how real life works.: You go to work, you make money, and you pay bills. The sooner you understand the cost of living, the sooner you will find ways to make sure you always survive." Mark showed them the Bible passage about if you do not work, you do not eat. With eyes wide open, they gave their nod of understanding and new-found appreciation.

THE STORE

2 MOM BUCKS each meal
2 MOM BUCKS dessert
2 MOM BUCKS snack
2 MOM BUCKS quarrelling
1 MOM BUCK for each item that is not put away
2 MOM BUCKS for each job not done on time
1 MOM BUCK per hour for free time
5 MOM BUCKS movie night
2 MOM BUCKS popcorn

100 MOM BUCKS= $10 real money

This system has brought such productivity, order, and peace into our home. They learn good work ethic, how to save money, and how to spend it wisely. One day Miles decided to take it easy. He is prone to laziness so we have to keep reminding him to stay busy or we will find something for him to do. I just let him loaf. When it came time for movie night, Miles did not have enough for admission to the show. I told him that the movie starts in 30 minutes so he'd better get busy earning some MOM BUCKS. That put a fire under my boy. He wanted to watch the movie, so he fixed his eyes on that prize and found some jobs to complete in time for the movie. Because he is the oldest, he thinks that this game is baby-ish. My answer to that attitude was, "No problem. You do not have to play, but you aren't going to eat unless you pay." It works. Now he is about 20 MOM BUCKS ahead. The kids feel good about getting work done, neg-ative behavior and quarreling is cutting back each day, and my house is always clean. They run around looking for things to do to make a quick buck rather than just sitting around picking at each other and driving me crazy. When I do their homeschooling, I charge them 1 MOM BUCK for each time they goof around. I am getting great results and everyone seems happier.

With the MOM BUCKS system, you can tell which kid is the most ambitious, who saves up, and which one will be the wasteful spender. The girls started making up snacks like popcorn, cookies, homemade crackers, and chocolate milk to offer in the snack shack. They enjoy having things for which they can save up. The boys are into airsoft BB guns, so Mark buys the little plastic bullets in bulk. They can buy the plastic BBs from their dad. The kids needed some clothing, so they paid for thrift store clothes with the MOM BUCKS they saved up. I would have bought them the clothing either way, but thought it would be fun to charge them 5 MOM BUCKS for each thing they picked out. It makes the shopping all the more fun for them! I hope this idea helps you and brings more order in your home.

Lessons in Etiquette
Time Etiquette

I am a firm believer in REAL LIFE skills. In real life, our children will have jobs that require them to punch the clock. They will have to be at the job at a certain time. If they roll out of bed too late and arrive at work past the required time, they could risk losing their job. As homeschoolers, we tend to be on our own schedule, just floating through the day with a "whenever it gets done" philosophy. Our children NEED structure if they are going to be successful in the real world. All the while we try to be flexible. Sounds hard to balance, but it can be done.

They need to understand *time*. They need to **be on time.** Being accountable is very important in our society. Who wants to hire someone who does not *keep* their word? I sure would not want to hire someone like that. I like to have someone who is where they say they were going to be when they say they were going to be there.

I used to be *late* all the time. My parents were so frustrated with me. They said I would be late for my own funeral. My parents are very timely people and they tried so hard to teach me how to be on time. As I got older I used the excuse of being "Fashionably Late." I started to hear people say, "Erin's always late. If you want something done, don't ask Erin, she will never get around to it."

I hated sitting in the principal's office every day while in high school, filling out tardy slips. I ended up getting an award for the best excuses for being tardy. Here are a couple of excuses just for the fun of it...

- **"Sorry I am late, there was a bird in my house and it was flying into the window. I had to help it, so I went into the garage and found a fishing net so I could catch it. By the time I finally caught the poor bird, I noticed that it was getting late." (They would laugh and hand me the tardy slip.)**

- **"Sorry I am late, I had my shirt stuffed with crumpled papers, I went over a bump and my folder fell out of my bike's basket. All of my important essays went flying in the wind and I had to chase them down as fast as I could. Then I put all of the papers in my shirt because I was in a hurry so I would not be late. Oops, I guess I am still late. Sorry :(" (They would laugh and hand me another tardy slip.)**

Well, I had many more stories and excuses for being late. They were all true stories from a very scatterbrained girl. I finally figured out, after I ran a wedding photography business, that I had to be on time. You cannot run a good business, especially in the wedding business, if you are *late*. If you are late for a wedding, you will miss the bride coming down the aisle. I had to be on time. It was mandatory. Being late was just not very considerate. Making people wait on you is just plain selfish and *rude*. **Be a respecter of their time!**

It is saying silently: "I really do not care about your time. You need to revolve your life around my clock! My time is more important than yours."

Of course, there are times when something really does happen that is unforeseen. I used to be late all the time when I had little ones; for instance, I would pack the van, and then one of the kids would fill their diaper while another child was falling into a puddle getting full of mud. Maybe you are driving down the road, and realize you forgot the diaper bag or your purse. I know. I have been there. It was poor planning on my part. I should have known to expect a ton of things to go wrong at the last second and learned to pack the car sooner. It was my fault! Now I am always on time. I hate being late. I will go out of my way to plan ahead so I can be right where I say I am going to be when I say I will be there.

I thought I could never get a new reputation. But, I did. I have overcome in that area and people comment instead, "If Erin says she will be there, she will be there. Erin is never late. Erin is someone you can count on for anything, she keeps her word!"

Keeper Tip...
- Do not make your lack of planning ahead someone else's emergency!
- Plan ahead.
- Consider others by being respectful of their time.
- Do not waste your time or other peoples' time.

Teaching your children to be accountable should be paramount in your home. We have to prepare them for the life they will live apart from us. They are only ours for a short time. Just because we like to be lax and have the freedom to do whatever, whenever, does not mean we should train our kids to be that way. It will handicap them in the future.

Do them a favor. Make them a schedule. Help them to be accountable to it. As stay-at-home mothers, homeschoolers, and housekeepers, it is important to not be too rigid to enjoy the little things in life. It is the principle that I am trying to convey. We should try to, in some way, teach them about time without taking away the beauty of creativity and flexibility that the home life offers them.

In other words, make time for fun! I like to schedule in a few hours of play/fun/run-around time each day. This way, I have all of our school done, the house is clean, and dinner is made, so we are free to be creative and go on adventures! And the best part is, we can come home to a clean home and a hot dinner ready to serve.

"So teach us to number our days,
that we may apply our hearts unto wisdom."
Psalm 90:12

"See then that ye walk circumspectly, not as fools, but as wise,
Redeeming the time, because the days are evil."
Ephesians 5:15-16

Recipe to be a GOOD WOMAN

Proverbs 31:13—A good woman is a willing, eager, hardworker. She LOOKS for tasks that will be an asset to her family.

"She seeketh wool and flax, and worketh willingly with her hands."

Key words: *seeketh, worketh willingly*

Industrious, hardworking, busy, diligent, patient.

A Good Woman Is a Prudent Woman.

Consider this:

- A prudent wife is not dumb.
- A prudent wife is not lazy.
- A prudent wife does not waste her time.
- A prudent wife is a learner.

Men value hardworking women who are eager to learn how to do new things. No man wants to be saddled with a slow, incompetent wife. I have often heard my sons and their friends talking about what they wanted in a wife. They all agreed that they did not want to marry "a high-maintenance chick." No young man wants to marry "a lazy, visiting, 'gotta eat out' gal."

All men agree on this one point: **A good woman is a helper, not a hindrance.** A help meet works, learns, and helps with the daily tasks of life. When a man gets home from work, there should be an obvious, visible, tangible difference in his house, his children, his food, and even his income, which she has helped generate. He knows his lady makes things happen, gets things done, and is not just a sweep-the-floor and wash-the-dishes gal. She is a true entrepreneur, an initiator.

Perhaps you have heard a man say on occasion about some other man's wife, "He's got a good woman." If you ask that man to define the woman he referred to as *good,* he would be describing a Proverbs 31 woman. It is a general blueprint of how a woman seeking to honor God should fashion her life. It is the kind of woman a man most admires.

~Debi Pearl

Time-Tested Wisdom...

Is Frugality a Good Thing?

Yes, it is a good thing. The dictionary defines frugality this way:

The quality of being frugal or prudent in saving; the lack of wastefulness: many people who have lived through periods of economic deprivation develop lifelong habits of frugality and are almost never tempted by wasteful consumption.

Our society is extremely wasteful. We have so much. We don't know what it is like to go hungry. Even a lot of the poor in our country are overweight. As believers, we need to be good stewards of this earth, our money, and our possessions. But, you can be so frugal that you become selfish and that is completely opposite of how Jesus wants us to live. There are many verses about being generous and helping those in need. We reap what we sow.

The Bible doesn't say anything about being frugal, but it does have a lot to say about being generous. It is very easy to become stingy and selfish when you want to be frugal. I know. I became that way when I was caught up in being frugal and it wasn't pretty. Here are some verses on being generous:

"Give, and it will be given to you. A good measure, pressed down, shaken together and running over, will be poured into your lap.

For with the measure you use, it will be measured to you."

Luke 6:38

"Be not deceived; God is not mocked: for whatsoever a man soweth,

that shall he also reap."

Galatians 6:7

"It is more blessed to give than to receive."

Acts 20:35

"One gives freely, yet grows all the richer; another withholds what he should give, and only suffers want. Whoever brings blessing will be enriched,

and one who waters will himself be watered."

Proverbs 11:24-25

"As for the rich in this present age, charge them not to be haughty, nor to set their hopes on the uncertainty of riches, but on God, who richly provides us with everything to enjoy. They are to do good, to be rich in good works, to be generous and ready to share, thus storing up treasure for themselves as a good foundation for the future, so that they may take hold of that which is truly life."

1 Timothy 6:17-19

We know debt is bad so we must live within our means and not be wasteful, but we must believe God. He says you reap what you sow. Treat others the way you want to be treated. Everyone loves being around generous people. Remember God is our provider. Trust Him from whom all blessings flow.

~Lori Alexander
From Blog: Always Learning

Chapter Nine
Virtuously Frugal

"She is like the merchants' ships; she bringeth her food from afar."
Proverbs 31:14

A virtuous woman is concerned about the health of her family

She is obtaining food from afar. She must care about what her family is eating. Upon taking this verse literally in modern times, I see a woman getting in her car to drive far to go grocery shopping. I am sure some of you have taken a weekly or monthly shopping trip to buy the finest organic foods that are only available at the Whole Foods Market. You do this because you want the very best for your family.

I have seen women more often than men concerned about eating healthy foods. I am prone to regularly concocting all kinds of healthy recipes and brews for my family. I will spend hours on the internet researching foods that heal various kinds of issues. If I have to drive a hundred miles to obtain a box of coconuts—I will not think twice about it. I never have done this, but I think I would go anywhere to get something if I knew it would help my family. A virtuous woman actually puts a lot of thought into her journey. She would make sure she did not waste the trip. Planning ahead is a virtue in itself. Making sure you get all the things needed in one trip will also save precious resources.

Searching for the finest foods to feed our family shows that we care. We do not run to the store to buy the easiest, instant, and processed foods that do not build health in the body. It is a blessing to a husband when he has a capable wife who feeds a well-balanced diet to the family. He trusts they are getting the nutrients they need while she figures out how to prepare it so it also tastes good.

Getting "healthy" food to taste good is half the battle. Make sure your healthy food tastes good. For instance, no one in my house likes to eat a bowl of fresh kale, even though I know kale is really good for them. I hide it in foods so no one knows it is there. That is fair game in my book. If I cannot grow kale, I will drive far to get some good kale. I put it in my blender with some water, grind it to very small particles, and add it to different entrees. I add it to spaghetti sauce, meatloaf, baked goods, smoothies, soups, casseroles, or salads. No one knows. They do not ask. I do not tell them. Case closed. Health without the fuss.

Everything in balance, ladies! Healthy foods are great, but we can push it too far. I have pushed the health thing until I became the "Health Nut." Early in my marriage, I was like a tyrant in my own kitchen, rationing and commanding, controlling and getting downright angry when they did not like my healthy food. I would force my family to eat strange things that just did not taste good. It literally forced my husband to have a secret stash of goodies that he could eat when I was not looking.

I would cry buckets of tears over the caffeinated soda, the boxed cereals, and the sweets in the glove box of his work truck. That was a sorry mistake. I was not being a virtuous wife. I was being a brutish woman, treating him like a child. That was not okay. It is not okay to cry over simple things like food. A typical conversation would go something like this…

"Did you drink _____ today?" as I glared at him. "Yes," he would say reluctantly, knowing I was going to give him a good scolding.

"Why? Why would you drink poison? Caffeinated soda is filled with poison, high fructose corn syrup, and all kinds of preservatives! You are going to kill yourself, slowly over time, not to mention what a horrible example you are being to your children. Next thing you know, they are going to be drinking that garbage!"

It drove him crazy and it nearly ruined our relationship. Wow. What a waste—to think garbage food was making our marriage garbage. A woman can trash her relationship without even realizing it over the most foolish things that do not matter in eternity. It was after I decided to get a grip, and let him eat what he wants, cook what he likes, and be more forgiving when he would sneak bad foods that our relationship blossomed into something wonderful. Years of me laying down my own will for his loving lead, gave fruits which were far more valuable than ones I could have concocted by force. Eventually, my husband began enjoying healthier options and he even asks me to add kale into the smoothies for that extra health benefit! He knows I add it to things and he actually buys it or grows it because he wants me to make sure I do add it to things. It is truly amazing how a sweet and submissive spirit can soften the hardest of hearts. It is a miracle he stuck with me when I was such a difficult woman to begin with.

What is a "merchant ship?"

A *merchant ship* is a large vessel that carries goods from one place to another on major waterways. These merchant ships carried precious cargo for others to buy. When this passage was written, a merchant ship was a very special thing. People could not grow certain things, so exotic fruits from other lands would come via these ships, and people could enjoy the strange luxury of eating foods that were imported. Now, we have grocery stores that carry food which has been imported from all over the world. It seems like a luxury to buy locally-grown foods.

The minivan or the sport utility vehicle is the modern equivalent of the merchant ship. We have such a luxury to be able to get into a car and drive to the store. The virtuous woman from a thousand years ago could only dream that something like driving to the market would be possible. It is ours with a turn of the key. I guess we take for granted the smallest details and how easy we truly have it.

Being frugal

A virtuous woman is concerned about being frugal. It costs a lot to buy fine organic foods. Some ladies are members of co-ops and travel a distance to unload the truck and divide the goods. They buy in bulk to be more frugal. It is a lovely thing to be frugal. Watching sales and being a good steward of the money you have been given is a good thing. If a husband is working a job that provides income to his family, it is an honor to him that his wife spends it wisely. She makes wise decisions on purchasing food that is both nutritious and inexpensive at the same time.

Keeper Tip...
10 ways you can Be Frugal...

$ *Frugal Tips* $

1 PRICE MATCH
Cut coupons or save ads from other grocery stores.
Most grocery stores will match a competitor's discounts.

2 BUY IN BULK
Buy staple items like grains, flour, and spices in bulk to save
big-time. Here is an example:

$1.98 $50.00

8 OZ. RICE
1 LB = $3.96
50 LBS = $198.00

versus

50 LBS RICE
1 LB = $1.00
50 LBS = $50.00

YOU SAVE: $148.00
WHEN BUYING RICE IN BULK. SAME WEIGHT.

The price tags are deceiving. BUT, you will not have to buy rice for a
long time. Even for a big family, that 50-lb. bag of rice can last about a
year.

3 STOCK UP
When you notice something on sale, stock up. If you can purchase
anything with a large discount, buying multiple items can save you
a lot of money in the long run.

4 BUY OFF-BRANDS
Just because it has a name brand, does not always mean it is a
better product. Most times an off-brand has the same ingredients
and tastes the same, but is half the price. Stop spending money for
a name on a pretty box.

5 MAKE YOUR OWN

Most things can be made from scratch. When you buy supplies and make your own version of a product, you can save a lot of money. You can make your own toxic-free cleaning supplies, baking mixes and everything in-between. Vinegar is cheap and it cleans almost anything.

6 RAISE YOUR OWN

Many people want raw organic homegrown meats and dairy but have to either drive a long distance to obtain them or else pay through the nose. If you live in an area where you can grow a garden or raise some chickens, you will save a lot of money. Some cities allow people to have a few hens for eggs if they have a small coop for them. Even on an apartment patio, vegetables can be grown in containers. Make sure you can the extra vegetables you grow.

7 BUY USED

A brand new vehicle depreciates quickly. If you try to sell a brand new car that you used for several weeks, you will never get what you paid for it. You will lose thousands. Craigslist, eBay, and other by-owner sales venues will offer used items that do not require sales tax to purchase them. You can get some pretty good deals that way.

8 USE IT UP, WEAR IT OUT, MAKE IT DO, OR DO WITHOUT

Make the most out of everything you have. If you can not afford something, do without. Distinguish the difference between WANTS and NEEDS. Some things are luxuries. Use what you have until it is gone. Fix things that are broken instead of replacing them. Repurpose things instead of throwing them away. Get a sewing machine and learn how to fix your clothing. Take care of things so they last longer.

⑨ Shop at Thrift Stores or Garage Sales

A lot of your clothing, decorations, furniture, kitchen equipment, etc. can be purchased at thrift stores. I have found really nice things that appear brand new for just a few dollars. People buy things on an impulse and later discover they did not like it so they donate it to the local thrift store. Now it becomes available to you, at a fraction of the price.

⑩ Be a Good Steward / Conserve

Get rid of credit cards. Save up for things instead of buying on impulse. Stay home; stop going out to eat, to the movies, to attractions and expensive vacations. Save on energy by turning lights off when not in use. Line-dry your clothing. Hand-wash your dishes. Carpool. Ditch cable TV. If possible, use the library for the internet, checking out movies, books, or magazines. "Do-It-Yourself" projects are also a good thing. Learn how to do anything from the internet.

What I learned from grandma

I spent a lot of time with my grandmother. She lived through the Great Depression. Being frugal was one of her highest virtues. I remember Christmas and how grandma would carefully unwrap the paper, peeling the tape ever so gently, so as to save the paper for another wrapping. She saved everything and wasted nothing. I can remember rubber band balls made from hundreds of stray rubber bands wrapped around each other until they made a ball. Plastic bags drip-drying over the sink to be used again and again. Hundreds of old twisty-ties bundled together in her junk drawer alongside neatly-stacked pencils of every size. She would have that catsup bottle turned upside down until the last drop could be coaxed out. Later, when it was all dripped out, she would fill it partway with water to grab the last juice to add to a soup.

When clothing wore through, she had her mending station forever set up. She would darn up old socks where the toes wore through. When her stockings had a run, she would get out the clear nail polish to keep it from getting out of hand. If the hole was beyond the repair of the polish, she would close the hole up with some kind of matching nylon string. Pants were patched and repatched. Dresses were made to fit several sizes.

She would take out the hem several times for me so I could wear it more years as I was growing. Rags were precious. They were used for making braided rugs or quilts. She found a use for everything. Even the eggshells would be repurposed to amend her kitchen garden soil.

Anything she did not serve fresh from the garden was canned. She had hundreds of jars of tomatoes in her cellar. She made sauerkraut from the cabbages and also made pickles. Grandma was known for her picked beets and eggs. Everything was made from scratch. Even in her eighties she was making big batches of bread with her bare hands. When it was berry season, she would be out there picking with the rest of us young hens. Freezer jam was made to spread on her fresh bread.

She refinished or reupholstered any furniture that started to look old. On holidays, she went all out. She saved her little decorations from half a century ago and made them do. She had a place for everything and made sure to ration her stores. When her children were little, they all wore cloth diapers with pins. Grandma used an old wringer washer and hung everything out to dry.

I was so blessed to learn from her. She taught me how to be frugal in so many ways. I will never forget our hands together, punching into the dough for the first time. I was learning a skill that would feed my family for a lifetime. Now I bake bread with my girls and can (preserve) our harvest. It is such a satifying feeling to know you did it with your own two hands. She inspired me to use cloth diapers, refinish old furniture, and learn to sew. After her passing, I felt that I had lost a good teacher. Her example fuels me each day. I know I am carrying on a legacy each time I teach others how to make things from scratch.

Eventually, I found other people to teach me. I was able to learn how to mend, sew, can, butcher animals we raised, make noodles, soap, and many other things from the Amish. They still live very much like my grandma. Somehow, if just for a moment, it made me feel like the world was standing still when I was sitting in their homes in quiet splendor, where the only sound you could hear was that of the treadle sewing machine clacking away or the tea kettle singing.

Little by little our world loses touch with its roots. They grab for their smart phones instead of that old-fashioned cookbook to find a recipe. Times are changing, but some things will never change. There will always be a need for people to be frugal and live by the old saying that Grandma always lived by, "Use it up, wear it out, make it do, or do without."

My metaphor: fashionable or old-fashioned?

- I would rather be a Rag Doll than a Barbie Doll; my cloth is worn from hours of working on the homestead. My hands are wrinkled from washing clothes and dishes, scrubbing pans, and baking bread. I would rather my hands be withered and my fingernails broken off to the nubs, than painted to perfection, and have a hard time grabbing things because my nails were too soft and pretty. I would rather that my hair was frizzy and wispy, held in a bun because it is practical and the hair doesn't get into the food I make, than to have my hair perfectly wavy and golden to attract. My eyes are wrinkled from hours of smiling and working in the sunshine, not darkened with makeup. I rub the eyes and they do not smear. Barbie can have her chiseled and boney figure while I will keep my fluff. It is much softer to hug!

- I would rather live in a shack than a mansion on a hilltop. The creaky wooden floors would be filled with many hours of sweeping, baking, and children underfoot. The shack would be tiny, and only a few could fit; but it would be cozy, while the mansion would be cold and lonesome. The electric bill for the mansion would be enormous while the shack would be free. More money to buy things to raise on the farm. Oh, and by the way, by the time you pay interest on a nice home, you could have bought one shack in that year, had it paid off and the rest of the money you make is a bonus. Of course, you would not need as much income, so you could have a small business raising chickens or produce to pay for any other expenses. Plus, you would have more time with family. I think most of us would rather that. The bigger the house, the more house to clean and the more <u>stuff</u> you acquire. And <u>stuff</u> just takes up space and is seldom used. I

like to think of the home as a digestive system; you take things in, but in most cases you do not get the waste out. Keeping your stuff going out makes life simpler. Only keep what is needed. When I spring clean it is such a relief to get rid of things. It makes life more organized and simple.

- I would much rather eat homegrown food than eat at a restaurant. I like to know where my food comes from. I like to prepare it. I put a lot of love in my cooking, and I love to share it with my family, knowing they are getting the very best I have to offer. Cleaning up is fun too, when everyone pitches in. It is fun to live through the seasons, growing food and raising livestock. It is very satisfying.

- I would rather ride in a horse-drawn carriage than in a fancy car. You can keep your car. I know I do not have a horse-drawn carriage, but I know that I would like it a lot. I would even take a beater over a fancy car. As long as I can get from point A to point B, that is all that matters. I guess I like to be home most times. The older I get, the more I want to be with my family and stay home. I am content with that! How about that! There is so much to do at the homestead that running around is just not as fulfilling to me anymore. I like to keep life simple.

- Keep it simple.

Keeper Tip...
- Use it up.
- Wear it out.
- Make it do.
- Or do without.

Tales of Victory...

Working Together, Doing Things Right

John and I have not always worked together when it comes to finances, but we do feel it's best if we communicate together and we are both on the same page and know what's going on. We do not sit down and pay the bills together, I (Beth) do all of that and at the end of the day let him know what I did and how much money is left. I know some husbands do pay all the bills and handle the finances and that's great, my husband is just busy and appreciates me willing to keep up with this and to keep the lights on. Now my husband trusts me! Yes, I just said that; there was a time in my marriage when I would sneak money and buy a new outfit or spend money on nails or a new purse, and then he was always wondering where in the world all of our money went! After I got saved and learned that my husband should trust me and I should be honest, I started the practice of involving him in the bill paying and grocery budget process. It lets him know that I'm being honest and that he can trust I have our family's best interests at heart. We are a TEAM!

With that said, we are by no means experts, and I'm sure it could be done better; this is what works for our family of 12 (we have 10 children under the age of 12! Yes, you read that right!). I know we have a lot of children, and we love it. A big family is so much fun; not easy, but fun.

My husband runs an automotive shop from our home, and so our monthly income varies. It's feast or famine around here, we always say! I have no idea week-to-week how much money I will have for groceries. When times are good I try to prepare for the hard times, buying extra beans and rice, flour, popcorn that I keep in buckets and other dry goods that can extend the food a little longer while we wait to be paid. We are "boring" eaters, I have learned you do not need to have a fancy menu plan to make everyone happy. We eat the same things all the time. I have a Mr. Steady husband and he is just fine with that! We eat lots of Mexican-style meals and a lot of just meat and veggies. I bake a treat once a week and we have non-GMO popcorn as a snack most days—just some coconut oil or real butter and sea salt with a little sugar and—BAM!—KETTLE CORN. My kids love it and it's cheap, easy and healthy. Many of you young mothers out there get caught up (as I did) in trying to keep up with the latest and greatest this or that when it comes to food. I say, "keep it simple"—it makes life so much easier and you will have more time to spend loving on those babies that grow up so quickly. And, when meals are simple, they learn to cook them, too, and that is such a great help!

Our regular house bills are all due at basically the same time. And in a stickler, we make sure we save the money to pay the bills first, and then I shop for food with the rest. God always provides just enough! We do not do a lot of extra things, but we love playing together and hanging out with friends and family! That's what life is all about: God, family and friends!

I have mastered figuring out how to make a meal out of the strangest things! And with the internet today, you can too. It's a wealth of help in times of need! We are currently living in an RV with all 12 of us! We are living the dream, working as a family to build a home in the middle of 64 acres, debt-free! It's not always quiet or easy, but we are working towards a goal of learning to work together and teach our kids the importance of faith and family. We are able to teach our children the value of money, what things cost, and the importance of hard work. We pray and ask God to provide. The kids see God's provision for our family time after time, and it has no doubt made an impact on their life already. Remember to involve your children in prayer time. It's such a sweet thing to hear a little one pray!

Erin has been such an inspiration for me to work harder and keep on going, even when it's hard and the road is tough! Smile through the pain and just keep doing what you can. Her zeal for life is contagious! You can't help but be excited when you're around her. I'm so blessed to call her my friend.

~Beth Determan

Making a simple monthly budget

If you desire to be more frugal, you might consider creating a budget. When you write down where all the money is going, you get a better picture of your financial situation. You can cut expenses here and there to free up more money which can be used for the more essential needs of your family.

Simple Monthly Budget		Actual Expenses	Over/Under Budget
PROJECTED LIVING EXPENSES			
$	MUST EXPENSES		
$800.00	Mortgage or rent		
$120.00	Insurance (home & car)		
$	MUST VARIABLE		
$50.00	Gas/Transportation		
$400.00	Food/Groceries		
$150.00	Electricity/Water/LP		
$60.00	Medical Expenses		
$	OPTIONAL FIXED		
$60.00	Landline telephone/Cell phone		
$60.00	Internet Service		
$	OPTIONAL VARIABLE		
$50.00	Clothing/Toiletries/Misc.		
$50.00	Leisure Activities		
$1800.00	TOTAL PROJECTED EXPENSE		
$3000.00	TOTAL INCOME	$1200.00 TOTAL SAVINGS	

How it works

Add up your paychecks and find your total monthly income. Project what you think your living expenses will be. As the month goes by, jot down the actual expenses. Remember to save all your receipts so you can have an accurate account of what is actually spent throughout the month. After you have gotten through the month, write down the differences in whether you went over or under your projected budget. It is fun to see how much money you can save by being careful with your spending. All the money that is saved can be used for an unexpected building expense or a vacation you have been dreaming about, for example. When you have more money, you can give more when needs arise within the church or on the mission field. Having a financial cushion is vital.

Being wise with your money gives you more flexibility. You can slowly pay off your debts, if you have them. Becoming debt-free should be a desire for every Christian family.

> *"Owe no man any thing, but to love one another:*
> *for he that loveth another hath fulfilled the law."*
> **Romans 13:8**

The envelope system

The envelope system dates back to when my grandparents were first married—but it never gets old. Some time-tested wisdom is still passed on to future generations. When you put your allowed money into an envelope, there is less temptation to go over your budget. If you walk into the grocery store with an envelope holding a one hundred dollar bill, you will also arm yourself with a calculator, pencil, and paper. You have to be careful with every penny when you know you have a limit. This is a great way to stay within your budget. If you do not use all of the money in the envelope, you can save the remaining balance. You will start to feel less strapped when you have a system in place to keep you from spending money impulsively.

Helpful resources on budgeting: www.daveramsey.com and www.crown.org

"The best things in life are free"

It does not have to cost anything to make a memory. Build family memories doing things that are FREE. To name a few...

- Go on a bike ride.
- Go fishing.
- Go for a hike.
- Go on a picnic.
- Make smores.
- Cook over a fire.
- Go camping.
- Play a card game.
- Play kickball.
- Go to the beach.
- Visit a historical site.
- Have a movie night with popcorn.
- Go on a field trip.
- Go on a scenic drive.
- Play a fun board game.
- Have an art contest.
- Do a theatrical skit.
- Hold a concert in your living room.
- Have a pillow fight.
- Make a cake or cookies.
- Go on a walk.
- Make a fort inside or outside.

Recipe to be a GOOD WOMAN

Proverbs 31:14—A good woman is prudent. She is a capable, wise shopper.

"She is like the merchants' ships; she bringeth her food from afar."

Key words: *is like, bringeth*

Frugal, not wasteful, using economy and good management.

Time-Tested Wisdom...

Raising Kids on a Tight Budget

Raising four children on a tight budget requires everyone to live within their means—parents and children alike. We implemented a system with our children, beginning when our youngest was in first grade, where everyone got an allowance twice a month on payday. This money was not tied to any chores or behavior expectations. The kids were taught how to budget the money because they were responsible for paying for their clothes, school supplies, gifts and entertainment.

Attending Christian schools, they wore uniforms, most of which could be purchased used from other folks in the school community. To stretch their dollars even further, we found families which had children a year or two older than each of ours and got to "shop" through their clothes as they outgrew them.

The kids learned that school supplies could be reused from year to year and the plain items worked just as well as the fancy ones.

As far as gifts went, the four of them exchanged names at Christmastime and had a set limit on how much to spend on each other. We didn't expect them to buy gifts for us, but they did have some birthday parties for friends throughout the year, and also used part of this money to give back to the church or other charitable organizations.

When the family did fun things together, we covered the expenses for everyone. If the kids wanted to go to movies, eat out or do other activities with friends, that was their responsibility. If there wasn't any money left in their envelope for the pay period, they either didn't go, found a way to earn extra money, or negotiated with another family member for a temporary loan.

All of the kids are now successful young adults with college degrees working full-time in their chosen fields and live in different areas of the country. They are excellent money managers. It takes some work to implement this system when children are young but it definitely pays off in the end.

~Amanda Lauer

Time-Tested Wisdom...

What's for Dinner?

     I am a middle-aged mother with nine kids. I live on a farm and our meals are what you would classify as "Farm Fresh." My mama always had food on the table so it is just normal for me to keep that tradition. I am amazed at how many mamas out there have a meal at our home and tell me, "Wow. This is such a good meal. I never cook like this!" I ask them, "Well, what do you eat then?"

     I can't stress enough the importance of making meals. Just do it. If you are a wife and mother, food should be on your mind. Home-cooked meals are not optional here. We have a tight budget because we work on our family farm. If we grow it, we cook it. Many women buy boxed convenience foods, like biscuit mix. It may take a few minutes longer, but when you make the biscuits from scratch, you are saving so much money. Not only are you saving money, but more often than not, food that is made from scratch is far healthier for your family. In turn, it helps your husband. He can work less because it takes less to buy the food you make.

     People say they are too busy to cook. We are so busy on our farm. It is a different kind of busy. We work to eat in a different way. Some days we may be butchering 200 chickens for other people and other days we are processing our own chickens after raising them for a time. It is all work—some work pays in dollars, other work pays by literally putting food on the table. The end is the same—food to grace our table each day. Eating is basic and necessary.

     As the head cook on our farm, I strive to instill these principles into the lives of my children. We are always together as a family so they learn as a default. Most of our time is spent in the kitchen or around the table. The kids are always helping with something. My older daughters make biscuits. If biscuits are planned for the next morning's breakfast, I have my daughter mix the dry ingredients that evening. In the morning, all I have to do is put in the buttermilk and bake them. So simple!

     If you feel too busy to cook, I would recommend using a crock pot. You can put a few things in there, let it do the cooking for you, and later you have a nice meal to grace your table.

~Terri Taylor

Chapter Ten
Virtuous Hospitality

*"She riseth also while it is yet night, and giveth meat to her household,
and a portion to her maidens."*
Proverbs 31:15

A virtuous woman is ready to serve others at all hours

She is on-call. Whether it be waking in the night feeding babies, or nursing her sick children to health, she is ready for the task. No matter the cost, she gives of herself fully in the hour in which she is needed most. When her husband has a job that requires him to rise early, she is at his side making him breakfast and packing him a lunch. She is ready to serve even if she is tired. If a friend is having troubles, she is a phone call away. If she is lying awake at night, she is thinking about others and praying for their needs.

She is not selfish

When you become a wife, you become a helper. You are your husband's right hand. When I first got married, I was ill-equipped. I did not know the first thing about serving his needs. Looking out for ME was what I knew best. I was not raised in a home where the Bible was preached. There were no lessons on "How to be a Good Help Meet to your Husband." But if I would have just opened my eyes, I could have seen it. My mother worked a full-time job as a nurse, but she was always there for my dad and for anyone. Little did I know that she was a good example of a helper with a true servant's heart.

She never failed to have a meal on the table. Planning way ahead for each meal was something at which she excelled. I never had to worry that supper would be late. Breakfast was always available at the crack of dawn. The food was always fresh, always good, and always there. If my dad was planning a hunting trip, she would fix every meal ahead for him, so all he had to do was pop it in the oven to heat it up. I wish now I would have spent my days learning from her example rather than pursuing all the many things I had interest in while yet at home.

My mom was always on-call. She would stay up all night with me if I was sick. When my small children had an illness, she would help me nurse them back to health. She did not consider her risk of infection. She did not worry about getting dirty with vomit.

When I was young I did not appreciate my mother. I see now what a selfless person she was. She was always willing to serve. Always early, ready to feed anyone at any time. Everyone knew that they could count on her. People would call all through the night if they had a need or a question. When I had my accident, she took a leave of absence from work to take me into her home and care for me, day-in and day-out. When I would scream in pain, she would be right at my bedside, holding me. Every time I needed to go to the doctor, she would haul me around in my wheelchair. When I returned home to my family, she would make meals for the children and help clean our home.

I would forget to eat. That was always my biggest trouble. For some reason, I just do not feel hunger like normal people do. When I would have a friend visit for the day in my growing up years, I would never offer them food unless my mother had prepared it for us. I brought that into my marriage. I did not think about cooking or feeding my husband. I did not know *how* to cook. I resorted to macaroni and cheese or ravioli from a can. I could have learned from my mother, who is an excellent cook, but I just did not have an interest.

When I became a mother, I HAD to feed my baby. It was the best thing for me; becoming a mother taught me how to serve. God puts an urgency in our hearts to care for our wee ones. They look up into our eyes and we know that they are hungry. With a baby at my breast all day and night, I was being trained by God to serve. I learned to serve from the long nights with babies that needed me. I was the one who took them to the hospital and sat by their bedsides. Laying aside all things to be there for them was something that I did without thinking. God puts that desire in our hearts as mothers.

I started having a desire to learn how to cook and how to be a better wife. It did not come naturally to me at first, but I soon learned the art of being a wife and mother. I started visiting my grandmother each week to learn things like how to bake bread or how to slow-cook a roast in a crockpot. I still remember our hands punching into the dough together. Years later, my hands were punching into the dough with my daughter's hands. Our hands were intertwining for a greater purpose than just bread for a day. It was a skill that could feed my family for a lifetime. A skill that will come in handy for my daughters and their future families.

Meals

Making meals is something I love to do now. I love cooking. Little by little I am still learning to have meals ready at a certain time. My husband feels so much love when, after a long tiresome day at work, he walks into the door to the smell of food cooking. He has never made me feel bad about all the years he came home and had to help me figure out what we were going to eat at the last minute.

I have been working on having breakfast each morning for my family. My kids are old enough to make their own, but it sure is nice to have a meal waiting on the table. If there is a meal, there is a prayer; and that is a wonderful start to our day. Fresh buttermilk biscuits and eggs never get old. Making a practice of setting the table for a nice meal is such a good thing. Everyone feels relaxed and ready to get more things done in their day.

Planning ahead

The simple task of planning ahead saves a lot of frustration. Before bed each night, I am determined to think about what we are having for breakfast the next morning. After breakfast, I determine to think about what I will make for lunch. After lunch, I determine to figure out what we are going to make for supper. Sometimes I make more than enough food for lunch so that there is plenty leftover to eat for supper. When I make a BIG meal, I try to make it stretch for another meal or two. If I make a chicken dinner one evening, I fix a shepherd's pie for the following day. I have enough meat left to layer into the bottom of a baking pan with gravy poured over and mashed potatoes spooned on top. I store it in the refrigerator overnight. The next day, I put it into the oven an hour before mealtime. I reserve the bones for soup the following day. It is really easy when you plan ahead.

"The early bird gets the worm"

This is an old saying. My dad was always an early riser and taught me the wisdom of waking early. When you wake early, you have more time in the day. It sounds crazy, but it is true. For most of my life I have lived by this wisdom and it has proven to add a lot of productivity to my days. The days feel less rushed and I have more TIME. Time is precious. I want to wake early and give a portion to my dear husband and my children. I want them to remember me like I remember my mother—as a woman who was always ready and willing to serve.

"Cause me to hear thy lovingkindness in the morning; for in thee do I trust:
cause me to know the way wherein I should walk;
for I lift up my soul unto thee."
Psalm 143:8

"They are new every morning: great is thy faithfulness.
The LORD is my portion, saith my soul; therefore will I hope in him.
The LORD is good unto them that wait for him, to the soul that seeketh him."
Lamentations 3:23-25

MEAL PLANNING 101

Since this has been an enduring problem for me, I decided to make myself a 14-day meal plan that I could follow. It has revolutionized my world; to think it was as simple as having a game plan! I just open my cupboard door to reveal my meal plan, and I instantly know what we are having for each meal. I picked out meals that everyone likes and would not mind repeating twice a month. I mean, who could say no to pizza two days out of the month?

If you struggle with **"What are we having for dinner?"** questions, maybe you should jump on my bandwagon and make a meal plan. I am sick of having a blank face when I am called to give an account. No more of that in my home. I am getting control over the meals. Since I have been on our 14-day meal plan, there has been a renewed sense of direction, peace, contentment, and order. Instead of scrambling around in the pantry trying to throw something together, I am ready an hour ahead of time and the table is set!

My husband has been so blessed. He likes coming into a home filled with the aroma of food. With regular meals, I am able to teach my girls how to prepare each of the entrées with success. When I am busy, I can refer my girls to the list; they know we have the ingredients, and they happily make a meal. What a victory for me! If I could get ahold of this principle, there is hope for anyone!

14-Day Meal Plan

Sunday	Monday	Tuesday	Wednesday	Thursday	Friday	Saturday
Week #1						
Bacon and eggs Beans and rice for church Tacos and salad	Scrambled eggs and biscuits Cheese quesadillas Salsa Fettucini Alfredo with chicken Salad	Cornbread and honey Egg salad sandwiches Hard-shelled tacos Salad	Eggs with toast Hamburger, noodles and veggies Chicken dinner, mashed potatoes, green beans	Granola Chicken Soup Shepherd's Pie with salad	Cereal Pork, fried sliced potatoes, bell peppers Pizza	Dutch Babies Lasagna and salad Hamburger and fries
Week #2						
Cinnamon biscuits with scrambled eggs Beans and rice for church Tacos and salad	Egg bake Bacon bagel with cream cheese Meatloaf, salad and baked potatoes	Oatmeal bake with fruit or parfait Oriental stir-fry Beef roast boiled dinner	Sausage, scrambled eggs and biscuits Beef fajitas with salad Cheesy potatoes and grilled meat	Pancakes Cornbread and chili soup Mexican haystack	Cereal Mexican casserole with leftover haystack dinner Chicken, rice, broccoli, and cheese casserole	French toast Chicken Curry with lentils Grilled cheese and popcorn

How to make a meal plan

Making a meal plan is simple. Just sit down some afternoon and start thinking about all the meals you have ever made. Scribble down all the meals that stand out in your mind as "successful." Successful would mean that it went over well; your husband likes it and the kids like it. Then, if you have a computer with a calendar program, you can type in your meals for each day of the week just as I have. If you do not have a computer, take a ruler and make a calendar on a sheet of paper. Fill in your meal ideas by hand and you are now in business!

If you do not remember how to prepare each meal, you'll need to grab your recipe cards and have them handy. You could even put them in a photo album to keep them safe from mess and in a place where you can get them FAST! I know everyone has their own tastes; but if you like what I have on my meal plan, use it, by all means!

The shopping list

When you have a meal plan, shopping is more productive because you know what is actually needed. Whatever is on your 14-day meal plan, you can add the ingredients you need by food group, so it is easy to find at the supermarket. Here is my **Week #1** Grocery List for an example:

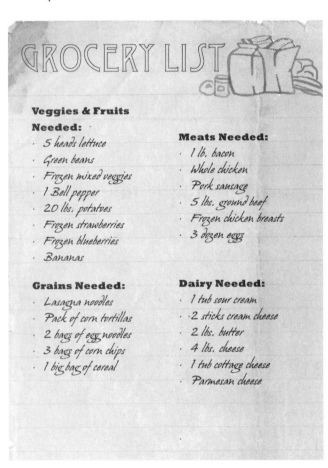

GROCERY LIST

Veggies & Fruits Needed:
- 5 heads lettuce
- Green beans
- Frozen mixed veggies
- 1 Bell pepper
- 20 lbs. potatoes
- Frozen strawberries
- Frozen blueberries
- Bananas

Grains Needed:
- Lasagna noodles
- Pack of corn tortillas
- 2 bags of egg noodles
- 3 bags of corn chips
- 1 big bag of cereal

Meats Needed:
- 1 lb. bacon
- Whole chicken
- Pork sausage
- 5 lbs. ground beef
- Frozen chicken breasts
- 3 dozen eggs

Dairy Needed:
- 1 tub sour cream
- 2 sticks cream cheese
- 2 lbs. butter
- 4 lbs. cheese
- 1 tub cottage cheese
- Parmesan cheese

Lessons in Etiquette
Hospitality

Hospitality or Hosting Etiquette is something I have always had a hard time mastering. Because I do not want people to fuss over me, I find it hard to know what is the proper way to host a guest. All throughout history, hosting guests has been an important part of life. It was a time when you could show respect to your neighbors or people of importance.

Medieval hospitality

For instance, when a king would visit his Lords and Ladies, special attention was made to every detail. Nothing went amiss. The fattest hog was slaughtered and the banqueting table was set so that the king would have all the luxuries of home in a far away land. The king would travel with his queen, along with his knights, squires, and the other members of his court. Preparations for their visit began weeks before their arrival. The manor home had to be cleaned from top to bottom, the rooms readied, and provisions had to be gathered for the great feast. The Lords' serfs would hunt for game and the Ladies' servants would help grind the wheat for the baking. The hogs and deer were turned on spits, and great big pots of boiled stew would be bubbling over fires on the kitchen hearth. Entertainment was worked into the plan. Jesters, dancers, and musicians would all practice for the great event.

When the King and all his people came, the trumpets sounded and a red carpet was rolled out. He sat down to the great feast while listening to the music and visiting with all his extended royal family. If this feast impressed him, he would be back again next year at the same time.

The evolution of hospitality

The emphasis of making a home ready for company has changed over the years in the United States of America since its foundation.

Colonial times

At the founding of our nation, women enjoyed entertaining her guests. She would take pride in showing off her home, and also provide tea to her guests. All the way back to the colonial times, the woman of the home would be ready at all times for a call. There were no phones, so you could not plan when someone would pop in for a house call. She made sure her home was presentable each afternoon. All her work would be done before lunch and the tea kettle on. As she sat in great anticipation for a possible guest, she would do some needlework. The children were to be quiet and reserved during calling hours.

When a guest arrived, they would be greeted and offered the nicest chair in the parlor. The lady of the home would place her finest china cup and saucer in front of the guest and begin pouring the tea. Soon she would set a plate of tea cakes before her guest as she knew the guest may have come a long way and would need refreshment. The guest felt a warm welcome and every need was met. Things were quiet and visiting was commenced. They may have talked for an hour until the calling hour was up. The guest did not want to stay too long or wear out her welcome since it was common knowledge that a woman had dinner to prepare, and that was to be respected.

Civil War era

During the times surrounding the Civil War, women practiced a great measure of hospitality. It was a measure of who you were if you could provide good hospitality to your friends and neighbors. The home was prettied and cleaned. The tea was on. The food was prepared. This is where the South gets their long-standing reputation for hospitality. It is known as *Southern Hospitality*. They would open their homes to anyone, offering fresh beds for sleeping, and hot meals for the filling.

Southern hospitality at its finest

We recently had the experience of Southern Hospitality in Mississippi. We were traveling down for a wedding of a close family friend. We were coming from afar, and thought we would have to spend a bunch of extra money on food, gas, and lodging. The bride's parents let us know there was a nice man who went to their church offering his home to anyone who needed it. I accepted the offer and we headed down the road. I had no idea who this man was, nor if we would be sleeping on a floor or in a back room. Visions of potential situations ran through my mind as we rolled through the beautiful countryside.

When we arrived, Mr. Travis greeted us with a warm smile and a handshake. He brought us into his home and it was just beautiful. He had spent days cleaning it with his family helper, Miss Ann. Miss Ann had been their helper her entire life. Her mother was a help to his late grandparents and parents who owned the family farm. Mr. Travis grew up with Ann and they became like family. The beds were made with fresh bedding. Fluffy white towels were stacked in the bathrooms. Soap and other bathroom provisions were available to us. And the snacks—we do not usually buy snacks and sweets, but it was a fun treat for the children. It was the highlight of the entire weekend for them. And soda—they never get soda. They could hardly believe their eyes. He opened his refrigerator to reveal all the food he bought for us. Wow! Mr. Travis did not even know us but he treated us with the highest regard. He wanted us to be blessed and well-fed. And then he asked us if he could have Miss Ann come and fix us some breakfast. I could tell it would thrill his heart to bless us like that so I said, "Yes, thank you so much!" My husband felt so guilty with all Mr. Travis did to make us feel welcome. I told him that this man probably enjoys blessing us much more than we understand. We should just relax, be blessed, and be thankful.

I learned so much more in that short stay at the home of Mr. Travis than I have learned in a long time. I have never been the best person for hospitality. I often forget to ask someone if they need a glass of water. I never serve tea and because I often forget to eat, I forget to offer snacks as well. We enjoyed hearing Mr. Travis' stories about the old dairy operation and all they did to keep it going in hard times. The views were spectacular and Miss Ann's biscuits were second to none. Listening to her tell of how she helped the family all these years just melted my heart. I wished I could have sat and learned from her for many more days. She is a good example of kind serving and a thankful heart. Watching her make breakfast was the highlight of my weekend, besides the beautiful wedding. She is a treasure. What an example of the love of Christ. We felt like royalty at this home and I want to take something from that experience—a lesson on hospitality.

Hosting short visits

- Before your guest arrives, make sure to carefully inspect the home, especially the bathrooms. Pay close attention to the toilet paper supply, have a fresh towel available for drying hands, make sure there is soap, that the sink and toilet are clean and operational, and the garbage is taken out.

- Tidy the home and make it as presentable as you can so there are no items on the floor that your guest will have to trip over.
- Make sure the home is a comfortable temperature. If you have air conditioning, turn it on for guests as some of us try to be careful how much we use expensive heating and cooling features. Make sure to have a fan on if you do not have air conditioning in the hotter months. If it is in the cooler months, make sure you have the heater going so your guests do not get a chill.
- Prepare a little snack in advance and arrange it on a fancy plate, if you have one.
- When your guest comes to the door, greet them and invite them into your home.
- Ask to take their belongings and put them in a safe place, or hang up their coats for them.
- Present them a comfortable place to sit down.
- Offer them a glass of ice water. If you have other things like tea, milk, soda, or juice, offer your best to them.
- Bring the plate of snacks out for them to enjoy while you are visiting.
- Do not get uptight about a mess or the noise of their children. Try to focus on them. Treat them the way you would want to be treated. A nervous look can make a person feel unwelcome. Just take a deep breath. You can clean up everything after they leave. Try to relax and make your guests feel at home while they are with you.

Hosting longer, overnight visits

- Before your guests arrive, make sure their bedroom is deeply cleaned, fresh sheets are on the bed, and the bathroom they are using will be extra clean. Provide them with enough bath towels, soap, and washcloths necessary for their stay. Show them where extra pillows and blankets are in case they need them for some reason.

- Offer meals at regular times. Find out when they are used to eating because some people are very worried about nap times for smaller children. You do not want to throw off their eating and napping cycles.
- Make sure to ask what they can and cannot eat. Some people have allergies to certain foods, and you would not want to have them hungry or in the hospital.
- Find out if they enjoy movies and see if there is anything they would like to watch. If they do not like to watch movies, then make sure you do not have the TV on at any time while they are there so as not to become a stumbling block for them and their standards.
- Try to adjust to them so they feel at ease in your home. Make sure they have plenty to eat at all times, providing snack times throughout the days they are there.
- Have drinks available at all times. Show them where the glasses are and where they can find drinks if they need them.
- Let them know they are welcome to do laundry if needed. Show them where the laundry facility is and how to use the machine.
- Allow them use of the phone if they need to make a call. Give them keys to the home if they are out and about, and need access to the home at some point. The last thing you would want is your guest sitting outside waiting for you to let them in.
- If they need Internet, share your Wi-Fi code with them.
- If there are things going on in the community, make sure to invite them along.
- Give them directions to shopping centers and restaurants or other places of interest so they that can take an afternoon break if they would like to see things in your area.
- Above all, make them feel rested. Do not get uptight if they do not do things your way. Allow them the freedom to be whomever they are. Enjoy your time with them.

Giving someone the royal treatment is a blessing. Making your home a fun place to visit is a good feeling for any housekeeper. What is even more special is that our Lord is preparing a place for us. He has his banqueting table set, and he will welcome us one day to dine with Him. What a feast it will be!

TABLE MANNERS 101

Yes, there are table manners still today. I never had table manners. When I was growing up, I would actually sit on my knees or lean back in the chair with my knees propped up onto the table. My plate was on my knees. Sounds more like a gymnastics routine of balancing than eating a meal! I was not that interested in food, so apparently I did not care about behaving properly when seated at the dinner table.

When I got married, I was introduced to a whole new way of eating. My mother-in-law would sit very tall at the table—very proper, indeed. I did not get the real concept until she started trying to train my children how to be polite and have table manners. They were used to grabbing food from the middle of the table. We would reach across another person to get the salt shaker, and there were sudden bodily noises that would burst forth from time to time. Talking with our mouths full was not uncommon. We did not eat out often or have many dinner parties, so it was easy for us to fall under the radar. Because I am intuitive, I was able to take what instruction she was passing on to the children and train myself. I started watching British drama movies and observed their table manners.

Many of these same silent rules apply today. We may not talk about it with others but we all notice when someone is rude or inconsiderate. Some people are downright revolting to eat with. I have seen it all. One person I know clears their throat so loudly, you can hear them pulling up whatever is clogging their sinuses. They will even do this in a nice restaurant. The other guests in the restaurant look like they have just lost their appetite after hearing that noise. Yet I have seen others blow their noses into their napkins—gross! Dripping food down their front is another issue!

Noticing others' behavior at the table has been one of my best teaching moments on etiquette. You see things that make you cringe and you know you'd better not do the same. When you practice table manners, you are actually learning to be more considerate and treating others the way you would want to be treated. It is within the law of unlimited love and kindness to offer that kind of respect and consideration to others.

Table setting

First things first: There is a proper way to set the table. This has somehow been made optional in our modern culture, but 50 years ago you would have made a fool of yourself if you did not place the utensils in the correct order. Everything has order. There is a place for everything needed in a meal. Try this just for fun sometime. When we have Thanksgiving Dinner at our home, I enjoy getting out Grandma's old china dishes. You can find really pretty, old china dishes at thrift stores for very little money. They sell them for less because, oftentimes, several of the dishes from the set are missing.

Formal place setting

Before placing the dishes, you need to cover the table with a linen tablecloth (or whatever you may have available). Table linens are traditional in setting for a dinner party. You see them more commonly at fancy restaurants and wedding banquets. Now place your dishes in the proper order. A large dinner napkin is folded in half, with the fold facing your body. A luncheon napkin should be opened completely. All tableware is placed about 1½ inches from the edge of the table.

Napkin etiquette

Place the napkin on your lap after everyone is seated, and after the host has placed his/her napkin. Never wipe your mouth with the napkin; instead, you blot or gently touch your mouth with the napkin. Never use the napkin for blowing your nose! The napkin should remain on your lap during the course of the meal. If you need to get up from the table, place your napkin in your chair, and push your chair back under the table. Upon returning to the table, return the napkin to your lap.

Salad is served

When practicing formal table etiquette, note that you will use each piece of your silverware working from the outside in toward your plate. You begin eating *after* everyone has been served and after the host says their grace. Sit up straight and bring the food to your mouth, instead of pulling your head over your food. Pace yourself. Do not seem ravished. You do not want to finish your food before the other guests. To them, you may seem desperate to eat, which is not a good thing.

Pass the bread, please

When the bread is served, take one, **never two,** and pass the bread basket to the person beside you. Never reach across another guest or across the table when you need something. Be polite; ask, "Please pass the bread." When buttering the bread, add butter to your bread and butter plate instead of double-dipping into the main butter dish. You will want to break the bread instead of cutting it. Butter one bite-sized piece at a time. Never butter the entire slice of bread or slice the roll in half to butter the half. Take your time and enjoy this formal experience.

When sharing sauces or dips at your dinner party, NEVER dip your food into the sauce dish! Instead, take a small amount and spoon it on your bread and butter plate. Now you can apply the dip one bite at a time.

The salad fork is to the outside of your place setting. It is there for you to use first, since in most fine dining experiences the salad is served first. After you have eaten your salad, the dinner will soon be served, so you will place your salad fork across the top of the plate to signify that you are finished.

The main course

When the main course is served, you will take up your dinner fork and your dinner knife. Yes, there is a proper way to cut your food. You achieve this by placing the fork in your left hand and the knife in your right hand. Using your thumb and index finger, begin cutting with the knife. All food should be cut with the knife into bite-sized pieces before taking it to your mouth. Do this by holding the food with the fork and cutting with the knife. It is inappropriate to shove large pieces of food into your mouth, or bite off from a larger slice. When feeding yourself, place the knife on the edge of the plate with blade facing in. You will switch your fork from the left hand to the right hand when putting the food into your mouth. Keep in mind, once you pick up a piece of silverware from the table, it should never touch the table again.

Table talk

There will be times when you will engage in conversation while eating. It is best to set down your utensils while speaking. You never want to start talking with food in your mouth. While talking, you will place your knife in the one o'clock position with blade turned inward, and your fork is placed at the four o'clock position with its tines up. When you are done speaking, you can pick up where you left off on your plate. Remember, never seem hurried.

Keeper Tip...
Conversational Etiquette...
- Maintain eye contact.
- Avoid dominating the conversation.
- Keep the conversation positive.
- Don't bring up controversial topics.
- Don't ask personal questions.
- Be relaxed and friendly.

Now that you have finished your meal, place your utensils back onto the plate all lined up at the four o'clock position. The fork will be placed with its tines up and the knife with its blade faced inward. When everyone has finished their meals, loosely place the napkin to the left of your plate. I must confess, I am still learning to mind my manners! There is still hope.

The Concept of Handmaidens

"She riseth also while it is yet night, and giveth meat to her household, and a portion to her **maidens.**"
Proverbs 31:15

A handmaiden is historically a female servant. When I lived in Peru, South America for three months, I found it very interesting that almost every family had a handmaiden. It is actually very common in many cultures around the world to have a live-in maid. In our country, we seldom see this. You tend to see it more with the upper class. They hire nannies or cleaning ladies to help with their homemaking.

In Peru, the maiden has her own room in the home and is paid to help. She wakes up early, before the family, and begins preparing breakfast or setting the tea kettle to boil. I would watch as she filled the tubs for laundry and washed all the laundry by hand. She kept busy all day long and sometimes had time off when she would go out with her friends. Sometimes the lady of the home where I stayed would work alongside her maiden and fix a meal with her. The virtuous woman in biblical times is actually serving her servant, which I find fascinating.

Being the maid is a paid position in most countries. In some cases these women are out on the street; they will gladly serve if they can have room and board. This is common in other countries, especially where they do not have government programs to assist the poor. When you are poor, you are destitute. They would be happy if someone would give them a place to stay. It is all in your perspective.

To serve or not to serve

In our country, if someone has a maid, they are judged. Why? Ask yourself why someone would judge this. Some of the main reasons for becoming offended are jealously or lack of understanding. I choose to allow people the freedom to either serve or be served.

I prefer doing things myself. I have a hard time asking for help and I like things done a certain way. I once had a sweet girl offer to give me a hand and it did not work out because I was not good at telling her what to do. I am the type that works alongside people better than having someone do things for me. Everyone is different. Some women have a husband who needs them to help with their family business. If they are able to provide a substantial income, they have a right to hire someone to help in any way they choose.

It is a blessing to be a keeper of the home but the way keeping the home looks in one lady's life may look different in another's. It is never a place to cast judgment. I know several ladies in my community who hire handmaidens to assist with homeschooling their children, help with meal preparation, and do some housecleaning. These women may be keeping up their home in ways which I do not. Maybe they have more time to pursue business endeavors for their family or alongside their husband. Not all women can handle multitasking.

There may be a time when you are ill and need to have help. I used to judge harshly women who had nannies or cleaning ladies. I thought, "Why would they need help? They should be doing that work themselves. How lazy!" Then the Lord allowed me to have some trials which caused me to be bedridden for several years. My home was trashed for awhile. I would hobble and scream in pain while I would frantically try to do some cleaning. My husband would help me back into bed and tell me I could not help clean anymore. That was so difficult. Having him do the cooking, homeschooling, and cleaning was a low blow for me. I felt so useless and terrible. My mother would come and clean for me on the weekends to get the major cleaning caught up. God was merciful; He gave me the help I needed when I needed it the most. It was a gift to be able to be in a spot where I had to be served so that I could have a level of understanding in that area. It was good for me. God knows what is good for us.

Now I am getting better at asking for help. I am also not willing to judge others when they have to ask for help. If I hadn't gone through that time, I would never know.

Preparing handmaidens of the Lord

There are times when other ladies in the community call and ask my girls to help watch their children or clean their homes for them. They get paid to help and they are learning how to be handmaidens. For young ladies, I think it is good for them to learn to be servant-minded. While they are unmarried, they can be a handmaiden for the Lord and do many things to make a difference. I know young ladies who help out missionary families in a foreign land. They enjoy helping at the orphanages. Other girls stand out in the street holding up signs against abortion outside the clinics. Some rally against human trafficking. Helping moms with newborn babies, making meals, and giving them a hand around the house is another great way to serve. Life is more fulfilling when you do something to make a difference. These young ladies have such purpose, and God is also preparing them to be wonderful wives and mothers at the same time.

"And be not conformed to this world: but be ye transformed by the renewing of your mind, that ye may prove what is that good, and acceptable, and perfect, will of God."
Romans 12:2

Recipe to be a GOOD WOMAN

Proverbs 31:15—A good woman gets up early and serves others.
"She riseth also, while it is yet night, and giveth meat to her household, and a portion to her maidens."
Key words: *riseth, giveth*
Self-starter, energetic.

Time-Tested Wisdom...
Training Handmaidens

After my first child Jeremiah came along it was a little more difficult working full-time, being a mother, a wife, and best friends with my man. James kept telling me that we worked hard, made money, and that I needed to spend that money to help make my life easier. I grew up poor and it was difficult for me to spend money. I knew I was having a hard time keeping up with housework, cooking, and I was stressed trying to balance work as well. It put stress on our marriage. That is when I realized that I was sacrificing being his Help Meet by trying to be Miss Prudence, and in truth it was not prudent. So, I hired a girl to help with everything from cleaning to handing me vitamins. I spent time teaching her how to keep my life organized, keep us fed, help homeschool and care for my children, and anything else that would give me more time with my man (and family). Jeremiah grew up strapped to me or playing in our office as we worked.

Years have passed and Jeremiah will soon turn nine years old. I have trained many young ladies in how to serve through the passing years. I love investing in their lives and I am grateful for each girl who has acted as my servant. I have paid them well; but they also earned something that money can't buy—experience!

James and I are best friends, work partners, and "people" who never seem to stop growing. He knows his heart is safe with me. I want what is best for him. I want to help him be a man of greatness. I want to de-stress and bring joy and happiness to his life. I want him to thank God for me. It is wonderful being a Help Meet when you truly choose to be. I am so happy, so fulfilled, so blessed, and I look forward to the next ten years with my wonderful, smart and handsome man!

~Shoshanna Easling
Author and Herbalist
Bulk Herb Store

Tales of Victory...
Serving God as a Single Young Lady

As a young, single girl, there are three verses in the Bible that really stick out to me. These three verses are:

Mark 16:15, "And he said unto them, Go ye into all the world, and preach the gospel to every creature."

Proverbs 29:18, "Where there is no vision, the people perish:" and

1 Corinthians 7:34, "There is difference also between a wife and a virgin. The unmarried woman careth for the things of the Lord, that she may be holy both in body and in spirit: but she that is married careth for the things of the world, how she may please her husband."

Being a single girl, I feel called by God to go into the world to preach the Gospel. Now this doesn't mean I have to go to the mission field, although I have; this simply means that we as Christians are supposed to be sharing the Gospel every single day we can. I do not want others to perish without having heard. I feel it is my duty to give the good news of salvation to the lost souls of this world. I want to be wholeheartedly willing to do whatever the Lord should ask of me. His will should be first priority in our lives.

There needs to be a vision in our lives towards serving others and not just ourselves. Especially as young women, we should have a vision to serve God fully, whether it is serving our families with a happy attitude, serving on the mission field, being a pro-life activist, volunteering at a pregnancy center, etc. We need to have our eyes and heart set on the goal to please God in all things. If we are fully serving Him before we are married, then we will be even happier as wives, as we give ourselves completely into serving and loving our husbands the way God wants us to. I can tell you from experience that there is nothing sweeter than growing closer to my Lord and serving Him with my whole heart! It's the most exciting, satisfying (and scariest) thing I have ever done and I can't wait to see what He has for my life in the next 60 years! I am very much looking forward to it! Serving my Lord is amazing and I would NOT exchange it for anything the world has to offer!

Since my conversion three years ago (when I was 16), being a missionary has been on my heart. My main goal is to go as a missionary into Asia; but right now, I am helping fight against abortions here in the US. I go to Nashville every week to stand in front of an abortion mill with my fellow sidewalk counselors, holding up signs and pleading with the women going inside to have mercy on their babies. Some weeks we are rewarded with a couple of girls who change their minds, but we will usually only get 3-5 babies (if that many) saved in a month. This mill does 20-30 abortions three days a week—you do the math! No, this is not easy; we weren't promised that serving God would be. In fact, he calls us blessed if we are persecuted (Matthew 5:10). It's not going to be easy, but it will be the most rewarding and satisfying thing you'll ever do.

Want to get motivated in this area? I recommend the Ray Comfort/Kirk Cameron witnessing series, Way of the Master Training Course. It's well worth the money and effort it takes to become effective in witnessing! Don't wait to start getting the Gospel into the hands of people who have never heard! You will be surprised if you ask people in the streets of the cities and towns if they have ever heard the clear Gospel presented to them in a way they can understand. Most will know the name of Jesus and have some knowledge about God, but how many actually understand their need for a Savior and why? There are a lot of people who will never hear if you don't tell them!

So, I encourage you, if you are a single person, male or female, to get involved in ministry of any kind. Guys, for me, I know I wouldn't consider a man who wasn't actively involved in some kind of mission work. Someone who is out on the front lines sharing their faith; who wants God's will in their life no matter what. As Christians, our main goal in life should be to please the Father in everything—thought, word, deed, etc. Nothing should come between us and doing His will, and His will is that none should perish
(1 Peter 3:9). You may be their only hope; don't let them down.

Get out there; tell someone about Jesus. Their eternity may depend on you telling them.

~19-year-old, Cameron Taylor

The Crown

"A virtuous woman is a crown to her husband: but she that maketh ashamed is as rottenness in his bones" (Proverbs 12:4).

A good woman is a crown to her husband. She can make a mediocre man be as honored as one wearing a crown.

➤ *A good woman might be married to a man who is lazy or just does not make much money. Yet, because she is a wise shopper and does not waste her time or their money foolishly by eating out or indulging in expensive entertainment, and because she is a keeper at home, she makes his "little money" go a long way. As a result, he appears wiser and wealthier than he really is and is looked upon with honor because of it.*

The Ball-and-Chain Woman

"...But she that maketh ashamed is as rottenness in his bones" (Proverbs 12:4).

➤ **A ball-and-chain woman** *is one who spends her husband's modest wages, five dollars here and ten dollars there, on things of no permanence. At the end of the day, she is "too tired to cook" or "there is nothing in the house to eat," so she wants to eat out. There just never seems to be enough money to get ahead. He appears to be a poor man, and she makes him feel the lack of every penny. He gets discouraged easily, because no matter how much he makes, it never seems to stretch far enough. When it appears that they might be getting ahead a little, a vacation or new furniture that she buys eats up their reserve. Others often look upon him as a loser. Rather than being a crown to him, she brings him shame and is as rottenness to his bones.*

~Debi Pearl

Chapter Eleven
Virtuous Consideration

"She considereth a field, and buyeth it:
with the fruit of her hands she planteth a vineyard."
Proverbs 31:16

Consider means:

- To think carefully about (something), typically before making a decision: each application is considered on its merits.
- To think about and be drawn toward (a course of action).
- To regard (someone or something) as having a specified quality.
- To believe, to think.
- To take (something) into account when making an assessment or judgment.

The virtuous woman *considers* a field. She does not make a snap decision; rather she uses wisdom and considers whether the purchase will be a worthy investment. She is careful.

Impulsive

Being *impulsive* is the opposite of taking time to consider something. I know I am guilty of being impulsive; it is my nature. I jump into things without giving them much thought. My husband is the opposite. He takes a long time to make a decision, while I am impatient. I want the ball to keep rolling. Mark will pause for a long time while I look at him and snap my fingers and say, "What is the holdup?"

He says in return, "I take time to figure out the depth of the water before I jump. You jump before you realize the water is only two inches deep." **Wisdom is precious**. That is why God gave me a husband who can warn me and stop me before I jump. I have learned to wait on him. I may speak of all my ideas, but I know now not to act on them unless he gives me the green light. Because he is careful, he protects me from making big mistakes.

Before my husband buys anything, he reads dozens of reviews and comparison shops several stores before he makes a purchase. He asks counsel from me because he values my thoughts on things. There have been many times when I did not want to make decisions with him. I wanted him to make the decision, and I would love whatever he loved. I have a husband who loves what I love, too. He considers me before he does anything, because he wants to please me. At the same time, I want to please him, and I want to follow him to the ends of the earth and back. So when we consider something, we also must consider how it affects one another. I think that is key to a happy marriage: Taking time to consider the other person no matter what you are planning.

The virtuous woman is not impulsive. She does not buy the first thing that she sees. She shops around and considers all the options. We know she also considers her husband and family because, ***"The heart of her husband doth safely trust in her, so that he shall have no need of spoil"*** (Proverbs 31:11). And because her husband knows that, ***"She will do him good and not evil all the days of her life"*** (Proverbs 31:12). He *trusts* her to make decisions about business. I cannot read this verse and say that it is not about a woman being somewhat of an entrepreneur.
She is a working woman.

How does she juggle it all?

She juggles it all by planning ahead as seen in the next few verses. ***"She seeketh wool, and flax, and worketh willingly with her hands"*** (Proverbs 31:13). And, ***"She is like the merchants' ships; she bringeth her food from afar"*** (Proverbs 31:14). ***"She riseth also while it is yet night, and giveth meat to her household, and a portion to her maidens"*** (Proverbs 31:15).

We have to take this verse in its context. She is faithful to her husband, she is hardworking, and she plans ahead. We can all take something from her example. Many of us have a home to keep up, a husband to please, children to teach, mouths to feed, and food to buy. We must care for sick children or take time to get to know our spouses and our children. It all takes a lot of time and it is a lot to juggle. Being a wife and mother is a lot of hard work and perseverance; but as we take time to consider how precious our role is, we know we must give it our all. In giving our all, we will reap some pretty amazing rewards.

She BUYS it with the fruit of her hands

The "fruit of her hands" is her *increase* or *profit*. She has made some money and now she is investing this money. It is money she made with her hands, working diligently. This is not money that was given to her. When it says she buys this land, she buys it *because* she has money from her own hands. She does not spend the money she made foolishly. She is taking time to use that profit to make more money.

She plants a vineyard

A vineyard is a long-term investment because you do not get a return on it for a long time. It takes years before you will see the fruit. This virtuous woman knows this. She is careful in her planning. She knows that if she just buys the land and does not plant it, she will not ever get her money back out of it. It needs to be planted so that it can yield a fruit that one day can be sold. As the fruit is sold, it will pay down the initial investment. Once that sum is met, the rest will be profit for her and her family.

What does this mean for us?

Most of us do not have money to purchase a field. I do not know about you, but I sure do not! What we can take from this passage is that we should be a good steward of whatever God has given us. If your husband works to provide an income, you must consider all of your purchases. You must spend the money he works hard for in ways that will not leave you penniless. Learn to pinch your pennies. Pinching your pennies is a good virtue. Making wise purchases is a good thing. Now, on the flip side, some husbands provide a considerable income, and they would feel slighted if you didn't buy the things you wanted. They take pride in spoiling their wife. In all things, consider your husband and what would please him. Do not spend money foolishly—that is the bottom line.

I have always worked. I have started businesses and made money

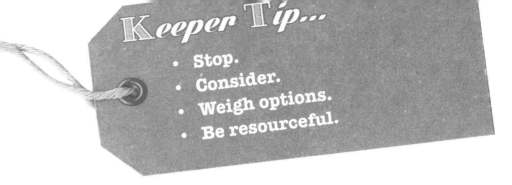

while I was also cleaning my home, serving my man, taking care of little ones, cooking, and keeping all my clients happy at the same time. Sometimes I have worked over 60 hours a week in my business. I know some of you would just love to throw the first stone. But first, before you judge me, know that I have a lot of energy. I push myself. I plan ahead. I want to spend time with my family, so I have figured out ways to juggle it all. My husband gave me free rein in business because he trusted me. I went to bed early and woke up way before the others just to squeeze my work in, and that was easy because I always worked from home. I worked during nap times, but I never let my work interfere with my first calling—my calling as his help meet and as a mother. My husband cherished that about me. Many times I did not want to work, but he kept lifting me up, showing me that I could do it. He knew I was born to be a hard worker; I was when he met me, and he never wanted that to change. He loves that I am creative and business-minded.

Now, some of you have a husband who would not want you to work for money. Consider that a precious gift. So many times I have wished I was in your shoes, where all I had to do was that half of my responsibilities. You do not have to work on customer relations, or deal with marketing competition, all while you are changing diapers, wiping noses, and helping one of your kids figure out another math problem. I feel like it would be such a relaxed lifestyle compared to what I have always known. But my husband knows what is good for me. He knows I thrive on being busy. It is like fuel in the tank. The harder I work, the more I love and serve others. It may be strange to others, but it works for us.

You must always consider what is best for your marriage, your family life, and whatever is the Lord's will in your life. God makes us so incredibly unique, so being a virtuous woman could mean a lot of things.

You can be a virtuous woman just by doing what your husband leads you to do. I think the main idea is that we apply ourselves, wholeheartedly, to the most important things God has given us. It is all an investment. When we invest in the lives of our husband and our children, we are investing in eternity. One day we will get to see the fruit of our labor of love. It may take time, but it will be worth its weight in gold.

"And let us consider one another to provoke unto love and to good works:"
Hebrews 10:24

"Finally, be ye all of one mind, having compassion one of another, love as brethren, be pitiful, be courteous:"
1 Peter 3:8

"And the Lord said, Who then is that faithful and wise steward, whom his lord shall make ruler over his household, to give them their portion of meat in due season? Blessed is that servant, whom his lord when he cometh shall find so doing."
Luke 12:42-43

"As every man hath received the gift, even so minister the same one to another, as good stewards of the manifold grace of God."
1 Peter 4:10

Recipe to be a GOOD WOMAN

Proverbs 31:16—A good woman is enterprising. She buys property, plants a cash crop, and multiplies her investments. She is not afraid of getting her hands dirty.

"She considereth a field and buyeth it: with the fruit of her hands she planteth a vineyard."

Key words: *considereth, buyeth, and planteth*

Enterprising, daring, yet cautious, and resourceful.

Time-Tested Wisdom...

A Trip to the Grocery Store

When I first got married, we had a tight budget for groceries. I had to learn quickly which foods were wants and which ones were needs. I had to weigh which foods would actually nourish us newlyweds. I knew how to bake, but didn't know much about cooking. So, I started by learning some basic culinary terms and prepared a few meals. When I shopped, I began looking closely at the food in the store and realized just how much money could be saved if we made some of this food ourselves! So that's what I began to do. If we wanted fruit salad, I would buy the fruit and cut it up. If we wanted macaroni and cheese, we would cook the pasta and use real cheese!

Over the years, this became more habitual and I began paying attention to the ingredients used in prepared foods. Mayonnaise, for instance, commonly contains genetically-modified oils like soybean or canola. So we began making our own. Things on our list that used our budget quickly were soon replaced by homemade versions. Our paper towels and napkins were now towels and rags. Lotions and soaps were made at home and with better ingredients! Pancake mix was made at home, as well as our laundry soap. We enjoyed taking a trip back to the days when convenience was not available.

As I shopped with the children, we would walk down the candy, chip, and soda aisles and discuss how the colorful and bright packages were designed to catch our attention and make the product more appealing. "Which one catches your attention?" I would ask. The children would point out the one that attracted them and would explain what grabbed their attention. We might see two bottles of shampoo that were seemingly identical in size and cost but, which one was the better deal? Then we would look at the amount in the bottle and make our decision.

Lots of schooling takes place in the store! Many trips to the grocery store taught me to be frugal without compromising our health. It's a wonderful thing knowing exactly what my family is eating and that we're saving money doing it.

~Daisy Farrales

Chapter Twelve
Virtuous Strength

"She girdeth her loins with strength, and strengtheneth her arms."
Proverbs 31:17

What does it mean to gird your loins? In the time this passage was written, people wore long robes and tunics. When they were at work in a field, they would gather the excess fabric up and tie it under or around them in such a way that allowed them to work freely. Any loose fabric could slow them down or could offer a risk of tripping over. It is a practical thing to do.

This virtuous woman has carefully considered a property, purchased it, and decided to plant a vineyard. Now that she is at the task of planting, she needs to dress for the occasion. Not in finery, nor long gowns; she must ready herself for the labor ahead.

As for me, if I am ready for a big, messy job, I tie on my apron!

Girding her loins with strength

She is showing her enthusiasm for every good work. Her head is held high with a strong resolve to finish the project she has started. She is not murmuring or showing signs of defeat. Her arms are strong. In contrast, so many of us look to the work ahead and we hang our heads low. We sigh and groan because we see this grand mountain standing in front of us.

There was a time when my body was so weak and so full of pain that I could do almostnothing. I took 38 pain pills each day, and that barely cut the intense nerve pain. My foot felt like it was in burning hot oil all day and all night so that I could not even sleep because of it. And this persisted for nine months. I felt so useless just lying there. Not knowing if I would ever be productive again, I had to find things I could do. I set out to do a few small tasks to make myself feel like I had accomplished something each day.

Most days, I felt like it was a mountain of work just to hobble around my bed to pull the covers up. It was a major accomplishment for me to make my bed and set the pillows up straight. It took me 30 minutes of all of my strength and endurance to make that bed—blood, sweat, and tears. After making the bed, I would wheel myself into the living room where I would find a chair to sit in. Just getting out of bed made me feel good. What I wanted more than anything was to have the strength and freedom to get up and sweep or wash a sink-load of dishes, but I could not even do that. I wanted to serve my family. I wanted to play with my small children. It took a huge measure of strength to gird my loins and set out to make my bed. I know it sounds pathetic that I thought making my bed was such a huge accomplishment, but I tell you, it was one of the things that kept me going. Just that little thing made a world of difference to me when I could do nothing but lay there in agony.

There are many of you who feel overwhelmed because you see your mountain sitting there in front of you. Get up and gird your loins today! One little task gives a lot of encouragement to do more little tasks. It is a blessing when you have strength and you are able to do things that other people cannot do because they are sick or in pain. Even now, I struggle to do work because my foot will never work as a normal foot. Things are harder for me than for most people, yet I just try to remember the time when I could only make my bed in a day. Those days will never be forgotten. I have courage to overcome because I know how much pain I used to have and how thankful I am that God has given me my second wind. I now have strength to do so much more than I thought I would ever be able to do when I was lying in that bed for so long.

I look at the hours differently now because of my accident and what I went through. I see time as such a precious gift. I used to scream in agony and pray that God would get me by for another minute; now, I see each minute as a gift to me. No longer am I in agony. God is giving me time to do things. I can gird up my loins each day and I can accomplish many things in the time that I have been given. So can all of you. You have the same measure of time that I do.

The moral of the story

Do what you can, to the best of your ability—with a smile on your face!

A lot can be accomplished when we put a value on the time we have been given. If we appreciate time and the ability to do things, we will have strength to accomplish them. It is all in our attitude. And it is all a matter of perspective. When we understand that all it takes is a cheerful and thankful spirit, we can go forth with strength and purpose. We can have Virtuous Strength.

HEALTH & WELLNESS 101

If you are a busy lady, you need to spend a little time thinking about your health so you can stay strong! Here are five ways to stay well…

1 **Drink plenty of water.** Try to drink at least two quarts of water each day. Keeping hydrated is so important. Because our body is composed of about 60% water, it takes water to keep the body functional. Drinking water aids in digestion, weight management, helps energize your muscles, is good for your complexion, and helps flush impurities out of your body.

2 **Eat a well-balanced diet.** Eating raw fruits and vegetables gives your body the vitamins, nutrients, fiber, and fresh enzymes your body needs to keep your body healthy and strong. Most of your leafy greens and other brightly-colored fruits are loaded with antioxidants, which help ward off disease and keep the body feeling youthful. Don't grab the greasy potato chips; instead, grab a stick of celery or an apple. Eating a fresh side salad with each meal is a good habit to make. If you have a hard time eating greens like kale, for instance, try mincing it up and adding it to your soup or meat. It does not carry a strong flavor so the kale can be added into a fruit smoothie. Kale chips are a great crispy snack. Grass-fed meats are great, as well as raw dairy. Nuts and seeds are very healthy snack alternatives which help with brain function and heart health. Stay away from white flour and sugar. If you are used to white flour, try whole wheat, spelt, or a variety of gluten-free flours. When you grind grains fresh they retain more nutrition. Instead of white sugar, try raw honey, rapadura, stevia, xylitol, or maple syrup. When choosing oils, make sure to stay away from hydrogenated oils. Instead, use coconut oil, butter, and olive oil. Coconut oil and butter have CLA (conjugated linoleic acids) which help with brain function and metabolism. They are considered healthy fats. Try to get some probiotics into your diet like yogurt or kefir. If you are allergic to dairy, you can buy probiotic supplements. Probiotics help build the good bacteria in your intestines that aid in immune function and proper digestion.

3 **Exercise.** Get plenty of exercise. Try to walk a little each day. If you can get outdoors for a little walk, you will also get some vitamin D from the sunshine. Do some sit-ups each day as well as some stretching exercises. Keeping your body moving will make your body last longer. Do not be afraid to walk the steps several times a day. The more you exercise, the better you will feel, and the stronger you will become.

4 **Get plenty of rest.** Rest is very important. You want to be sure to get at least eight hours of sleep each night. Take breaks when you need to during the day. Take a ten-minute power nap each afternoon. That will get you energized for the rest of your day.

5 **Minimize stress.** Stress is a killer. Try to pick your battles. Do not overexert yourself by putting too many irons in the fire. Pick one thing to do and finish it before starting another. Avoid toxic relationships. If someone is dragging you down with their bad attitude, avoid being around them. Their poison will start affecting you.

6 **Hygiene.** Maintain good hygiene. Brush and floss your teeth regularly. Keep yourself clean by bathing daily. Wash your hands frequently; washing hands can prevent the spread of disease. Change your undergarments every day. Clean under your nails, behind your ears, and between your toes. Look presentable. Comb your hair, wear clean clothing, and freshen up. It is a blessing to your husband if you look nice and smell nice. When you look good, you feel good—it is psychological.

7 **Balance.** Moderation is key; in all things learn a measure of moderation. A little processed food is okay; do not eat it all the time. Make yourself a dessert every now and then. If you eat sweets with every meal and in-between meals, you will eventually have health problems. Be wise with your time. Balance work with relaxation. It is not good to work all the time; spending time with your spouse and children is very healthy. Be lighthearted. Having a merry or cheerful heart is like good medicine.

"A merry heart doeth good like a medicine."
Proverbs 17:22

"All the days of the afflicted are evil: but he that is of merry heart hath a continual feast"
Proverbs 15:15

Recipe to be a GOOD WOMAN

Proverbs 31:17—A good woman does physical labor and thus is strong.
"She girdeth her loins with strength, and strengtheneth her arms."
Key words: *girdeth, strengtheneth*
Physically strong, a hard worker.

Chapter Thirteen
Virtuous Confidence

"She perceiveth that her merchandise is good:
her candle goeth not out by night."
Proverbs 31:18

When the virtuous woman perceives that her merchandise is good, she takes pride in her work. She is confident in herself and what she is selling. There is an art to being a business person. If you lack confidence in yourself or the product you are selling, people will sense it. Why would someone want something that you do not believe is really good? What would the selling point be?

As Christians, we hear a lot of talk about being prideful. There are two forms of confidence. One is a good confidence while the other is prideful conceit. Some religious groups will come against the spirit of pride. In order to find the difference one would need to examine pride. What is the spirit of pride? The spirit of pride is a haughty kind of spirit. It is when a person believes they are better than another person.

Here are some Bible verses to illustrate prideful conceit:

"But he giveth more grace. Wherefore he saith,
God resisteth the proud, but giveth grace unto the humble."
James 4:6

"Every one [that is] proud in heart [is] an abomination to the LORD:
[though] hand [join] in hand, he shall not be unpunished."
Proverbs 16:5

*"Not a novice, lest being lifted up with pride he fall
into the condemnation of the devil."*
1 Timothy 3:6

"Pride [goeth] before destruction, and an haughty spirit before a fall."
Proverbs 16:18-19

*"The fear of the LORD [is] to hate evil: pride, and arrogancy,
and the evil way, and the froward mouth, do I hate."*
Proverbs 8:13

To have prideful conceit is wrong. It is a cocky spirit. Anyone who has this kind of pride has no fear of God. They feel they are above God. I have seen women get on their high horses and look down their noses at others. They also look down their noses at their husbands. The kids will pick up on that nasty spirit. It is a will to control and be supreme. The end is that God will resist you. You will FALL.

I will never forget when I was young and prideful. I thought I was going to have the most well-behaved children this world will have known. I had it all figured out—before I had children, of course—that I would have them trained to sit quietly, never throw tantrums, be content in all things, and be extremely talented. One day I saw this lady with a screaming, kicking, crazy little two-year-old in a shopping center. I sat there gazing down my long nose, thinking, "My kids will NEVER do that!"

Since God can hear the secret thoughts of my heart, He resisted my pride and gave me my own kicking, screaming, crazy little two-year-old. I brought my little boy, Miles, to a doctor's appointment, as I recall. Things started off great. He was a cute little boy and relatively content. But this day he decided that he would embarrass my socks off. He sat there playing with a toy on the floor and soon our name was called. I looked at my sweet boy and told him that it was time to put down the train and come with me. He threw himself on the floor, kicking and screaming, telling me "NOOOOOO!" His soft, angelic face quickly turned into a hidious snarl. I thought I was in the presence of some demonic spirit. I did not know kids could be that bad, and it was MY KID!

I made my way over to the nurse and said, "I am so sorry for all this screaming. God is teaching me a lesson." She looked a little confused. "You see, I used to judge the mothers who had kids like this in public places. I was so prideful. Well, now it is my turn to eat my words!" The nurse started laughing because apparently she had never encountered a young mother grasping a concept such as this. From that day forward, I thought twice before casting the first stone. That was my big fat FALL. When I became aware of my faults, it became the first step in conquering them. When you conquer things by the grace of God, you can justifiably have confidence.

In contrast, godly confidence

The opposite of pride is humility. Humility is when you realize the greatness of God. The definition is: A modest or low view of one's own importance; humbleness. Anytime we measure ourselves against the perfection of Jesus, we see how small we really are. He knows everything; he understands the intents of our hearts and judges them justly. We certainly cannot judge others when we do not know the things in someone's heart. We can only know in part. Rather, we can trust God and put confidence in Him. The Bible offers some verses that pertain to confidence…

"But Christ as a son over his own house; whose house are we, if we hold fast the confidence and the rejoicing of the hope firm unto the end."
Hebrews 3:6

"For we are made partakers of Christ, if we hold the beginning of our confidence stedfast unto the end;"
Hebrews 3:14

"Cast not away therefore your confidence, which hath great recompence of reward."
Hebrews 10:35

"And now, little children, abide in him; that, when he shall appear, we may have confidence, and not be ashamed before him at his coming."
1 John 2:28

"Beloved, if our heart condemn us not, then have we confidence toward God."
1 John 3:21

"And this is the confidence that we have in him, that,
if we ask any thing according to his will, he heareth us:"
1 John 5:14

Confidence in truth

When you have confidence in the **truth** of God, you can better give an answer to those that seek it. How do you answer the tough questions from the lost without a good measure of confidence? Questions like, "Why do bad things happen to good people?" I know how to answer this. I answer with confidence, "Bad things happen to good people because it makes them stronger. God uses death to bring forth life. How could we cherish the rain unless the earth has been dry? We would not appreciate the sunshine if there was no rain. It is easy to take things for granted." Often, we do not know what we have until it is gone. Many times people show up at funerals full of regret. "I should have done this, or I should have spent more time with this or that person." When you go through loss you understand a little better. You can offer strength and comfort to the weary. You can confidently offer support.

I think of merchandise as anything you are trying to promote, whether it is a product or something as important as your faith.

This kind of confidence is good. It edifies others and builds our own faith. So many people doubt that God's grace is sufficient to save their souls. They waver because they think somehow they have not done all the things which they ought. Their sins are innumerable and they shrink in the sight of God, knowing anything they did right is nothing compared to the righteousness of God. Yes, they are correct, but they are putting confidence in their ability. To God we are all rotten sinners. However, He designed a fool-proof plan—a plan in which we can put our confidence.

Passover pictures

It wasn't until recent years that I was really exposed to the Passover. I was reading the story about the Passover in Exodus to my children from the Bible. I saw it as a picture of the gospel. The Israelites were enslaved, just as we were enslaved to sin. It did not take a revolution for them to break free just like it does not take cleaning up our lives to set us free.

These slaves were given some pretty outlandish instructions one evening in Egypt. After they had seen Moses plead for their freedom, each time the Pharaoh would say, "No," God would unleash a plague that would put the pressure on. Imagine frogs by the millions, or flies and sores from head to toe. Grievous plagues. The one that caught my attention more than any other was the final plague. The death plague of the firstborn in Egypt.

Moses warned all who would listen. God instructed them to kill a perfect, spotless, white lamb. A lamb was to die in place of their first-born child. The blood was to be collected and painted on the doorpost of their dwelling place. When the wrath of God, in the form of death, came to consume, it passed over the dwellings that were covered in that blood. Simple. Easy to do. I am sure there were some of God's own people who did not trust that the blood was sufficient and they found out what all of the Egyptian families found out—that the wrath of God visited their homes that evening and stole the life from their firstborn. The blood was a covering and protection. It took faith to believe that by applying the blood they were saving themselves from the wrath of God.

Christ was the spotless lamb of God. He died in our place. His blood was shed to cover our sins and make us free. Just like the wrath of God passing over the homes that were covered in the blood of the lamb, one day His wrath will pass over all who trust in the sufficiency of Christ's blood to cover their sins. Christ's blood is real and it is effectual to cover all sins.

So many people do not trust in something this simple. As humans, we make things into our own image—in our own understanding. We try to fit God into a box and define faith. We do not believe it can be that simple. We must add something to it to make it better—to make it ours. We refuse to trust that Christ's blood is enough to save us. We cannot understand that we are partakers in Christ's death, burial and resurrection. We just cannot believe our sins are dealt with. It is an ongoing waxing and waning of believing and confessing our sins, doubting and trusting, wondering if we did enough, and challenging our hearts to meet our own standard, but it is void of a sufficient rest. Void of confidence.

"The next day John seeth Jesus coming unto him, and saith,
Behold the Lamb of God, which taketh away the sin of the world.

*This is he of whom I said, After me cometh a man which is
preferred before me: for he was before me."*
John 1:29-30

Jesus was the perfect lamb of God and he takes away the sin of the world. No matter how much we aspire to live a sinless life, no matter how holy we think we are, we can never be good enough. I tried to be good enough, to do enough right things in order to please God; yet in all my striving, I knew I failed miserably. I fell short. We all will fall short.

*"God looked down from heaven upon the children of men, to see if there were
any that did understand, that did seek God.
Every one of them is gone back: they are altogether become filthy;
there is none that doeth good, no, not one."*
Psalm 53:2-3

God made a plan in his commandments that offers a way to please Him. All who can keep the commandments fully can be saved. The only trouble is, no one can. Who can say they are without sin? He sent His only son who was the only one capable of keeping His law. He was the perfect lamb of God. Until Christ came into the world, people had to sacrifice animals to pay for their sins. This was the only acceptable payment. Christ shed his blood for our payment—once for all. He was the perfect substitution. He took the punishment we deserved, and it was acceptable and sufficient to God. Why do we think His sacrifice is insufficient? It is because we do not have confidence in God's ways, which are better than our ways even when they do not make sense. Even when we doubt, the offer still stands, for those who will believe.

Death, burial, and resurrection

I chose to believe and trust in the finished work of the cross. I no longer labor to win a spot in heaven. I rest in God's plan and His perfect solution to sin. Because I am in Christ, and His spirit lives within me, I have access to God. I actually have more access to God than King David himself. He had to go to the Holy of Holies, behind the veil, to commune with God. I have God with me every second of the day. It is real to me. I have confidence that, because I have Christ's blood applied to my account, when the wrath of God passes over mankind, I will be safe. His wrath will pass over me. He will not see me as a rotten sinner deserving of hell for all the many, many mistakes and failures I have in my past. When He looks down, he will see that precious blood which was applied. He will see me for something I am not—a sinless daughter of God. Christ died and I died with him. Christ was buried as my sins and life were buried with him. He was resurrected and I was made new. I am a new creature in Christ. I trust in that. I wholeheartedly believe in it. I am alive in Christ. I am ALIVE! I put confidence in the finished work of the cross. It is such a wonderful, powerful, victorious life when you are living in the newness of life. And this kind of simple faith is counted as righteousness according to God's Word.

"What shall we say then that Abraham our father, as pertaining to the flesh, hath found? For if Abraham were justified by works, he hath whereof to glory; but not before God. For what saith the scripture? Abraham believed God, and it was counted unto him for righteousness. Now to him that worketh is the reward not reckoned of grace, but of debt. But to him that worketh not, but believeth on him that justifieth the ungodly, his faith is counted for righteousness. Even as David also describeth the blessedness of the man, unto whom God imputeth righteousness without works,
Saying, Blessed are they whose iniquities are forgiven,
and whose sins are covered.
Blessed is the man to whom the Lord will not impute sin."
Romans 4:1-7

Confidence in the gospel

When you fully grasp the concept of the gospel, you can more effectively share the "good news" of salvation with others. If you, yourself, are unsure of the plan of salvation and how it works, and you have doubts, no one will want what you have. You have to perceive that the message is good and have confidence that others would benefit from the finished work of the cross when they believe.

You can be effective in the kingdom of God when you have confidence. When you perceive your merchandise is good (the message of

Jesus), you can find ways to minister to others. You don't have to make a huge commitment to make a difference. You can plant small seeds along the way. We need to do something. Jesus left us with this instruction:

"Go ye into all the world, and preach the gospel to every creature."
Matthew 16:15

Here are some ways in which you can minister:

- **You can send a missionary money to do the work of spreading the gospel.**
- **You can hand out tracts.**
- **You can tell someone what Christ has done in your life.**
- **You can go on the mission field.**
- **You can buy Bibles and give them to others who need them.**
- **You can pray for eyes to be opened to the truth.**
- **You can read missionary stories to your children so they get a vision for ministry. Teach them by example in ministering to others.**
- **If you are an aged woman, you can teach the younger women how to minister to their family and keep their homes.**

Because of what Christ has done in my life, I confidently share that truth and victory with others. It is our duty to share what we know. You are in ministry if you are a wife and mother. It is your highest calling. You can also minister the gospel to others when given an opportunity. Promote Jesus, not a church or denomination.

Promoting your product

Besides having confidence in the gospel that you promote, the same rules apply in promoting a business or a product you believe in. You can sell more products if you have confidence that they will fill a need.

MARKETING 101

The virtuous woman is proud of what she has made. She may work long hours to produce it. It is okay to take pride in something you worked hard to create. If you baked a good pie, you get confidence the more you hear from others that it is good. When you perceive that pie as good, you will be better able to market that pie.

Here is how it works

Okay, you have a product that you want to sell, be it a pie, or a quilt, a service, or a health product. I will use a pie-making business as an example, but it can be anything. There are a few simple steps to successfully market your product…

1 Test it out. You need to test it out on some of your family and friends and see what their honest reactions are. If they like the pie, their eyes may roll back into their heads and they may hardly be able to speak because they are actively enjoying it. If you get a false positive you need to keep perfecting that pie recipe. The false positive is the "people-pleaser" who will say it is good just so they do not hurt your feelings. Once in a while you will get that honest person who will outright tell you that your pie stinks. They may even have the guts to spit it out in front of you. If you have a high percentage of people who really like the pie, you can have confidence that it is sellable.

2 Know your competition. Find every pie maker in town and start analyzing whether they are successful in business. Some key things would be: Do they have employees? (If they have enough money to hire a staff, chances are they are selling a lot of pies. You have to sell a lot of pies to be able to afford full-time help.) Are they in a store front? (If they have a successful pie shop, they can afford a store front.)

3 What are they charging? If you intend on being the next best, or the best pie maker in town, you need to keep your prices competetive. Many business people fail because they think that they can undercut the competetion to zero them out. More often than not, you make your product seem cheap if you go too low on your pricing. When people pay more, they think they are getting a better product. The old saying, "You get what you pay for," rings into their mind. When they see the next-door pie maker selling pies at half price, they are thinking you must be using poor quality ingredients to make it that price. They were used to getting pie for X amount of dollars and they trust that is what a pie should cost. It would literally take years to convince people that your pie is better even though it is half the price.

4 **Who is buying the pie?** Who is walking out of their shop with boxed pies? Are they men? Are they women? You need to know your target market. If there are more women buying pies than men, you need to keep the name of the pie, the look of the pie, the store front, the logo, and even the color scheme feminine-looking, so as to appeal to the women. Make your pie shop look like a French pastry or candy boutique. A lot of women love pink, lace, and antiques. Putting a little parlor table with a vase full of pink roses would add a very lovely touch. If you are seeing more men buying pies, you know that they might like a country, rustic look. They want Grandma's pies. That smell takes them back to when they were a child. You have to think like they think. The more you know your customer, the better you can serve them and keep them coming back for more.

5 **Start small. Grow by word of mouth.** Some businesses can be done on the side, or while you are homemaking. You could start by making pies for your friends and family. If you friends like the pie, they will share a slice with another friend, who will in turn tell their friends that you sell pies. Gradually, you will build up a reputation. In the small town of Little Chute, Wisconsin where I grew up, there was a man who started making pizzas in his garage. Eventually, he was delivering pizzas around the neighborhood. Everyone wanted Jack's original pizza. Later, he began making them frozen to sell in the local grocery markets. He outgrew his old gargage and opened a pizza factory. That pizza factory popped up right next door to my parents' dog kennel. Years later, Jack's pizza was in every grocery store in the state of Wisconsin. He had hundreds of full-time employees, and when he was tired of the business, he sold the company for millions of dollars. Just think, he started in a little garage down the street.

6 **Brand your product.** Think of something classic. It has to stick in people's minds. If your pie is going to be sold nationwide, you have to stand apart from all others. The logo must be catchy and easily identifiable. No one is going to buy a just a "PIE," but they may want to buy a "Tastee Brand Pie." If you have a catchy logo with a sketch of a chef holding a pie—well, that is more appealing to your potential client.

7 **Advertise.** Using the internet, you can market your goods and plug into social networks. Taking beautiful photos of your product is also important. Declutter the background and set up a stage for your pie so it looks homey and delicious. When you can afford it, purchase ads in certain newspapers, magazines, or on websites. If you can figure out how to ship that pie, the sky is the limit. It won't just be "pie in the sky!"

Keeper Tip...

Take pride in your work
Do a good job. Have integrity. Be honest. Humbly admit when you are wrong. Be teachable. Have confidence that you have produced a good product. Do not be ashamed to feel good about your hard work.

Her candle burns bright

The virtuous woman has a candle that is not snuffed out by night. She works long hours, sometimes creating her merchandise in the wee hours of night to get her orders out. She is not afraid to push herself when the need arises.

Running a photography business for eight years of my life, there were times when my candle burned all throughout the night. I had to put in sometimes 60-80 hours a week to fulfill a print order. Pushing myself during the Christmas rush was inevitable. I had clients waiting for their beautiful storybook albums. Customer service was very important to my husband and me. He would tend to the meals and the homeschooling so I could spend a couple of weeks finishing out all my orders. It was teamwork. Most of the time, I was able to wake up several hours before my family to work, and then was still able to manage the homeschooling, the cleaning, the cooking, and laundry. I worked full-time, but no one ever knew it because I slipped those hours in while everyone was asleep. The Christmas rush was an exception to my normal busy schedule.

I would give my brides the opportunity to choose their favorite photos for the storybook. More often than not, they would get busy, forget, and wait until a couple weeks before Christmas. They wanted to give out keepsake albums to their parents, so now they were frantic. I would have about 20 frantic brides who were counting on a miracle. I did not like to spend those weeks pouring into my job instead of my children but I knew it had to be done—it could not be helped. Sometimes things have to get done and you just have to stick it out, no matter how much you would rather do other things. It is good business practice to meet your deadlines and follow through with what you have promised to the client. I, in turn, had a very good reputation because people knew they were going to get my full attention. I was confident in my merchandise because I knew I would not stop at anything to make sure my customer was 100% satisfied with my service. I made it happen.

Be careful not to burn yourself out

The thing with going strong and pushing yourself is that you can burn yourself out. Burnout happens when you get completely overwhelmed and worn out from stress and stretching yourself too thin. People get burnt out from being nice to people that take advantage of them time and time again. You can burn out by not getting sufficient rest. I have gotten burned out several times in my life. It can be unwise to push yourself for too long. You need to know when to quit and how to pace yourself. I am usually *hard-core, pedal-to-the-metal,* but my body will sometimes cry out, "STOP!" Sometimes I fail to know my limitations, and I literally burn my physical body out to where I cannot even get out of bed. It has happened on numerous occasions. My mind is ramped up but my body is weak. I am learning to say, "No," when I know I cannot handle too many irons in the fire. Finding balance is always a good thing. Work hard, do it right, but do not BURN your candle from both ends.

Should a woman have a career?

Some women have no other choice. They may be single or widowed and have to provide for their children. Other women have their children in a private or public school all day and work a part-time job while the children are away from home. Some husbands require their wives to work. My mother worked full-time as a nurse while I was at school each day. She still looked well to the ways of her household. I graduated from college the day after I had my first child and started my first teaching job the following school year. I stopped working after the first week because I wanted to be home with my baby. I found out that staying home with your children is hard work, too. It can be more exhausting than working a full-time job elsewhere. When you are a full-time homemaker, you are working around the clock. It is a career where your payment is not in dollars but in the relationships you gain with your children and the satisfaction that you are investing in something eternal.

Some women never have children, or perhaps remain single. They work a full-time job. Can a woman work a full-time job and take care of her home? Yes, but some things will suffer as a result, and it will put more stress on the family. When children are grown, a woman still has a lot to do. She can work a job, or she can minister to the younger wives and mothers, teaching them how to manage a home and how to minister to their families. Ministering is a big responsibility, a lot of work. Work is anything into which you pour yourself. If you have a full-time job outside of the home, you may still have opportunities to share your faith with others or minister to them in some way.

It is not a cut-and-dried issue that I can judge. Each family is on their own journey. I have seen "stay-at-home" women who are lazy and do not look well to the ways of their household—they have rotten kids, a horrible marriage, and a dirty home. I have also seen the opposite—other ladies have a career; yet they always have a meal on the table, a clean home, happy children, and an excellent marriage. I would like to see all the stay-at-home moms be better examples of order. That is why I have written this book; to encourage women who stay home, as well as women who have a career, to rise to their calling as a wife and mother, and do it well.

Recipe to be a GOOD WOMAN

Proverbs 31:18—A good woman is competent; she takes stock of her work and is satisfied that she has done things right. She is dependable.
"She perceiveth that her merchandise is good: her candle goeth not out by night."
Key word: *perceiveth*
Willing to work long hours.

Time-Tested Wisdom...

Should Older Women Have Careers?

There is a woman who has been commenting on my blog for many years. She is a working mother and wife. Her children are all grown but whenever I teach about women being keepers at home, she has to add her two cents about how beautiful her life is even though she works outside of the home.

Recently, she made this comment on a post . . .

"As I lay in bed this morning I contemplated my choices. I could decide to stay home today (and from here on) and have a sleep-in, lazy day as the housework is all done, reading, watching movies, sewing, blogging, cooking—putting my feet up—or I could get up and go to work. I have no children at home, so life at home would be a breeze." ~A reader

Yes, some older women who stay home can choose to do those things, but they can also choose to mentor young women as they are commanded to do. They can babysit their grandbabies, cook for families who are suffering, help clean a young mother's home for her, serve her elderly parents, teach Bible studies, listen to sermons and read books to learn more to teach younger women, help her husband in his work, plus many other very beneficial things that our society desperately needs but is losing out on with all the older women having careers.

Paul gives a job description for older women in Titus 2:3, "The aged women likewise, that they be in behavior as becomes holiness, not false accusers, not given to much wine, teachers of good things; that they may teach the young women . . ." Sounds like a great job description to me!

If the older women can run a home, care for their husbands, and teach the young women, along with lodging strangers, washing the saints' feet, relieving the afflicted and following every good work as 1 Timothy 6:10 states, then I am sure the Lord wouldn't mind if she had a career.

~Lori Alexander
From Blog: Always Learning

Tales of Victory...

Proverbs Cookie Mama

When I first married, I moved to a town where I knew absolutely no one, and lived in a tiny apartment downtown. A couple months of boredom passed before I took the few dollars I had and carefully spent them on the ingredients in this recipe. With the fresh, hot cookies on a plate (the first time), I walked to the nearest businesses and told the employees that I was going to bake cookies once a week and sell them for 50 cents each.

Most of my faithful clients bought their first cookie that day. One bite of a hot chocolate-chip cookie sent even the grouchiest old sales person back to memories of childhood, and they were ready to make orders for cookies by the dozens. After Joe Courage was born, I put him in a carrier on my back and continued to carry fresh cookies around downtown. My favorite places to sell were businesses with a lot of employees; in this way I could sell 200 cookies in the course of one hour. Businesses such as laundromats, non-profit organizations, work crews, towing companies, and pawn shops grew familiar with "The Cookie Mama."

I soon had more business than I could manage, and limited my sales to orders and pick-ups only. My clients would come right to my door to pick up their orders once a week. If I had wanted to grow, I could have obtained a business license, hired a helper, added fresh bread, pies, cheesecake, oatmeal cookies, homemade deli sandwiches, etc.

My little cookie business lasted for three years, until I began to write for various magazines for additional income. My son always helped me sell the cookies, and he became a popular little fellow with the diverse group of people to which we sold. We often had the opportunity to pray for a buyer's health, tell a dry-cleaner lady about Jesus, and give away a cookie here and there to a child on a street corner.

It has been two years since I sold any cookies, but I still see people occasionally who call out across a street, "Hey, there's the cookie mama! How come you don't sell cookies anymore? I want to make an order."

Cookie Recipe

Beka's Chocolate-Chip Cookies
(makes 48-52 large cookies)

Cream together:
1½ cups softened butter
½ cup oil
1½ cups white sugar
1½ cups brown sugar
5 eggs (add one at a time)

1 Tbsp vanilla
1 tsp lemon extract
Stir in:
2 level Tbsp baking soda
1 tsp salt
2 cups wheat flour
2 cups white flour

Knead in:
12–16 oz. package semi-sweet chocolate chips, 1 cup chopped almonds, pecans, or walnuts. Add more white flour, kneading it in until the dough is stiff like bread dough, and the chips just begin to fall out as you knead. Shape into golf-ball-sized balls, flatten slightly between palms, and lay the thick disks on a cookie sheet to bake about 10 minutes at 350 degrees. Remove from oven before they begin to brown.

Cool on sheet for about 5 minutes before removing. Cool completely on flat surface before storing them in an airtight container (zip-lock type bags by the dozen or two dozen) and sell within 48 hours.

~ Rebekah (Pearl) Anast

Time-Tested Wisdom...
Content & Emotionally Stable

Do these words describe you? They are supposed to if you are a believer.

"But godliness with contentment is great gain."
1 Timothy 6:6

"For God hath not given us the spirit of fear;
but of power, and of love, and of a sound mind."
2 Timothy 1:7

Many women are controlled by their emotions and hormones. If they feel well, they are friendly and happy. If they are not feeling well, they are grumpy, mean, and discontent. This is why it is so important to be continually renewing our minds with God's Truth.

He tell us that we have everything we need for life and godliness. He reminds us that all things work together for good to those who love Him. His Spirit gives us self-control. We must remind ourselves of these truths continually and believe them.

Every one will go through many trials on this earth. Every one has their own personal struggles but when those around you see you going through them with peace and joy, God is glorified.

Therefore, be content with the husband with which the Lord has blessed you. Be content with the home in which you live and the way in which it is decorated. Don't go looking for another husband or home. Be content with how much money your husband makes and learn to live within your means. Be content with the weather and your neighbors. Learn to be content!

Let the Word of God dwell in you richly, so when trials come you will have a sound mind as you remind yourself of all of God's promises. Don't dwell on the news and the stuff going on in the world. That will just lead to depression. Remind yourself of who wins in the end.

From now on, tell yourself you are content and emotionally stable. Speak positive words to yourself, not negative ones which come from our enemy. Start believing God and His life-giving words—and not the words the world wants you to hear—for they are life and give life abundant and free.

~Lori Alexander
From Blog: Always Learning

Chapter Fourteen
Virtuously Content

"She layeth her hands to the spindle, and her hands hold the distaff."
Proverbs 31:19

The virtuous woman is content in her daily grind. In times past, spinning was considered a lowly job. It was the job given to the handmaiden. In the Victorian Era, spinning factories were full of unmarried women, women who did not have the social status to marry. They confined themselves to work as spinners for those of nobility. Hence the term "spinster" for women who get old and never marry.

The virtuous woman was right in there, spinning wool with her maidens. She was not above such a thing. It shows me that she was real. She cared about her working staff and about her business so much that she would work alongside them to ensure things were running smoothly. It was not degrading for this woman to do jobs which maids were accustomed to doing. I see her as humble, sweet, patient, hardworking, and confident. She was content to do whatever needed to be done, no matter what the job was.

I have met people who will live off the government for years because they refuse to take a lower-paying job doing work that they feel is beneath their dignity. I admire my husband for his humility. When we needed work, he was willing to work for minimum wage at a dirty, greasy junk yard just to make ends meet. Most men would feel degraded to work for someone else sorting other people's scrap metals and trash. Not my husband. He realized it was a job, a blessing to have income, and he would do anything he needed to do to provide for his family. If the only job he could find was flipping burgers at the local fast-food joint, I know he would do it. Knowing that my husband is a very talented woodworker, can build an entire home—from pouring a basement to delicately crafting all the trim by hand—you can see that he is not high on himself or his talents. He has always known that there are many guys out there doing good work and the competition is steep; so, whether feast or famine, he will take whatever work he can get.

When I worked for my dad in his dog-grooming parlor, I would help do the final touches with scissors. That is like sculpting a work of art. You have to cut so the hair lays in such a way that it does not look uneven or choppy. There were several other woman working in the shop. They clipped the dogs, cut their toenails, brushed, and bathed them. When I would enter one lady's work area, there would be a foot worth of dog hair on the floor around her grooming table. This particular lady told me, "It is not a part of MY job to sweep the floor. I groom dogs." I never forgot that. While the rest of the staff would sweep up the hair from their stations, hers would pile up. They did not feel like it was their job to sweep up her hair, either. My dad, who was the owner of the business, would frequently come down there and he would sweep up her hair for her, if I did not get to it first. I asked him why he did not just *make* her clean up after herself. He would tell me, "I just do what has to be done. If that means cleaning up after others, that is what I will do. The lady already feels she is below her pay grade." When the blow dryers were running, if the hair was not cleaned up, hair would go all over the entire shop, making it hard to breathe, hard to see, and the hair would get lodged into every little corner making it harder to clean up later. He was willing to do whatever needed to be done to ensure that his business ran more smoothly. He was the boss and was also the servant to his employees. I find that a wonderful example.

Days of the week

When I first got married and we bought our first home, I had no idea I would be where I am today. Walking through an empty home in town with my belly expanding from the growth of our first son, I dreamed of what I would fill each room with. As I walked through room after room, I just could not believe how "huge" our home was. My husband would lovingly remind me of my rose-colored glasses and that the reality was that it was a nice house but that it was *not* "huge." It was a five-bedroom, 1½-story home on a regular city lot (1,200 square feet). To me it was a palace!

I came across a box that was shoved into a closet. As I opened the dust-covered box, I felt like I was stepping back in time as the aroma of old book hit my nose, and I was transported. I remember sitting there for hours paging through these 1920s encyclopedia books, called *Wonderland of Knowledge*. One in particular stood out to me; it was the book on mothering! The encouragement on mothering was just what I needed since I was expecting my first child and I did not know the first thing about being a mother. I found this picture of little Dutch children working through the week (see page 216). It fascinated me beyond words. Even to this day, I look at this picture and it inspires me. Both of my grandmothers are from Holland, and they were both keepers of the home. They did certain jobs on certain days. It was the order of life in their era, not to mention the way it had been for centuries before them.

They maintained a certain weekly routine because it simplified life.

My Amish friends had the same routine every week. They always washed on Mondays, ironed on Tuesdays, shopped on Wednesdays, mended or sewed on Thursdays, baked on Fridays, and on Saturdays they would clean the home from top to bottom. You could drive down the lane in Amishland and see the wash in everyones yard just waving in the breeze, and you could hear the occasional snap of a towel being caught with a sharp change in the speed of the wind. Blue pants, pink and green dresses, little white diapers, and towels—just seeing it makes a woman feel good. I do not know what it is about the wash line, what it is that gives me such a good feeling. Maybe because it makes me feel the presence of yesteryear or maybe it is the stirring up of the senses—the sweet smell of fresh laundry mixed with sounds and colors. At any rate, the Amish still do their wash on Mondays like my grandma did and my great grandma did before her. It is a custom that is lost in our culture today.

The invention of the electric washing machines made it easy to throw a load in each day rather than making a day of laundering. When I lived in Amishland, wash day was a very big deal. It was an all-morning affair. You got up early, made your piles of whites, darks, and colored clothing. Other piles were of towels or sheets, blankets, coats, or socks. The wringer washer would splash and slosh the clothing back and forth while you filled the rinse tubs. Load after load, you would wash, then wring, rinse, and then wring out. After the girls would hang each piece on the line or the drying rack, wow, such a good feeling would come over me. I could relax in the afternoon and know that as the sun was setting, my wash was ready to be taken down and folded. Simple. More work, but simple.

Content with the daily grind

Repetitive work is glorious to me. Some women dread it. They see the laundry as a neverending mountain, and the cooking as continual as the shining sun. Even though we can do most of our daily chores in a fraction of the time that woman did for the past thousand years, we still become discontent. Imagine having to gather your water at a well. You may have to walk a mile and then turn back and walk home with a five-gallon vase propped up on your shoulder. This task may have to be done several times a day if you are not wise with your use of water. Imagine how dirty that water would be if you lived in Bible times and you were washing clothing that was full of dust. You only have a small tub in which to wash five robes. You cannot even see through the black water to your hands agitating the cloth. Not to mention cooking food over a fire three times a day, or grinding your flour with a millstone.

We can take a clean pan out of the cupboard, stick it over the stove-top and simmer our food slowly. After that, we can rinse it out with fresh, hot, running water from our kitchen sink. Our toilet is indoors; all we do is flush it to remove the waste. The laundry machine is in our home; we just stick in the clothing, add soap, and push a button. The machine does the washing; we can read a book while it does the work for us. Instead of using a tiny cup to pour clean water over our head for sponge-bathing, we can turn on the shower and enjoy a luxurious flow of hot water cascading over our entire body. We do not have to spin our wool to weave our fabric, so in turn we can sew all our clothing. We can run down to the local thrift store and buy garments that cost way less money. Fabric is so expensive, it is hard to afford the hobby of sewing your own clothing. Instead of lighting the lamps in the evening to reveal light, you can flick a switch. Your food lasts longer because you have a refrigerator while the virtuous woman had to rely on what she could raise and eat fresh.

Let this virtuous woman be our example as we find contentment and joy in the monotonous work that being a homemaker provides. With all the modern conveniences at our fingertips, we surely do not have it that bad. It is all in your perspective.

"Not that I speak in respect of want: for I have learned, in whatsoever state I am, [therewith] to be content."
Philippians 4:11

"[Let your] conversation [be] without covetousness; [and be] content with such things as ye have: for he hath said, I will never leave thee, nor forsake thee."
Hebrews 13:5

"But godliness with contentment is great gain."
1 Timothy 6:6

"But as God hath distributed to every man, as the Lord hath called every one, so let him walk. And so ordain I in all churches."
1 Corinthians 7:17

"But seek ye first the kingdom of God, and his righteousness; and all these things shall be added unto you."
Matthew 6:33

Recipe to be a GOOD WOMAN

Proverbs 31:19—A good woman is willing to do repetitive, boring work. **"She layeth her hands to the spindle, and her hands hold the distaff."**
Key words: *layeth, hold*

ALL THE DAYS OF THE WEEK

On Sunday we go to Church.

On Monday we wash.

On Tuesday we iron.

On Wednesday we go to market.

On Thursday we mend.

On Friday we sweep.

On Saturday we bake.

There is freedom in structure

Map out what you need done in the course of your week. You have to figure out what works best for you. Anything is doable with a system in place. A couple of hours each day go a long way. Here is an example…

Monday Wash Day. Laundry is sorted into piles. Bedding is stripped from beds. Bedrooms are picked up and cleaned. All bedding is washed and beds are made. Clothing is folded and put away. Towels are washed and dried.

Tuesday Bathroom Day. Wipe down the entire bathroom. Sweep and mop the floors. Scrub out the toilet and wash the entire fixture. Clean the shower and vanity. Take out the trash, replace the hand towel, neatly stack your clean, folded towels, and restock toilet paper and soap.

Wednesday Shopping. Go to the grocery store to buy the food items needed for your week. Stop at the bank, post office, hardware store, or library while you are out. If you are going to be gone long, bring a cooler for any grocery items that need to stay cold.

Thursday Living Room Day. Pick up and sweep/vacuum the floor. Make sure to move all furniture out to clean under. Vacuum furniture upholstery and under cushions. Dust all tables, baseboards, trim, and knickknacks. Mop floor if needed and shake out any area rugs.

Friday Kitchen Day. Declutter, wipe down cabinet doors and counter-tops. Clean the stovetop and other kitchen appliances. Sweep and mop the entire floor. Touch up the walls for splatters. Wipe down the window above sink, wash sink and fixtures.

Saturday Project Day. Any jobs that need attention can wait until Saturday. This could include weeding the flower beds, raking leaves in the fall, mowing grass, painting a room, baking bread, sewing, crafts, or organizing your pantry. It is a day to get caught up on other things.

Sunday Family Day. Take time to spend time with your family.

Chapter Fifteen
Virtuous Compassion

"She stretcheth out her hand to the poor; yea,
she reacheth forth her hands to the needy."
Proverbs 31:20

The virtuous woman is compassionate. She stretches her hand out to help others who are suffering or in need. When someone is sitting alone, looking sad, she is the one who sits beside them and asks them if they are okay. She feels what others feel. The virtuous woman does not just feel sorry for others and say she will pray for them, she is actively doing something to solve the problem.

In our modern culture, people seldom notice the bum on the street corner. They avoid the hands that are holding the cardboard signs begging for food. There have been so many scams on the internet that when a real situation arises and an email is sent out trying to raise money for someone in need, even the most compassionate person will not trust it. They will inevitably see it as a possible scam and hit delete. Too many people have saturated the internet with these made-up stories about great suffering and how they need you to wire them thousands of dollars. It is understandable that people are careful when they see another person asking for money. It is sad, because some people actually do have a real need, like a medical procedure that can save their child's life, and it will get ignored. The family will then have so much debt caused by an unforeseen event that they have no way of fixing it on their own.

The Good Samaritan

Jesus illustrates a story of the "Good Samaritan" in the Bible.

And, behold, a certain lawyer stood up, and tempted him, saying, Master, what shall I do to inherit eternal life?
He said unto him, **What is written in the law? how readest thou?**
And he answering said, Thou shalt love the Lord thy God with all thy heart, and with all thy soul, and with all thy strength, and with all thy mind; and thy neighbour as thyself.
And he said unto him, **Thou hast answered right: this do, and thou shalt live.** *But he, willing to justify himself, said unto Jesus, And who is my neighbour?*
And Jesus answering said, **A certain man went down from Jerusalem to Jericho, and fell among thieves, which stripped him of his raiment, and wounded him, and departed, leaving him half dead. And by chance there came down a certain priest that way: and when he saw him, he passed by on the other side. And likewise a Levite, when he was at the place, came and looked on him, and passed by on the other side.**
But a certain Samaritan, as he journeyed, came where he was: and when he saw him, he had compassion on him,
And went to him, and bound up his wounds, pouring in oil and wine, and set him on his own beast, and brought him to an inn, and took care of him.
And on the morrow when he departed, he took out two pence, and gave them to the host, and said unto him, Take care of him; and whatsoever thou spendest more, when I come again, I will repay thee.
Which now of these three, thinkest thou, was neighbour unto him that fell among the thieves?
And he said, **He that shewed mercy on him.**
Then said Jesus unto him, Go, and do thou likewise.
Luke 10:25-37

My "Good Samaritan" story

While I was lying in bed for nearly nine months in the most intense pain, I did some research on the internet of possible cures for my disease. Every doctor and physical therapist told me that they had done all they could to help me. Therapy was not helping, drugs made me feel worse, and the pain stimulator implanted into my spine was not taking the edge off anymore. I learned that the disease I had was incurable. Complex regional pain syndrome (CRPS) is a chronic pain condition most often affecting one of the limbs (arms, legs, hands, or feet), usually after an injury or trauma to that limb. CRPS is characterized by prolonged or excessive pain and mild or dramatic changes in skin color, temperature, and/or swelling in the affected area. Through all my many hours of research, I found something I thought could help. It was stem cell implantation. It was not practiced here in the United States, so the cost of travel and medical treatment was very high.

We just did not have the money for it. I looked at the computer screen and just wept, knowing I could do something but money was in the way. I just wanted to take care of my family. Being bedridden was stressful enough on the entire family. My husband had to quit work to care for me and the kids and it about killed me that I could do nothing to help. I took a chance and asked a close relative in our family to lend us the money. I cried out to her for help because I knew it was within her means. It was so hard to ask her because she was so careful with her money and I respected her for that. She answered, "I will have to pray about that." She never got back to me and I realized then that I had done things in the past to put a strain on our relationship, so I could understand why she was hesitant. There I was, crying in pain all day and night; I could not care for my children or my home, and someone in our own family refused to stretch forth their hand in our great need.

Five years before I had my accident, I slandered a friend from church. I told another lady information about this friend and in turn it was exaggerated and it got back to my dear friend. You know how that works. I had been a busybody and a bad broadcaster. She was so hurt; she told me she had to forgive me, but she never wanted to see my face again. I spent the next four years in regret and with so much shame. I wished I could have done something to change my spoken words. I was reviled and I spent years without having a friend at all for fear of hurting others with my prattling. She did not ever want to trust me again and made it known that I would never be her friend. When I would see her around town, I would walk away and hide as if I were a disease.

I carried that burden of spoiling my testimony until I could bear it no longer. I finally called her and told her again how sorry I was and that I couldn't stop feeling bad about what I had done. She said, "I have not even thought about you in years. And no, I forgave you, but I still do not wish to be your buddy. You do not have to feel bad; I have moved on with my life." The burden lifted as I realized I carried that burden alone. I could have given it over to Christ, but I chose to carry the guilt and shame. She moved on with her life and I needed to let go.

About six months after my accident, she heard that I was really bad off. She invited me to her home. She and her husband asked me if there was anything that could help me so I could walk again and take care of my family. I told them what I had found but that I would have to save up to go. That is when her husband declared, "Go. I will pay for you to go. You need to be able to minister to your family. You do not have to pay me back. I just want you to get better." Here this family that I hurt so badly and that never wanted to see my face again were the very people to stretch forth their hand and give me the miracle I needed. My own people refused to reach out and help, but the Good Samaritans, my enemies, were the ones who showed virtuous compassion. What a miracle.

Not only did this heal our relationship, it taught me to be very careful of my words. Words can do so much damage. By God's grace I was given a second chance. After the treatment in Mexico, I was able to walk again and also help minister to my family with a brand new outlook on life. I was not cured, but I had a lot less pain. Just being able to do half of what I used to be able to do was such a miracle. I am so thankful for mercy.

Virtues in Charity
BEARING ALL THINGS

"Beareth all things, believeth all things,
hopeth all things, endureth all things."
1 Corinthians 13:7

"Bearing" in the English language means to endure, to support, to carry. In the original meaning (Greek: στέγει/stegei) it means to cover. We could say we bear a burden or bear a child. If the original means to cover, we can think of how Christ bears our burdens by covering them—paying for our sins.

How can we cover or bear one another's burdens?

We can do this by caring for them in their greatest hour of need. When someone is hurting or having a crisis, we can bear all things by coming to their aid—a helps ministry. In the body of Christ, we have many members and when a member is suffering, the entire body feels it.

When I had a major nerve damaged in my right leg, it sent a signal to my brain that there was an emergency. My sympathetic nervous system kicked into overdrive to help. It sent the needed blood supply and the needed warmth. Because the injury was in the center of the nerve that controlled the foot, my foot swelled up and turned dark purple. All the pain and throbbing was in the right foot and lower leg even though the injury was by my hip. My brain was smart enough to know what part needed the help even though, to my mind, it was not the correct area. I was confused about why my foot hurt when it was the sciatic nerve in my pelvis which was injured. It did not make sense to me. The human body is a wonderfully-designed machine which repairs and heals itself. The brain sends the signals and kicks on the immune system or the adrenaline needed to survive.

Our bodies are built to survive

If a person gets slammed under a car, the brain will send a message for the adrenal glands to secrete enough adrenaline to lift off the car—a car that is not humanly possible to move, yet in that situation, the body becomes able to bear the weight of it for a short spurt of time. You hear stories about amazing things the human body is able to do when it is trying to survive.

In the Body of Christ, when a member is suffering, the other members should figure out ways to bear the burden so that they will survive. It is to the Church's benefit if its members can function as a whole, as a wonderful, well-oiled, working machine. The purpose of the church is to minister, heal, protect, edify, and most importantly, to spread the good news of the gospel.

Bearing all things in grief

When someone loses a loved one through a tragedy, the church should come to their aid. Going though tragedy is hard enough on its own. When you are grieving, it is hard to think about preparing meals or paying bills. If other people are assisting in that time of great grief and sadness, they are carrying some of that burden, thus making it more bearable for a seemingly unbearable situation.

Knowing you have a support system is helpful when you are grieving. People should not have to ask for help. We need to be better at recognizing the imminent needs of other people. Try to have compassion and understand how you may feel in that situation. Loving your neighbor as yourself through grief is offering…

- **A shoulder to cry on.**
- **A listening ear.**
- **A warm meal.**
- **Something alive, like flowers or plants.**
- **Groceries.**
- **Money.**
- **Prayer.**
- **A nice card or letter of sympathy.**
- **Cleaning their home.**

Bearing all things in sickness and pain

When a member of the body is sick, or has been in some kind of accident, or is laid up in pain, we can help by assisting in some way, by doing things for them that they are no longer able to do. People become sick with fever, or with a terminal illness, or they break their leg in a fall. These are situations out of their control and they are frustrated because they either have to stop working or they cannot do the things they normally do. It can be a very depressing situation for some. When you get used to being useful and helping others, it can be a very hard thing to get used to being an invalid.

I went through this for a time. I felt like such a burden because I was bedridden for so long and needed so much help. I am very sympathetic to other people suffering in pain because I went through it; I can relate. Some people have a long road ahead to get well. Others, sadly, will never get well. Yet some are sick for a short time. Sometimes they will lose a job, and have no money for the things they need. Loving our neighbor as ourselves through sickness or pain is offering…

- **Rides to appointments.**
- **House cleaning.**
- **Money to buy things they need.**
- **A card or flowers.**
- **Prayer.**
- **Meals.**

Bearing all things in financial crisis

People enter into financial crisis in so many ways. They lose a job or loved one and it seems like they have no money to survive. Our government is there to support people if they have a real crisis with their finances. It is called Welfare. So many people are on welfare for many different reasons. It is a corrupt system that helps people no matter what their integrity. For some, it is a miracle; for others, it is a crutch. But in the Body of Christ, if we pool our resources to lift a brother or sister up during a difficult time, it could help them get back on their feet.

It is hard to judge whether it would enable a chain of bad choices or truly help a person of integrity to get off to a new start. Because welfare does not care about whether or not a person has integrity, people who make foolish choices get rewarded and remain foolish their entire lives.

As the Body of Christ, we can help a member to the point that they do not have to be dependent on welfare. We can lift them up by…

- **Helping them find work.**
- **Buying groceries when needed.**
- **Providing clothing for which you no longer have a use.**
- **Donating money for a time.**
- **Fixing things around their home.**
- **Praying.**
- **Making meals.**
- **Offering a place to stay.**

Bearing all things in family crisis

There are situations which may come up, like child abuse, abuse, neglect, divorce, struggle in sin, or abandonment. These are things which may come up in the lives of people we know and love. Even in the Body of Christ, we find out that members get into a crisis in their homes. It is best to bear this burden more privately if possible. Part of bearing another's burdens is not broadcasting stories to everyone. If broadcasting it to a certain person would help the matter it would be okay, especially if they have been through it, and know how to comfort. The difference would be to just tell everyone for the sake of a good gossip.

Going through a family crisis can literally suck all the energy from you. I have been through many different crisis situations. It feels unbearable at times and the thought of walking through the day can be overwhelming.

Sometimes it requires getting the law involved if someone you know is being abused, and other times it requires prayer. People who are hurting because they have been abused or rejected need help. They may be struggling with overcoming sin in their life or figuring out what to do next. You can help bear their burden by…

- **Recommending a book or scripture verse.**
- **Helping them find a good counselor.**
- **Offering a listening ear or shoulder to cry on.**
- **Helping them figure out what options they have and choices they can make.**
- **Providing a safe place for them to go if they are in danger.**
- **Praying for them.**

There may be many more things that I did not even touch upon. The general idea is that if we practice Charity, we bear all things in love. I want to help bear all things by helping in a time of great need. It is not always easy to do, but it makes a big difference to others when they know people care. Because I have been shown such mercy, I in turn want to be merciful toward others.

When you are trying to comfort others, you may need to pay them a visit. Did you know there is proper visiting etiquette? Well, if you know how to be a good visitor, you will make their burden even less.

VISITING ETIQUETTE

When I was a young mother, I would visit old folks' homes and my grandmother's home with my baby. The elderly just love looking at little babies. They probably see something eternal about new life. They are at the end of their days, with every page of their story written. Stories of years gone by, different times, risks taken, joyous moments of raising families, and the regrets of dreams never fulfilled—it was their life lived out. Their children are old and their grandchildren are too busy to visit. Through their old worn-out eyes, they see something so wonderful about a baby. A life full of empty pages and stories untold. Their dry and withered hands stretch forth to touch the softness of the baby's hand, and they are lost in the moment.

My weekly visits were much anticipated. The older ladies would look forward to my visits. Grandma could not wait to hold the baby. I could take them anywhere and the elderly would just hold my contented baby for hours.

As Miles grew, so did his behavior. By the time I had three little ones, my oldest was getting into the toddler years and I was not ready for the fight ahead. He would beg and plead, dragging my skirt with him, begging for a toy in the store. My sweet little Miles would lay down in the aisle, kicking and screaming. I became that frazzled mother I once had the arrogance to condemn. My kids were not so cute anymore; they were a pickle. When I would take the three over to the old folks home, I learned quickly how nervous the poor old ladies would become as my child would tear around the room. I eventually had to stop going because I knew it was causing more harm than good.

I needed to train the children how to behave properly so we could be a blessing when we visited others. I started giving them little lessons on how to act. We would pretend to sit quietly on the sofa, or tiptoe around the house like "little Indians" (my grandfather, who was a native American, taught me this when I was little). We were so quiet that not even a mouse could hear us. It was a fun game for us. If the children did not get their way, they would scream. I would then tell them how I would not give them anything if they fussed, making sure I NEVER gave in to their fits. Amazingly, the fits stopped and life became more peaceful again. I could start visiting others again!

Etiquette in children

Train your children to be "good company." Teach them to be quiet when you are visiting with others.

When they are with you, train them to be respectful of your conversations with their daddy or other people. There is nothing more frustrating than an out-of-control child when you are having a conversation on the phone or in person. The child demands your attention. Every couple of minutes you have interruptions to answer their demands. No. That is not okay. The child can learn manners, and above all, patience. Have you ever wondered when you would attend to your child's needs for 14 hours a day and then they would wait until you pick up the phone to start demanding things? It is because you trained them to do that. I had signals to my children for being silent. I would place my finger over my lips for a warning. Next, I would hold up my index finger, showing them that they will have a consequence.

This is not a license for moms to sit and gab for hours on the phone. I am talking about the times you need to make an important call that only lasts a few minutes. Do not tempt them by spending too much time on the phone. If you do want to visit on the phone, pick a time when the children are napping. My children learned that it was not in their best interest to interrupt their parents. Rather, they would learn patience and wait to ask their questions until I was free to answer them. It is unseemly behavior to go to someone's home and have your child demand, demand, demand. It is not their fault, it is yours for not teaching them patience. It reflects poorly on your mothering.

I have had many mothers visit who have a child that demands their continual attention. For example, I cannot talk with this mother for a few minutes without her child asking her questions. The mother stops the conversation in which we were engaged to answer the child. It is understandable when a child has a genuine need, but it is not okay for them to hijack the entire conversation. Why try to talk when you know the child is soon going to inturrupt? The child is used to having the undivided attention of her mama. They may as well stay home and talk to their three-year-old. If they are needed that much, they should refrain from visiting others.

Training children to behave unseemly

If your children jump on the furniture and damage toys in your home, they will do it at others' homes. If you do not teach value or stewardship for things they own or respect for things you own, they will not learn to be respectful of others' things. I have had people visit that allow their kids to pound on our piano, jump on our beds, and open our refrigerator. They wreck stuff and I feel like kicking them off my property. Instead, if you train them to take care of their toys when they are little, they will take care of your things when they are older. They will learn how to be a good steward of the things with which God blesses them.

What amazes me is that some mothers have no discretion at all. They hear their child pounding on the piano, and smile. They see their child jumping on the bed and just laugh. Their child sits on the floor, ripping pages out of a book, and they just ignore it. Have people no respect? If my kids were tearing stuff off shelves at my home I would make them clean it up or at least teach them not to do that. When I would visit others, if my child would stand on the furniture, I would immediately take them down and scold them.

I have had people visit who allow their kids to barge into our home without waiting for their parent's instruction. They run through the house and have no reguard for our family or our property. One time a lady walked over to my home with her children and their dog. She was outside while her three-year-old was up in *my* bedroom jumping on *my* bed. Make sure you know what your kids are doing and where they are. The lady was trying to be respectful by staying outside because she knew I was busy with my writing. Meanwhile, her dog was incessantly barking and I had to stop writing to help her train her dog to stop the barking, since it did not seem to bother her. I had to make the barking stop because it bothered me!

I would give preparatory instruction before entering someone's home or a store. Children need instruction, period. Before you enter any new place, you must tell them what they can and cannot do. Tell them what the consequences will be and what you expect of them. If we were going shopping, I would tell the kids in the car, "Do not ask for anything. Do not run around in the aisles. Do not climb on the cart. Do not yell or talk loudly. Finally, do not touch anything! If you do not obey, we will immediately leave the store."

When we would visit someone, I would instruct the kids in the car, "Do not ask for food. Do not climb on the furniture. Do not touch anything unless the other children share with you. Do not interrupt my conversations. Place your hand on my arm if you have a question and I will know you need something urgent. If you do not obey, we will leave immediately." It may sound like I am a mean mama, but I never had to leave. They learned to obey and respect. Sure, I have had many situations come up where my kids behaved unseemly; it is to be expected occasionally. Kids are kids, after all. I am a kid-friendly person. I let the kids be kids; I let them run and play. Now that they are older, I instruct them to play outside if they want to be wild and free.

Visiting etiquette

If you are planning a visit, always bring food to contribute, unless the hostess instructs you otherwise. If you have a larger family and you are invited to eat a meal at someone's home, ask a few simple questions:

- **"Can I help with anything?"**
- **"Is there something I can contribute to the meal?"**
- **"Can I help clean up after the meal?"**

It shows you care, and if you show some simple courtesy, they will be glad to invite you over again.

Overnight or extended visits

If you are planning a trip and staying overnight at someone's home make sure you follow six easy steps:

1 **Laundry.** Bring your own bath towels and bedding, so your hostess does not have to do more laundry. If the hostess offers her washing machine, be very thankful. You could ask to use the machine, but bring your own soap if you are staying long, unless they offer their soap to you. The object of the game is to not cost your hostess more money and time. Bring your own soaps, toothbrushes, and other toiletries that you will need on your visit.

2 **Bedwetters.** If you have a bedwetter, make sure to buy extra diapers, a floor mat or rubber sheet, and a plastic bag in which to put soiled or wet clothing/bedding. Store the mess in your car. If your child accidentally pees in the bed, let your hostess know immediately and find out how you can fix the situation. Do not allow your hostess to smell your bedwetter's bedding or clean it up themselves.

3. **Bring food.** Always bring your own food so you can contribute. If the hostess does not want you to contribute, save your food for the trip home. It is better to have the option of contributing than to make an impression that you expect them to feed you. Always offer to assist in meal preparations.

4. **Clean up.** Clean up after yourself and your family: Make sure to pick up around your living quarters. Make beds, tidy up, and fold clothing. Do not leave your area a mess. If you are eating, make sure to help clean up after meals. If you have small children who play with toys, be sure to help them clean up the toys before bedtime or before meals. Especially before you leave, clean up to the best of your ability. Do not leave a pig sty or mess for your hostess. That is very unseemly. They were nice enough to offer you a place to stay, so you should not make it more work for them than is needed.

5. **Eating meals.** If you are invited to stay for all the meals, count it an honor. A perfect hostess will make sure to ask what you prefer, but it is highly unlikely. Expect your hostess to serve things that are not exactly what you are used to eating. Instruct your children to take very little so they can finish their plates. It seems very wasteful and ungrateful if your child leaves a whole plate of food sitting at the table uneaten. They should be taught to *never* complain about the food at home. If they do not like the food, they should not be allowed to yell, "I do not like this, this is gross, I hate this food, or I won't eat this!" That is just plain embarrassing for you and insulting to the hostess. If they do not like what they are being fed, instruct them to wait until the hostess is distracted for them to quietly let you know. Then you have time to scrape their food onto your plate or into a napkin. Try not to make a scene about it.

6. **Quiet time.** Try to make sure your hostess has some down-time, too. Do a family nap time or a family walk time. Give your hostess some

room to breathe. She is so glad you are there, but everyone needs a break from visiting. It helps you to unwind and talk privately with your husband for a bit. If your family wakes earlier than usual, make sure you keep everyone quiet. Teach the children not to talk loudly or slam doors. Before bedtime ask your hostess what time they usually get up. If they get up much later than your family, respect their sleep times. Make sure to pack breakfast foods along just in case. Simple things like granola bars, hardboiled eggs, fruit, or yogurt cups will help tide the children over until a meal is served. That way you can take a walk outside or drive around while the other family is sleeping. They are working hard after all on your behalf, so it is nice to make sure they have their rest.

Final thoughts

The important thing about visiting is to not wear out your welcome. Do not overwhelm your hostess. Be a blessing. Overall, just think of others before yourself! It is that simple and the rewards will be eternal.

Recipe to be a GOOD WOMAN

Proverbs 31:20—A good woman is benevolent; she gives to those in need.
"She stretcheth out her hand to the poor; yea, she reacheth forth her hands to the needy."
Key words: *stretcheth, reacheth*
Compassionate, merciful, generous, easily moved by the distresses and sufferings of others.

Time-Tested Wisdom...

Taken from Created To Be His Help Meet by Debi Pearl

Be Quiet and Trust Me

He plays golf every weekend and watches sports on television. He rarely plays with the children. She has talked to him about it. She tells him he is lazy and needs to father their children. Then she hears the Lord softly whisper to her,

"Be quiet and trust me."

He gambles and drinks a little too much. He holds a steady job and loves his children. She quotes Scripture to him about his foolish use of money and drinking too much. She is constantly angry with him. Then the Lord whispers to her,

"Be quiet and trust me."

There are so many habits of his that annoy her. He leaves the toilet seat up. He leaves the cap off of the toothpaste. He burps after he eats. She tells him over and over again how annoying he is and that he needs to have better manners. God softly whispers to her,

"Be quiet and trust me."

Why do we think we can do such a better job at changing our husbands than God? I think it is interesting that the Bible tells husbands to love their wives and not become bitter towards them (Colossians 3:19). It must be that husbands must be encouraged not to become bitter because wives have a great tendency to nag them which can easily lead to bitterness.

One woman commented that she had a friend whose marriage broke up after many years. She asked the husband why and he said he couldn't take the nagging and high expectations anymore. Think how much more a husband would be likely to change instead if he had a wife who was joyful and smiled at him often, who never nagged or tried to change him.

Let God change your husband. Tell your concerns to your husband several times and then leave it in God's hands. Pray earnestly for your husband, that you will love him just the way he is. Listen to that still small voice that whispers to you,

"Be quiet and trust me."

"Likewise, ye wives, be in subjection to your own husbands;
that, if any obey not the word, they also may without the word be won
by the conversation of the wives."
1 Peter 3:1

"In quietness and trust is your strength."
Isaiah 30:15

~Lori Alexander

From Blog: Always Learning

Chapter Sixteen
Virtuous Trust

"She is not afraid of the snow for her household:
for all her household are clothed with scarlet."
Proverbs 31:21

The virtuous woman is not afraid. She is not a "worry wart." Instead, she is simply prepared. When she sees the ominous skies encroaching, she is ready. Her family could be snowed in for days, but because this virtuous woman planned ahead for disaster, they are warm, clothed in the finest scarlet and fed. Thinking ahead is a virtue. There is no need for anxiety when you have a game plan. Even if the inevitable happens, she is wise enough to figure something out. She does her research, she works hard, and has good common sense.

Women are notorious for worrying. When we do not see our small child for a few seconds, we automatically assume the worst. Our heart starts pounding and our adrenals get ramped up, pumping adrenaline through our body. We think the worst first and fear rules our minds. **Fear is the opposite of Trust and Faith**. There are two different kinds of fear. Fear of God (to reverence God) and being fearful. Fearing God is healthy, whereas having fear is damaging to us. It is interesting to note that the phrases "fear not," "be not afraid," and "be anxious for nothing" appear over 365 times in the Bible. There are 365 days in the year. I find it very comforting that God saw fit to remind us to not be afraid enough to abundantly cover every day of the year.

*"Say to them that are of a fearful heart, Be strong, **fear not**: behold, your God*
will come with vengeance, even God with a recompence;

he will come and save you."
Isaiah 35:4

"Fear thou not; *for I am with thee: be not dismayed; for I am thy God: I will strengthen thee; yea, I will help thee; yea, I will uphold thee with the right hand of my righteousness."*
Isaiah 41:10

"And **fear not** *them which kill the body, but are not able to kill the soul: but rather fear him which is able to destroy both soul and body in hell."*
Matthew 10:28

"But and if ye suffer for righteousness' sake, happy are ye: and **be not afraid** *of their terror, neither be troubled;"*
1 Peter 3:14

"For God hath not given us the spirit of fear; *but of power, and of love, and of a sound mind."*
2 Timothy 1:7

These are just a few examples of the many, showing us that we should not fear or worry. Meditate each day on a verse about being afraid for nothing. Resist the temptation to worry. God is in control. Nothing changes just because you have some anxiety. When we have a healthy fear of God, we live life differently. If I saw God, I would fall on my face before him. Even though He sees the secret thoughts of our hearts, we still think bad things about others and give lots of occasion to bitterness and jealousy. He has command over the sea, over the clouds, over life, and over death. One day we will see God and He will be so magnificent, mighty, and merciful at the same time.

Fear of man
The fear of man is when you fear people will judge you, condemn you, hurt you, or reject you. We fail to share the truth with others because we fear offending them. We care too much what others think. When we care about what others think, we become a First Class People Pleaser. I

have been a people pleaser so much of my life it is not funny. I would never say no because I was afraid of letting people down. I let people take advantage of me because I was afraid to stand up to them. What could they do to me? What is the worst thing that would have happened?

- **They could stop visiting me.**
- **They could call me a bad name.**
- **They could hate me.**
- **They could tell people I am mean.**

These things are not that bad. It may be a bit uncomfortable at first but time passes and wounds always heal. Examine whether or not this person is your "real" friend. "Real" friends do not put expectations on you because they accept you for who you are. If God accepts you, then you need not worry about what others think.

Fear of circumstances

Lots of things can happen. A tornado can suddenly rip through your home, leaving you homeless. People get in car crashes and die. Cancer claims lives while diseases spread. Abusers lurk around the corner. Murderers take life while thieves break in and steal. Kids get abducted. People are snuffed out in house fires. Our freedoms are being taken away. Our food is being poisoned. And Satan is the god of this world, gaining more and more followers each day to join the dark side. What do we do? How do we hide? It is easy to allow fear to set in. Rather, Christ tells us…

"Take therefore no thought for the morrow: for the morrow shall take thought for the things of itself. Sufficient unto the day is the evil thereof."
Matthew 6:34

It is so easy to get caught up in the doom and gloom, what ifs, and being fearful. Information is powerful. I like to be wise and know what is going on so I am ready.

"Behold, I send you forth as sheep in the midst of wolves: be ye therefore wise as serpents, and harmless as doves."
Matthew 10:16

"Watch therefore: for ye know not what hour your Lord doth come."
Matthew 24:42

It is good to be ready, like the virtuous woman was ready. Note that she was not afraid when disaster hit because she knew what to do. Many people run around being fearful of war and what could happen. They spend thousands on preparedness gear and have a bug-out location. I heard of a man who died about ten years ago. He survived the Y2K scare and lived in fear until his last hour. He had surveillance cameras all over his property, which was nestled in a remote wooded area. This guy thought the end was coming. He had his guns loaded and was ready for the Apocalypse. Eventually he died from natural causes, but to think about locking yourself down like that is just plain sad. He could have enjoyed the sunshine, the roses, and being with family; but instead he looked at his stash of guns he never used, his hoards of rations that never needed rationing, and probably felt utterly alone. I bet his passionate drive against what could have happened drove all of his loved ones away. The stress he placed on his fearful heart caused him to die early. Stress is a killer.

Instead, I look at history. I see nations that have risen and then fallen, and wicked rulers who wanted to be like God in every generation. Wars and famine, pestilence and disease never stopped because of fear. We have a choice. We can either choose to fear the unknown or we can get wise. Life is unpredictable. People can lose their jobs. I was not prepared to lose my photography business. Stuff happens. People get sick. Storms of life come. Disaster strikes.

God instructs us to be wise but not fearful. When Joseph was suddenly abandoned by his own people and enslaved in Egypt, he never knew he was going to be used of God to prepare the land for famine. Through Pharaoh's dream, God gave this young slave a vision of what was coming. He was able to interpret this dream. Joseph, by the grace of God, was able to organize a plan to store up for the seven years of famine. While they were living off the fat of the land, they had such an abundance that they were able to put away enough to last for the hard times to come. When the drought came and the rain ceased from watering the earth, Joseph opened the storehouses. They were prepared. If it was not for his wisdom, they would have been destroyed. God gives us great examples in His word of how He took care of His people.

We need not worry. Being watchful and being prepared is a good thing. If you have a way to grow food, a way to cook it with no power, a source of heat and water, and some essentials stored up, you will be ready when the snow comes. Your home will be clothed in scarlet.

Being prepared

We have been homesteading for about twelve years now. Homesteading is a great life. Not only are you raising food that your family eats, but you are building strong family ties. The family that works and prays together, stays together. You do not have to live in the country to start homesteading. There are little things you can do to be prepared for whatever life may bring.

Keeper Tip...
- Be Not Afraid.
- Be Prepared.
- Be Wise.
- Relax.
- Trust in the Lord.

HOMESTEADING 101

Are you still dreaming about becoming a homesteader someday? Someday, when you finally convince your husband to sell the suburban home and move out to the country. A day when you can finally afford that pretty piece of God's country where you can plant your roots and start growing. You go online and fish around for properties in the country only to find yourself discouraged because the price is not one that you can afford. I remember those days all too well, while sitting in the kitchen of our city lot, watching cars buzz by every couple of seconds, dreaming of a quiet life. There they are—listings come up in your price range. You look at those properties with rose-colored glasses and a vision of what they "could be." A run-down trailer on a couple of acres with a promise hidden in your heart that one day you could tear down that old rat den, and build a little log cabin in its stead. Years go by and you are still in the city trying to make the days pass. Why not grow where you are planted? Find ways, today, to start homesteading. It is not that difficult to get started. You do not have to be out on the prairie to be resourceful. **Homesteading, in its true essence, is being resourceful.**

Here are 10 Ways to Start a Homestead or Prepare

1 **Plant a micro-garden.** If you have a planting bed around your home, you can plant all kinds of herbs or even vegetables. You do not need to have a garden plot to accomplish this task. If you want to start your own plants from seed, you need to make sure to keep them indoors or in a cold frame to start, until they have established a good root. Once they are hearty enough, they can easily be planted in your flower bed by digging a hole and placing the root system in that hole, and covering it with sufficient soil around the stem. The other option would be to buy established seedling plants at a local greenhouse shop. That makes it all the easier for the newbie.

If you live in an apartment, grow little potted herbs in your window sills where they get some sunlight.

All year long you can clip little sprigs of herb off your little potted herbs and it will give you a feeling of growing some of your own food. Some people have a patio or sun room. These are great places to grow all kinds of things. You can grow a cucumber plant on an old iron bench, or a tomato in a large clay pot. The biggest maintenance would be making sure you water your pots frequently.

Having a few things growing around and in your home, whether you are in the city and you grow a few potted herbs or in the country with a large-scale garden, you still get the same satisfaction—the satisfaction of growing some of your own food. Even the largest-scale home garden is usually incapable of growing ALL the food needed. It is a common misconception that the modern homesteader is able to grow ALL of their own food. Most of us still buy our grains.

Store up some bulk grains. Another way you can start the homesteading experience of being resourceful is to buy in bulk. Did you know that if you have a few buckets of dried beans and rice, you can survive on those commodities for up to a year without going to the grocery store? The cost of a few sacks of beans and rice would be less than $100. Of course, it is not ideal to eat beans and rice at every meal for an entire year, but it would keep you alive as long as you had fresh water to drink. What's nice about mung beans is that they are very nutritious, easy to grow, and do not need soil to sprout. People use mung beans to toss in a salad or just eat fresh. One tablespoon of tiny dried mung beans can make two cups of edible sprouts! These are just a great thing, all around, to have on hand. Think of it—you could have your city-dwelling children grow some of their own sprouts, and you are all becoming homesteaders at the same time!

In a survival situation, you could have your beans and rice....AND a side of mung beans for a vegetable! This is a healthy combination! All bulk grains can be stored in five-gallon pails for years to come, as long as it is sealed up well. Diatomaceous earth can be used to repel the creepers that may enjoy your stash. I have never had an issue with critters getting into my grain bins. I do not air seal them, I do not add basil leaves, I do not buy expensive mylar bags with oxygen absorbers; I just dump them into a $5 bucket I bought at a hardware store down the road and put a lid on it.

We buy 50-pound sacks of the following grains each year:

- Dried beans (Kidney, Black, Pinto, Great Northern, etc.)
- Lentils
- Rice
- Wheat berries (Spelt, Kamut, Rye, etc.)
- Corn
- Oats
- Quinoa
- Millet
- Barley
- MUNG BEANS

 Grind your own wheat. You can use a wheat grinder, which gives you that homegrown feeling. Grinding wheat can be done with an electric wheat grinder. If you do not have an electric wheat grinder, you should check out the one we sell in our store. We use our industrial-strength grain mill (The Country Grain Mill) which can grind a lot at one time. When you grind wheat fresh, you get all of the benefits from it. Flour really loses its nutrition the longer it sits on the shelf. Do not store up flour; you should always grind it fresh. Fresh-ground flour has to be used immediately because within about 72 hours it loses at least 90% of over 30 nutrients through oxidation.

Making your own breads, cereals, crackers, and noodles from scratch lends to the homesteading experience. If you watch our *Homesteading for Beginners* DVD series, you will find all kinds of recipes and demonstrations on how to make them.

 Canning and freezing produce. You don't have to have a garden to do canning or freezing. My grandmother lived through the depression, and canned everything she grew in her flower beds. She didn't live on a homestead or out in the country, yet her pantry was always filled with jars.

Farmer's Markets are great places to find produce in bulk, if you want to can something for the winter. Certain things can be blanched, put in freezer bags and stored in the freezer. Some folks just don't have the space for a garden, so buying fresh produce is a wonderful alternative that will give a great feeling of self-sufficiency. Some ladies do little one-batch canning projects and find it very fulfilling. It is not really hard to do and it can offer a selection of food to eat later in the year.

 Micro-clutch of laying hens. Nowadays, most city ordinances allow for a few caged hens for laying eggs. Many people do not realize the possibilities of this. You can house them like you would domestic rabbits, in little cages with shelter attached. They make very little noise, which is the reason they are allowed. It is fun for children to pick out some baby chicks in the spring and raise them to be laying hens. Each day they can run out and throw them some kitchen scraps or feed. Gathering eggs is such a delightful experience for people of all ages! You have your fresh homegrown eggs and a feeling that you are making it a little closer to the land. This is something within anyone's reach. Check out your county or city ordinances and start homesteading today!

Alternate lighting. Have flashlights. Become a collector of candles. They can be bought by the hundreds at thrift stores. Every time I go to the thrift store, I pick up a few half-used-up candles for about 25¢ each. In my closet, I have a couple of old shoe boxes that hold these old candles. When the power goes out, I have a way to make some light. Old-fashioned oil lamps are also good to have on hand. We have about five glass oil lamps and some extra bottles of lamp oil. If you had to, you could cook food very slowly over a candle or lamp. Fire is fire.

 Cooking. If you have some aluminum foil and some Styrofoam, you can make a little oven or hot box if you ever need to. We have one, and use it to save energy. If you bring a pot of rice to a boil, you can put it into an insulated hot box and it will finish cooking without any power. We incubate our yogurt this way as well. Get it to the desired temperature; then wrap a small blanket or several towels around the hot box to insulate, and it will keep very close to that temperature all day long. When you line your box with aluminum foil, you can set it out in the sun and it will cook food. Amazing!

 Water. Do you realize that it takes power to pump the water to your house? If you do not plan ahead for this, you could be without water for days in a storm that causes a major power outage. Buying distilled water in jugs is a good thing. Every so often when you are at the market, just grab a jug. Distilled water is best because it will not become stagnant or grow bacteria. It can sit out of sight and out of mind until a need arises. You will be glad you have it if you should ever need it. When using water in emergency situations, **conserve.** Every drop counts when you do not know how long you will be without it. No taking showers. Sponge bathing with a cloth will give you a fresh feeling without using too much water. Collect rain water for watering animals or washing dishes. It does not take much effort to have a rain barrel sitting under your downspouts off the side of your roof.

 Heat. If you have a power outage in the winter, heat is very important. Have lots of warm clothing and heavy quilts on hand. If you have a fireplace or wood burner, make sure you are never "out" of wood. I have known people who had to chop up their kitchen table and chairs to keep their fire going. When it is a life or death situation, people have used things like money or family heirloom antiques for burning just to keep warm. Nothing is as precious as your family's lives. Huddle together. When you put several people under a big quilt, you will generate heat together. Keep moving. When you move your body, you create heat as well.

10 First aid. Always have first aid supplies on hand. If someone gets a bad cut, you'll want to have something to clean out the wound properly and keep it bandaged. Think natural healing, because when you are in a bad storm you cannot get in the car to drive to the emergency room. Have natural healing and emergency first aid books in your reference library. Remember, the internet and your smart phone may not work if there is a major disaster. You cannot just look up the information you need. Be smart and prepare yourself.

First Aid and Emergency Kit Essentials

- Rubbing alcohol
- Hydrogen peroxide
- Bandages of all sizes
- Tweezer and scissors
- Needle and thread
- Antibiotic cream and Aspirin
- Essential oils (**Melaleuka**—kills bacteria, **Lavendar**—heals burns, **Oregano**—fights colds, **Frankenscense**—helps with pain and healing, **Peppermint, Ginger**—stomach relief)
- Benadryl, for allergic reactions
- Splints and wrapping bandages
- Bentonite clay and charcoal for drawing; charcoal for diarrhea
- Healing salve

- Immune-boosting herbs
- Matches
- Flashlight
- Hammer
- Knife
- Crowbar
- Saw
- Rope
- Hot water bottle
- Duct tape
- Latex gloves
- Filtered face mask
- Heavy-duty work gloves
- Resealable bags
- Pepper spray or gun

The moral of the story

Be prepared. It does not require any fear. You may never have to use your knowledge but it is good to have it just in case the need arises. I have taught my kids some safety drills, like:

- **What to do in case of a fire. We show them how to escape and how to stop, drop, and roll. How to crawl under the smoke.**
- **What to do when there is a tornado. Get to the lowest place possible, whether it is a basement, cellar, or under the stairs.**
- **What to do if a burglar is trying to enter your home.**
- **How to defend themselves against someone trying to take them or rape them. We teach them to stay together in groups.**
- **What is out there in the world. How wicked people's imaginations are and how to be wise.**
- **Gun safety and how to hunt for food. How to skin out an animal and cook it.**
- **Which plants are poisonous and which wild plants are edible.**
- **How to build survival shelters, build fires, and how to swim.**
- **Who they can trust and about not trusting strangers.**
- **How to drive a car—just in case.**

Believe it or not, all of these things are super fun to teach. Kids love learning how to do every one of these. Now they can be wise and prepared for anything that comes their way.

Do you have to join an Amish community to be prepared?

NO! In fact, I would highly discourage it. The Amish are a closed religious sect. They do not welcome "outsiders" into their circles easily. It is very complicated to join. They would ask you to give up everything and follow them. Even when you follow everything, they will not be satisfied. They will test and prove you until you feel like a failure. Your life will be under a microscope as long as you are trying to fit in. I know, because I tried to fit in. Because you are not born into this lifestyle, you will have a harder time shifting over to their primitive ways. We lived in an Amish community for one year and I can tell you, we were good at being Amish. We had been homesteading for twelve years before moving there. I knew how to make more things from scratch than they did! I used a wringer washer or washed our clothing with a washboard and a bucket of water.

We had candles and kerosene lanterns to light our home. Our water was manually pumped each day with a pressure tank and generator. When the water pressure went down, there was no water. We had a horse and buggy, a treadle sewing machine, I sewed all of our clothes in their appropriate fabrics and style, and I knew a good bit of their language. You could not tell that we were impostors.

The attitude of the Amish can be prideful just like any other human being. They sometimes believe they are better than the "English" people. Not all Amish believe this way, but it is more common than not. Our experience was that the Amish would gossip about our family and make fun of us when we were not around. They waited and hoped for us to fail. One winter, I invited 42 Amish people into my home for an ice cream supper. Ice cream suppers are monthly gatherings of the Amish with their close relatives. Since we did not have Amish relatives, I wanted them to accept us as family. The evening started out lovely. I had made an Amish-style dinner with all the many fixings. I had the whole thing figured out. I took down all the paintings I'd done of our children because I did not want to be a stumbling block, yet a few Amish girls begged to show them off. They are not allowed to have any photographs of people because they believe it is idol worship (making a graven image). The Amish girls paraded around the home with my paintings, one by one, after which, they began chanting, "Play the piano, Erin!" I told them that I was afraid it would be a bad idea because I knew they did not allow musical instruments. They loudly coerced, "PLAY, PLAY, PLAY!" I could hardly believe it. Being the people-pleaser that I was, I walked over to the piano and started to play. That was not enough to satisfy them. They wanted more. Out came the guitar and I played another hymn on the guitar as we all sang loudly together.

We were running a business selling my husband's wooden drying racks online, so we hid a computer under the stairs in our bedroom closet. They knew about the computer, so they asked me to play them one of the songs I wrote and recorded. So, here I was, crammed into a tiny bedroom closet with fifteen Amish people gathered around a little computer screen. I had a bad feeling about that night. My husband had the same feeling. We knew that we had crossed the line and it would be crossed forever. My husband and I went to the minister and said we were sorry for leading the Amish astray. He told us that he felt bad that it turned out this way, that the other members were not too keen on having us around, and that this incident would probably make matters worse. He suggested that we take the piano out into our front yard, smash it to pieces, and get rid of our vehicles. Even then, he told us it would take about five years to become accepted. The Amish church would not allow us to join until they saw some improvements.

I went home in tears and told my daughters that we had to smash the piano. They cried and said, "Why? What is so wrong with a piano?" I thought about it for a long time and realized how silly the whole thing had become. We decided that we would give up trying to fit in with the Amish. Besides, it had gotten to the point where they only called when they wanted a ride. I was not there to be a driver! They did not want us there and it became more and more obvious to me. We learned a lot living in their lifestyle during that year. The skills we acquired could be useful in the future but if I could do it over again, I would never have tried to fit in. That was a big mistake. All we really wanted was community life because we felt it was better for our children to be raised within a farming community.

I have a friend who is doing the same thing–walking in the same footsteps. The end will be the same. Unless you are born Amish, you will never be accepted fully as one of them. Right now they are suiting her up with all the dresses, patterns, head coverings, and whatever else she will need to "fit in." I remember that feeling all too well. It truly feels good to "fit in," but you do not have to join the Amish to find what you are looking for. You do not have to be Amish to homestead or have community life.

My community life is home

Many people would love to live in a community like the Amish do. So many of us crave that warm community life and all it has to offer. The singings, barn raisings, and canning bees. It is the over and over of living that seems so romantic, so simple—where there is no television set gleaming its cold stare, or computers that steal your attention for hours. Those hours turn into days and weeks when you lose count of them. We long for a simpler life, sitting on a creaky old porch, shelling peas while the breeze gently gathers our hair from our eyes—a time where life seems to stand completely still and free. Children running barefoot in the fields of clover, and you can hear their laughter. I dream and long for this in my heart of hearts, just as most of you do. There is something so void in our culture. As I embrace the musings of yesteryear, I take hold of something greater. If only just for a moment, I see meaning to this life more than my desire of the simpler life. For if I would be sitting on my porch shelling peas in the breeze, I would not be writing a "blog" or making homesteading DVDs.

I am the type that would want to run away fast from the grips of technology and the business of keeping up with the world. It would be my wish to say goodbye to all of it forever and step back into life as it was a hundred years ago. That is my flesh! You see, I used to covet the simpler life; and it was wrong for me to want it so badly that I lost sight of why I am here—NOW. I have had to realize that God created me in this present age to be of His service to the people He still loves and leads. He has a ministry for me—first to my husband and then to my children who also live in this present age. Children who will soon be on their own in this, the modern world as we know it. Daughters who may one day marry a man who works on computers, or sons who may marry wives who get a lot of encouragement about being good wives and mothers from reading Christian blogs.

It would be so much easier for me to walk away from it all. Instead, I work with it, not because I want to, but because I need to do whatever the Lord's will is for my life right now. Right now, we live in a modern, functioning old farmhouse in TN that runs on electricity. We are thankful we learned how to live off-grid, because we now know how to survive a bit more than before, just in case we need to survive. It is valuable information for anyone to acquire.

One of the main reasons people get a good feeling when they think about the way humans lived a hundred years ago is the community life that was a part of their daily living. I cherish the stories of my grandparents and how they lived in close farming communities. Aunt Janis would walk down the lane to help milk Grandpa Fred's cow with the short teats. Since she was young and her hands were so small, she was needed and was a valued helper on the farm. All the relatives who lived in that community as well as neighbors would meet for ice cream socials on Friday evenings, where they would sing and enjoy the time together. Girls would churn the cream in an old ice cream maker. Sunday afternoons after church were spent eating popcorn, laughing at all the stories people would tell, and just relaxing as a community. They were never shorthanded and they were always there for one another when they were needed.

The Amish are a good example of community in this modern society. They are the only ones, to my small knowledge, who can continue living the community life that all humans lived for thousands of years before them. It is rare today and that is so sad. The Amish have that similar community life which my forefathers enjoyed a hundred years before. They still have the ice cream socials, the Sunday afternoon popcorn visits, the community work of the fields and farming, and the women gathering for quilting bees and tea time. Amish community life is closed to outsiders and through my firsthand rejection, I now understand why. I had to accept it. In order to "keep" that culture and lifestyle, they have to fight against change. For to accept change, or other influences, would be to accept the end to life as they have lived for hundreds of years.

Even here, in our current community, there lives an Amish-type community. They are all outcasts from the Amish because one way or another, they changed their heart towards a deeper meaning in their life, and that change is very threatening to the steadfast Amish. Instead of trying to grow in understanding, their first instinct is to protect what they hold sacred—their community life. Therefore, they cast out the free thinker or the ones that seem different. The plain folk here are very warm to you if you follow their rules, but they will avoid you if you refuse to change to meet their standards. It is very similar to the Amish I lived around, just a different style of dress and mode of believing.

It is right to admire some of their age-old wisdom and hard work ethic—I know I do. I wished with all my heart one day to have a community like that with like-minded believers who love the LORD and want to work as a community, hand in hand. However, I soon realized, you would have the same end. Some people would move in and want to add more technology, or just have a bad attitude, and how do you deal with that? Maybe another family would move in and want to dress provocatively; then what? That is why, if you had a community, you would have to be like the Amish to "keep" it simple and "keep" it as righteous as you decide as a group it should be. The bottom line is that we know enforcing man-made rules is wrong as well. Today they are called communes or cults. You just can't win…That is why I gave up on it for this side of heaven. I still have a little homestead where we try to grow our own food. I still enjoy the fellowship community offers, like canning or butchering livestock with neighbors and friends when time allows and other ladies seem interested to give it a try. I know that is within reach for all of us. More importantly, I have cleaved unto my family for my community life, to my home. We are not all off doing our own thing. We tend to stick together all the time. We work together. We play together. We relax together. If we need more meat, we figure out a way to obtain it, cut it up and can it all. What a blessing to have a family. We are never shorthanded, nor are we ever too busy to lend a hand. When the hands are in close proximity and a need arises, they are ready to offer help. Still, "many hands make light work!" We still have our ice cream socials. My girls churn the fresh cream from our cow in our kitchen mixer. They pop popcorn over the electric range with our hand-crank popper. We have it. It is not all perfectly nostalgic with oil lamps flickering, but it is home. And it is my community right now. I find my community life so much more glorious and fulfilling today in my home with my family than dreaming of it somewhere else in years gone forever. I embrace the now. We are loving life no matter what life is at the time. That is the most wonderful thing about joy; it is wherever, whatever the circumstance, and whenever you choose it.

Recipe to be a GOOD WOMAN

Proverbs 31:21—A good woman is confident in how she has provided for her household. It is well-outfitted due to her management and hard work. She doesn't wait until the last minute to prepare dinner. A good woman plans and prepares ahead.

"She is not afraid of the snow for her household: for all her household are clothed with scarlet."

Key words: *not afraid*

She has made preparation for the future.

Letters from my Readers

Dear Erin,

    This post is so beautiful, and I needed to hear this. Sometimes I find myself wanting to escape the modern world so badly and live in the "good old days" that the thought just consumes me. I could give up all modern conveniences in a heartbeat for a simpler life...but at the same time, I am thankful for some of these modern things, like Christian blogs, for instance.

    Like you said...God put us here, in this time, for a reason. Perhaps He wants me to use my love of the old ways to inspire people to go back to a simpler, more fulfilling lifestyle? I realize now that coveting a life in the past is a sin, and I need to be thankful for all of the blessings that God has given me here, today.

~ Pauline

Dear Pauline,

    Amen. It is true that God puts us here for a reason and I am so thankful that you took the time to comment about your life. I think it is wonderful to pass on some old-fashioned values to the modern society. They need it desperately. Keep encouraging others!

In Christ,
Erin

Chapter Seventeen
Virtuously Skilled

"She maketh herself coverings of tapestry;
her clothing is silk and purple."
Proverbs 31:22

The virtuous woman is a skilled woman. She is able to make useful things. This woman is making her own clothing. She probably makes clothing for her entire family. When she is not making clothing, she is making other things. Today, women can start hobbies of all kinds. I know women who make baskets, quilts, curtains, and crafts of every kind. There are so many things for you to learn and enjoy.

Since the beginning of time, women were raised to be skilled in making useful items. They had to make everything from clothing to floor mats on which to sleep. They made clay pots in which to hold their water or cook their food. Baskets were woven because they needed a place to put things and something in which to carry things. Plastic totes and bags were not invented until the last 50 years. Where there were no entertainment devices like phones, computers, and televisions, people had to do other things for their pasttime, if they had any. You see evidence of what they did in paintings on stone walls or canvas, in ancient manuscripts, in sculptures and etched pictorials on clay pots. People played musical instruments, they painted, they had live theatre, and they engaged in sports.

The Jewish people had their feasts and celebrations; Egypt had their paintings on papyrus and stone sculptures; the Greeks had their Olympic games; the Romans had their Colosseum for violent entertainment; the medieval people had their grand castles and paintings; and the Renaissance gave way to art in every form. All throughout history people created great things and had ways to find enjoyment. During colonial times, women who were not spinsters or peasants were living a life of frivolity. The frivolous lifestyle involved sitting in a fine room, wearing fine clothing, having servants that brought them tea, and doing crafts. Women of nobility or wealth were afforded a hobby. They could learn how to read and write, play instruments, do needlework, or paint pictures or fine china.

These women did not have to make cloth or clothing like the virtuous woman of biblical times did. They could buy the fabric from a shop and hire one of their maidens to sew it. The Age of the Aristocrats in England was also a time of frivolity. The women were delicate and quiet, while the women of lower class were still making a lot of the things the upper-class citizens used in their glorious homes.

We have the luxury of both worlds today. I do both; I work hard making things and keeping my home as well as spending time doing artistic things like writing, painting, taking photos, or singing. Because we are created by God to love beauty and be expressive, we can do things to make our homes lovely.

Making a house a home

Most times when you see a single man living alone, you see the trademark "Bachelor Pad" or "Man Cave." Animal heads loom over big, padded chairs that have remote controls laying all over them. There are cups and other dishes laying out on various rustic tables. You won't see flowers, lace, or Precious Moments® sitting on their shelves. When a man marries a woman, she turns that cave into a beautiful home. She adds her special touches. Women like to decorate. Our God is a God of beauty, or else he would not decorate the grasses with pretty flowers. Our homes reflect the beauty and grace of God. We can use our skills to create a lovely home.

INTERIOR DESIGN 101

1 **De-clutter.** We can make sure our homes are tidy. De-cluttering our living space is a must. Having piles of junk laying around the home is not very homey or attractive. Get organized. Throw out stuff you never use. When you have a ton of stuff you never use, looking at it in piles is going to cause stress. You know it does not belong and you do not

want to look at it. Either find a place to store it, donate it, or trash it.

 Painting walls. Give the walls a fresh coat of paint. Pick a color that you can live with. Avoid bright colors because they will make you nervous after awhile. Think soft and complimentary. Instead of reaching for the fluorescent pink or blue, pick a soft pink or pale blue. Brighten up your trim with a coat of white paint and your walls with a contrasting color like tan or slate blue. If you have good quality wood, polish it and paint the walls a contrasting color that is lighter to offset the darkness of the wood. You would not want brown walls with brown trim, Or white walls with white trim.

 Balance. You want to make the room feel balanced. Center things on the wall.

 Window treatments. Curtains are a nice touch. If you sew, find a fabric that will work with your chosen color scheme. Do not have red curtains with pink walls! Wispy white curtains are very classy when you have white trim and tan walls. Think bright and cheery when picking curtains. You do not want to darken your room and close it in. The lighter and brighter the curtain, the more light that is allowed into your room. Roman shades or blinds are nice because, while they offer privacy and darkness during late hours, they can also be drawn back fully to allow light in.

 Tapestries and lace. Putting a little runner on your dining room table is a nice touch. Lace can be placed under a lamp for a little contrast against a wooden table. Whether you want a modern look or an old-timey look will determine if you use lace at all. If you are going for a modern look, ditch the lace. The modern look cries out for flat-colored, simply-patterned tapestries.

Furniture. Old furniture can be re-covered. Learn the skill of upholstery. I read a book and re-covered several antique sofas and chairs using my little sewing machine. Refinish wood furniture where the finish is worn. Cover old couches with a slipcover, if nothing else. Arrange the furniture so that your room comes together, instead of spreading it apart. You want people to sit in places where they can see each other and visit properly.

 Wall hangings. Find things that you really like. If you are into the outdoors, a painting of a scene is perfect for you. If you like something more modern, an abstract picture would be right for you. How about nostalgic? If you like to be taken back a hundred years, put a painting of a woman and child from a few hundred years ago. A picture of a basket of flowers or a lighthouse is perfect for the cottage look. Sconces with candles are always nice. Beautiful, framed mirrors are a classic. Photos of your family or children can be nice in certain rooms. Decals with verses of scripture or neat sayings are very fitting in some homes.

 Knickknacks. Some women love their knickknacks. They have a Hummel® collection, Precious Moments®, salt and pepper shakers from around the world, or maybe they collect farm animals. I am not a knickknack type of gal, but I have been in a lot of homes that are bursting with them. I see this more often than not, so I will venture to say that women like their trinkets and treasures. But having too many can give a very cheesy, cluttered feel. Here and there is fine, but if you want a home that is lovely, weed out some of your clutter. Less is more!

 Plants and flowers. Plants are great. They add a little color to your living space. It brings in an outdoor feel. If they are real plants, they are giving off oxygen, which is also a plus. Flower arrangements or bouquets are a nice touch. Pick colors that compliment or accent your room. For instance, I have a pale yellow kitchen with white trim. I accent with a bouquet of burgundy-colored flowers mixed with some pale yellow flowers. My curtain is beige with burgundy flowers and white hydrangeas in the fabric. The flowers are placed on the island in my kitchen and offer a great compliment to my color scheme.

 Lighting. There are many different light fixtures available. You can have a fancy chandelier, if you are going for that fanciful feel, or you can have a ceiling fan with a few sconces hanging down to give light. I like lamps. They give a softer, more ambient feel to a room in the evening. Candles are great accents. They smell nice and provide mood lighting. I have even seen women make their own chandeliers with sticks and canning jars. It had such a neat, rustic look. I have enjoyed putting strings of little white lights in my plants, for fun. It added a soft light at night. I have hung a string of lights from the rafters of my front porch for a twinkling light when you are sitting out there in the evening.

Pick up a hobby

There are many things you can do other than spending most of your free time on the computer, the phone, or watching television. Learn a new skill. You are never too old to learn something new. I have a desire to learn how to play the cello. I am already playing several songs. A few months ago in the spring, a neighbor lady brought me down to the creek to gather willow branches. We soaked them in water and the next day she was showed me how to weave a basket out of them. It was so simple and enjoyable. When the branches are soft from the water, they weave very easily. It took us about two hours to make one basket. What a fun use of my time and now I have a basket that I can gather eggs in!

Do not be afraid to try new things. You will never know how skilled you could become if you never try. Think of something you always wanted to do. Maybe you want to learn to sew. Buy a used sewing machine from the thrift store or from Craigslist. I have lessons on sewing on our *Homesteading for Beginners* DVDs. I show you how to make your own skirt or quilt. There are books you can read that have instructions. YouTube is filled with tutorials on almost everything. If you want to learn, there are a lot of resources. Just because your mom did not teach you a particular skill does not mean that you can't learn alongside your children today. Use your time wisely.

Lessons in Etiquette
The Time Thief

To start this lesson on social etiquette, I want to provide you a timely quote from a book written during the Civil War era.

"Frequent consultation of the watch or time-pieces is impolite, either when at home or abroad. If at home, it appears as if you were tired of your company and wished them to be gone; if abroad, as if the hours dragged heavily, and you were calculating how soon you would be released.
Never read in company."
~Louis Martine (Handbook of Etiquette, 1866)

If only Martine could see how our society has unraveled! Watches and time-pieces are a thing of the past, in most regards. People now have phones and pods that not only tell time—they do it all. Handheld devices have brought us to a whole new level of rudeness. People who own them will get a beeping noise or ringtone emitting from their pocket, which signals an incoming text or call. Even if they are engaged in conversation or in the company of others, they will plunge their hand into their pocket to pull out the device and look at it.

It shows a lack of patience and courtesy.

The lack of patience is evident in how they cannot wait until the conversation is over to find out about the text or call. It shows that they feel whatever that instant message is, it is more important than what you are saying at the time. They are not being courteous if they interrupt another person's thoughts to take a call or text right in the middle of the conversation. The person talking will lose their train of thought and forget the point they were trying to make.

I have seen this all too many times. In fact, when you see young people using these devices, you will most always see their faces transfixed upon its glowing light. Sometimes they may look up for a brief moment to be sure they do not stumble over things that are lying on the floor. Instead of picking things up, they will look up long enough to make a lunge over it and then resume their attention toward their little "world."

"I've got the whole world in my hands." It has everything I need...

- **On-demand streaming of television, movies, and YouTube videos.**
- **Texting and instant messages.**
- **Facebook and Twitter live feeds.**
- **Phone.**
- **Video games.**
- **The internet.**
- **A photo camera.**
- **A video camera.**
- **Software.**
- **Database.**
- **Calculator.**
- **Clock.**
- **Apps of a zillion sorts.**

Who could blame a person if they feel this is their world? It is everything they need in one handy little package. Twenty years ago I was dreaming of such a thing. I thought it would be so neat to be able to watch my favorite shows while I was sitting in my high school math class. It was a time when the internet was not yet fully developed. I remember sitting in a meeting in my high school. It was a meeting about our future in the business world. They said there was a way we could instantly communicate with a person in China from a new thing called the "Web." At the time, I can remember how far-fetched it seemed. How could it be possible? Now, not only can you instantly communicate with people around the world, but the most vile and evil sorts of entertainment are only a click away. It is sad that such a device can be such a huge time thief for people in our time.

People can be on these devices for hours without even knowing it. My son, Miles, wanted one in the worst way. He coveted that device for the past 5 years. We lived on our little homestead, working the land, yet he was somewhat dissatisfied. He would occasionally see other kids enjoying them and it seemed a grave injustice to him that we shielded him from these devices. For some reason, I could see it was a world of iniquity waiting to be played with. Eventually, when he saved up enough money, he bought one. He told me that he would be extra nice and extra helpful. The week before he bought it, he woke up around 4 am each morning to clean the entire house. I was smitten! It was a lovely manipulation tactic for a mom like me. I could easily get used to this new level of work ethic in my son.

He promised that he would continue this lovely habit of cleaning and helping me around the house. We thought it would be okay. About two days after he got the device, he stopped helping entirely. He became ornery to the other kids who wanted to get a glimpse of whatever was so enchanting in his hand. That device stole his time. It was gone. He would no longer have conversations with real people as he started texting and Facebook messaging others. He got busy downloading movies, apps, and video games. The indulgence of this device became my worst nightmare.

I would see kids in public places smiling down into their hand instead of smiling toward their friends. They were no longer talking to each other with their audible voices; it was all by the touch of their fingertips. They would be texting each other even when they were sitting right next to each other. That is so messed up! And now it was in my home all day long. I hated seeing my son looking into his hand instead of into my face. I missed our conversations.

We did what most parents do not have the guts to do. We bought it back from him. We wanted it to be his choice because having something taken from him that he worked hard to pay for would only grow bitterness in his heart. I tried to find a good alternative. I went on the internet to look for other cool things he could buy with that $300. He could buy an airsoft gun or survival equipment. He was easily swayed while I had that device in my hand. Soon we sold it and I could not be more happy with the step we took. We gained our son back.

Addictions

God did not create our minds to handle the amount of graphical stimulation that we get from modern technological devices.

Brain's Response to Stimulation

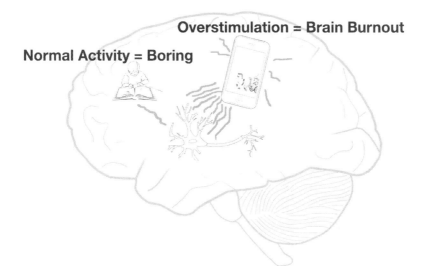

Flashing lights, action-packed scenes flashing in and out, music, instant gratification, and graphic images that overstimulate brain cause too many impulses to generate in the human brain. If your mind gets used to the constant stimulation, normal activity will now seem boring. When a person who is an overuser of these types of devices has one taken away, they will display similar characteristics of a drug addict. If you do not believe me, try it. When my kids were little, I took great lengths to keep them away from high-action cartoon movies. I felt it was too much for their little minds. Instead, my kids were content watching documentary films with a lot of narration. They found it fascinating.

In the past year, since we have been settled into a new community with parents who allow devices and lots of action-packed movies, we eased up on our convictions. I watched as the kids started becoming less interested in learning. It was crazy how fast this happened. If I told them we were watching a documentary about earthquakes (to my mind, very interesting and action-packed), they would roll their eyes at me and sigh in disgust. That was "boring." I cannot even get my kids to watch *Anne of Green Gables.* That used to be an all-time favorite in our home. They got used to watching action-packed movies in the evenings before bed, and since we had Netflix, they could watch a new one each time. Before, they would watch movies over and over again. Now they feel like they *need* to watch something fresh and more interesting. Lately, we have been trying to cut back, and they display withdrawal symptoms. They seem nervous and unsettled. They cry and beg. They start fighting and arguing. It gets ugly. I want to turn the clock back to a different time. Since we still live in a neighborhood where video games and movies are important to the kids, we have to find balance. It is hard to backtrack.

Weeks have passed and their brains are healing. I see the kids playing chess or reading a book again for enjoyment. They look forward to our family movie night. I think with some moderation we can have the best of both worlds.

The necessary evil

These handheld devices are very needful to the business people in today's word. I can see that they are practical for many. You can communicate with your business and research on-the-go. I can see them as being useful for keeping tabs on your kids when they are away. They can be used for safety as you can notify people of an emergency when one arises. It is a great missions tool. You can reach the lost souls all over the world from a social network on the Web. There is no end to the convenience and usefulness of these devices. The only troubling thing is when they become a *time thief.* Adults can fall into the trap. I think the word *web* is fitting. You can get caught up into it. Many adults are responsible; they know when and how to use them. When kids have them, they do not always have the discretion and moderation that an adult would have. They can get lost in a video game or movie for hours at a time. A young person can accidentally or intentionally surf into areas that are very inappropriate. It can be a device that will steal more than your child's time—it can steal their soul.

I suggest getting safety apps which will not allow certain things on the device. Spend time with your child to find out what they are looking at and spending their time on. It is important to keep your relationship REAL, and not allow them to slip into a virtual existence where everything they know is some digitized entity.

Although a device is needful for a lot of people today, etiquette can be observed. If you are a gal who likes to keep abreast of all the Facebook timeline feeds, make sure you are not looking at the device when you are engaged in a conversation with another person. You could turn the noise off when visiting so you are not distracted by the constant beeping of notifications. It is very rude. Rather, you want to esteem others above yourself. It is both biblical and a good benevolent practice.

"Let nothing be done through strife or vainglory;
but in lowliness of mind let each esteem other better than themselves."
Philippians 2:3

If you are placing others above yourself, you will listen intently to their words and show care for what interests them. In so doing, you are treating them the way you would want them to treat you. When you are talking to another person, you do not like it if they are is texting or looking at their phone. It makes you feel as though what ever you are saying is of little importance. I want to conclude with another quote from Martine's Handbook of Etiquette:

"To cultivate the art of pleasing is not only worthy of our ambition, but it is
the dictate of humanity to render ourselves as agreeable as possible to those
around us. While, therefore, we condemn that false system of philosophy
which recommends the practice of flattery and deception for the purpose
of winning the regard of those with whom we come in contact, we would
rather urge the sincere and open conduct which is founded on moral princi-
ple, and which looks to the happiness of others, not through any sordid and
selfish aim, but for the reward which virtuous actions bestow. The sacrifice of
personal convenience for the accommodation of others; the repression of our
egotism and self-esteem; the occasional endurance of whatever is disagreeable

or irksome to us through consideration for the infirmities of others, are not only some of the characteristics of true politeness, but are in the very spirit of benevolence, and, we might add, religion."
~Martine, 1866

The *Crown* of the house is *Godliness*

The *Beauty* of the house is *Order*

The *Glory* of the house is *Hospitality*

The *Blessing* of the house is *Contentment*

~old inscription

Recipe to be a GOOD WOMAN

Proverbs 31:22—A good woman is a craftsman. She is a skilled worker who creates beautiful wall and bed coverings for her house, as well as beautiful clothes for herself.

"She maketh herself coverings of tapestry; her clothing is silk and purple."

Key word: *maketh*

Has mastered skills of crafts and sewing, and makes dresses with beauty.

Letters from my Readers

Dear Erin,

I am a 24-year-old woman about to get married. I was raised in a Conservative Mennonite home. We did not have television for most of my childhood. I do not think I had seen more than two movies by the time I was 13 years old. When we left the Mennonite church we started off pretty conservative, but gradually got into more and more things of this world, like having televisions and computers.

When I was a little girl, I remember spending days setting up my playhouse in our living room made out of blankets and pillows. I would marched across the backyard and pretend we were on the prairie. I played and had a vivid imagination.

I am the oldest of ten kids. As I watch my younger siblings play today, I see something so different about them. They lack imagination and they are not as content to play in the living room for days like I did. It is not "bad" but it is "different." They'd sooner watch movies and play video games with their free time.

When I have kids, I wonder how it will be? I hope that I can keep them interested in the simple things of life. I am not sure if I will be able to fight against the latest devices and entertainment. I know these things will be hard to compete with.

Thank you for the illustration on the brain. It helps me understand the importance of moderation with things like this.

~ Amanda Martin

The Jezebel Profile

When the name Jezebel is mentioned, most of us see the painted face of a seductively-dressed woman gazing into the eyes of a man who lacks good sense. The Bible portrays Jezebel in a different light. Revelation 2:20 says that Jezebel "calleth herself a prophetess," and men received her as a teacher, showing that she was part of structured Christianity, "ministering" to the saints. Jesus warned the Church against the teaching woman, Jezebel. Any woman who defies the scripture's prohibition against women teachers in the Church is following in the grave tradition of Jezebel.

I went back to 1 Kings to see what the Bible had to say about the historical Jezebel. The first thing I noticed was that she was more spiritual and religiously devoted than her husband. She used her insights to guide him. He was a weak man, so she took the lead to motivate him. The Bible says in 1 Corinthians 11:3, "But I would have you know, that the head of every man is Christ; and the head of the woman is the man; and the head of Christ is God." Regardless of our circumstances, when we women take the spiritual lead, we step out from under our designated rightful head.

The second thing I observed was that Ahab was emotionally volatile—unstable. Is your husband prone to retreat? Is he bitter, angry, or depressed? When a woman takes the lead in marriage, her assuming of the masculine role makes a weak man weaker, to the point of "sending him to bed"—as did Jezebel to Ahab.

The third and most significant thing I noticed was that she used his emotional stress to endear herself to him—a strange way of lording over her husband. If you read the story, you will see how Jezebel manipulated and accused an innocent man, then had him murdered so that Ahab could obtain his vineyard. Ahab, in depression, kept his "face to the wall" and let her do her dark deeds. Today, if a woman is willing to play her husband's role in directing the family, her husband will lose his natural drive to bear responsibility. He will turn his face to the wall.

The fourth thing that jumped out at me was how Ahab was easily manipulated by his wife to suit her purposes. She stirred his passive spirit, provoking him to react in anger. Jezebel used him to set up images and to kill God's true prophets. Often a man becomes involved in the local church, not because God has called him, but because he is trying to please his wife by at least LOOKING spiritual. When a husband steps into a spiritual role at his wife's beckoning or emotional pressure, he is susceptible to her "guidance" in that role. Jezebel took steps to help promote her spiritual leaders. In the process, she provoked her husband to destroy those in spiritual authority whom she did not like. Have you influenced your husband to think evil of those in authority because you did not like something about them?

Jezebel knew that she was not the rightful head, so she invoked her husband's name to give her word authority. Have you ever said, "Oh, my husband will not let me do that," when you knew he would not care? It is a way to maintain control and to stop those who would question you. When a woman steps outside her divinely ordained nature and assumes the dominant role, she will soon become emotionally and physically exhausted, <u>and dangerous</u>.

~Debi Pearl

Chapter Eighteen
Virtuously Known

"Her husband is known in the gates,
when he sitteth among the elders of the land."
Proverbs 31:23

When I think of her husband being known in the gates, I think of her always giving good reports about him. The virtuous woman is actively promoting her husband so that he has a good reputation. He is known to all and trusted by all because of her glorious attitude and gracious words. If her husband is sitting among the elders of the land, he is in a position of authority. Elders are considered head over something. They are looked up to by the people of the land. She is careful what she says about him. She wants to build him up in his position, stand by him in his rulings, and honor him with her works.

Every king needs a queen. Every president needs his first lady. Ruling over people is so much easier when you have someone you love standing by your side. We can be that kind of wife to our husbands. I want my husband to be known in the gates as someone people can trust. In the same way we build up our husbands, we can completely destroy them.

About ten years ago I tried to counsel a married woman. She was hurt. Her husband was not as attentive to her needs as he should have been. He was into sports and she felt left behind. I tried to encourage her to play the games with him or become his cheerleader. Sometimes it's the little foxes that spoil the vine. She became jealous when he would talk with other women or watch movies that had love scenes. Those jealousies started small sparks in her mind. The sparks turned into fires of doubt and hatred. In her mind, him watching an R-rated movie turned into a full-blown accusation that he was using porn. Every bitter thought turned into fabricated truths. Yeah, he was not a good husband; even he would admit to that. He knew he did not love her the way he should have and attended to all of her needs. They both failed to love each other properly.

One evening I cried as I told her what these thoughts would lead to. She would go down a path of no return and her children will have to go along for the ride. She had poisoned her own mind until she could not see things as they really were. Instead, everything became a made up fantasy where revenge fueled her fires. She opened the door for the devil to control her thoughts and actions. I told her that she will be all alone and someday her children will figure out the truth. Once they figure out how she destroyed their chances for a relationship with their father, they will hate her. The ending is always broken. No one wins.

She continued on that slippery slope in her mind, and got counsel from other ladies who felt sorry for her instead of having discernment. They were not strong enough to encourage her to do the right thing, so she left her husband and took her children far away. She wanted to punish him and she was successful. The things she started to believe ten years ago had become a reality in her mind. Eventually, she did not allow her children to see their father. She managed to get an entire church to believe her false reality. Her vile accusations kept changing and getting more outstanding. She wanted him known in the gates. It amazed me how the men listened to her seducing spirit like Ahab listened to Jezebel. She knew how to play the game and how to get the men to see her as the poor victim.

After months of attacks at the pulpit and viscous fights in the church, she succeeded in not only smearing her husband's good name, but also took the church down in the process. The unsuspecting churchgoers who thought it was just a spat between husband and wife did not see the bigger picture and how it was actually an attack upon the church and upon their own families. Satan got a foothold ten years ago. He is so calculated. Not one shred of evidence could be produced to prove his guilt but forever this man will be known in the gates for his supposed sins. Even if he could produce the evidence to clear his name, it wouldn't matter. The damage is done and the bitterness is growing thick between them. The Bible says,

"A good name is rather to be chosen than great riches,
and loving favour rather than silver and gold."
Proverbs 22:1

Nothing new under the sun

My husband went through the pains of divorce. His mother was righteously justified to leave his father because of adultery. The divorce was bitter, with many nasty court battles. She believed the children needed to be shielded from their father's sins. He had betrayed his family, after all. Despite her efforts, he was allowed partial custody of the children. Even though he had them on the weekends, my husband told me his mother found ways around it. His father was bad in her mind. He was to blame for all her hardships. Eventually, my husband could see that his father was not the monster that his mother made him out to be. Being deprived of a relationship with his father was very difficult for him as a young man. It caused him to become withdrawn and lack confidence. It is important for children to have a father in their lives.

Divorce is final. It hurts. It affects future generations. The long, evil talons of divorce and bitterness reach out every time there is a family get-together. My husband and I fought hard to bring peace, and it was not easy. Sometimes I took in the poison and that same bitterness pulsed through my veins. I became bitter towards his mother because of it. My husband could see how the bitterness affected me. He told me, "Erin, you are ruining your life now. It is like a disease that is spreading and you are drinking of the poison. Your bitterness is not going to change anything about my mother, but it will destroy you and possibly our family. It is also creating a wall between you and God. Stop this madness!" I am glad my husband does not let me continue in sin. When I am weak, he is strong. At that point, I realized how evil my own heart had become and I chose joy and forgiveness instead. **Forgiveness is as healing to the person forgiving as it is for the forgiven.** When we forgive we loose the shackles around our darkened heart. It is like taking the antidote for the poison.

We live in a fallen world; no one is perfect. Our husbands are not perfect, and we as wives fail daily as well. More and more we understand our own need for a savior.

Edification

We build up others when we talk about their strengths and let the love we have for them cover the multitude of their sins. Find things to praise them about. When you give good reports about your husband you are actually giving yourself a good name in the process. People will either know you as the wife who bashes her husband or the wife who is so devoted. No one likes to hear about how bad your husband is. If they do, they are sick and twisted in their mind. Finish well by bringing honor to your family. Stay positive and be an encourager instead of a discourager.

Marriage would be a breeze of sweet, loving fellowship if both man and wife understood how to really love each other. If each would treat their spouse the way they would want to be treated it would cure the cancer they have growing between them.

Virtues in Charity
BEARING ALL THINGS

"Charity never faileth: but whether there be prophecies, they shall fail; whether there be tongues, they shall cease; whether there be knowledge, it shall vanish away. For we know in part, and we prophesy in part. But when that which is perfect is come, then that which is in part shall be done away. When I was a child, I spake as a child, I understood as a child, I thought as a child: but when I became a man, I put away childish things. For now we see through a glass, darkly; but then face to face: now I know in part; but then shall I know even as also I am known. And now abideth faith, hope, charity, these three; but the greatest of these is charity."
1 Corinthians 13:8-13

Unlimited love and kindness in its deepest form never fails. It is the kind of love that is so concerned for another person that it abandons all thoughts of self.

Knowledge

Since the beginning man and woman wanted to have "knowledge." Eve was tempted by the tree that bore fruit which unlocked the keys of knowing Good and Evil. This is the knowledge that would forever change the course of eternity. Knowing Good and Evil caused them to realize their nakedness. It caused sin to enter in and death to reign until Christ came to die for all sins. A man who "knew" no sin was sent to teach us how to love and to ultimately pay the debt of sin we owed. Man has always been and will remain in pursuit of "knowing." The more we know, the more we fill with pride, and yet it will vanish away. Knowledge is good. It is good to know how to read and write, and to understand how things work. With knowledge we can learn how to heal disease and how to make buildings stand for a thousand years. When we have knowledge, we have a key that opens doors to opportunities. Yet we know in PART.

God reveals things to be understood through nature

"For the wrath of God is revealed from heaven against all ungodliness and unrighteousness of men, who hold the truth in unrighteousness; because that which may be known of God is manifest in them; for God hath shewed it unto them. For the invisible things of him from the creation of the world are clearly seen, being understood by the things that are made, even his eternal power and Godhead; so that they are without excuse: because that, when they knew God, they glorified him not as God, neither were thankful; but became vain in their imaginations, and their foolish heart was darkened. Professing themselves to be wise, they became fools, and changed the glory of the uncorruptible God into an image made like to corruptible man, and to birds, and fourfooted beasts, and creeping things."
Romans 1:18-23

We know in PART. We can understand all things and yet be so foolish as to believe that God did not create all things. In society today, with so much knowledge, with so much wisdom, there are few who will glorify God. All this knowledge is in VAIN if it cannot produce eyes to see there is more purpose in life than to exist and return to the earth. The scoffer is not thankful for the breath and the life they are given. They have all knowledge so as to move a mountain, technology to make almost anything happen, but they fail to understand the greatest thing—love.

It is like looking through a dirty, foggy piece of glass. You cannot make out exactly what is behind the glass. Everything there is to know here on Earth is dim like that piece of glass. We can only see darkly through it. **God can make every attempt to relay the importance of loving our neighbor as ourself, and yet we can still not see it clearly.**

We are proud of our advances, whether it be knowledge or some spiritual gift of some sort. We are proud to be lifted up a bit higher than another person. If we cannot learn to treat others the way we would want to be treated, which is the greatest command of Christ, we cannot ever see clearly.

Why is it so hard to love your neighbor as yourself?

It is hard because most people are self-seeking. I see people who will charge top dollar for something that was given to them, while trying to get another thing they want for next to nothing from someone who is less fortunate than they are. People look down their noses at another person and then are shocked and hurt when someone looks down their nose at them. One person is hurt by rejection, yet they will reject someone else for the same foolish reason. People do not like being rejected, judged, condemned, used, and treated badly, yet they will manage to treat others in all those ways because they don't understand the most important thing—love.

> *"Thou shalt love thy neighbour as thyself.*
> *There is none other commandment greater than these."*
> **Mark 12:31**

There is no other commandment greater because, if we truly loved and treated others the same way we would want to be treated, there would be no sin. There would be no fighting or wars. There would be no divorce or abuse. No dissension, no quarreling, and no jealousy. We would be happy for others' success and sad when others fail. If we were poor and in pain, we would like for someone to comfort us and to help us financially. Yet when we see someone who is afflicted, we often ignore them because it is too much of a sacrifice of our time and resources.

I have had many people tell me that they helped enough and they have forgiven enough. Wow. To say you have done enough for someone after all that Christ has done and forgiven you in your life is beyond my understanding. Can you imagine if Christ were to look down to you and say, "I have forgiven you enough. You have taken advantage of my graces long enough. I have helped you enough"? We know that this would be out of character for Christ. If He is our example, why do we think it is okay for us to say such things? God is the author of Charity. He is more patient and merciful than what we could ever understand. He sees clearly enough into the hearts of all men so that His judgments are just. We would throw people in hell after the first or second offense, while God will allow a person the free will to sin their whole life through and then forgive them as they come to him in their last dying breath, like the thief on the cross. Jesus promised that he would be with him in paradise. None of this makes sense to us—it seems unfair that a rotten sinner should be granted eternal life and that is why God told us that we "know in part."

Treat others the way you would want to be treated, not how they have treated you. Most people like to treat others the same way that they have been treated. That is backwards. I had a talk with my daughter about that very thing. Her sister and another friend were excluding her. She wept with the pain of rejection. Yet, the week before, I remembered a similar situation in which she had rejected her sister. I said, "Why do you treat your sister this way? You know how much it hurts." She said, "But she treats me like that." It feels unfair to treat someone better than they treated you. It makes sense to return evil for evil. Christ teaches us a better way—to return good for evil. We are set apart, as a follower of Christ, by how we show love and mercy.

A good practice in loving your neighbor as yourself would be to question yourself before each action or word...

- **Would I like to pay top-dollar for something?**
- **Would I like to be made fun of for how I look?**
- **Would I like to be rejected by others?**
- **Would I like it if someone acted like they were better than me?**
- **Would I like it if someone made a nasty comment about me?**
- **Would I like it if someone made loud noises while I was trying to sleep?**
- **Would I like it if someone wrecked my stuff and did not replace it?**
- **Would I like to be treated like I am worth very little?**

Your answer to each of those questions would be NO. That is because no one likes to be treated in such ways. If you would not appreciate

such treatment, you should not treat others in such a way. I have found that many people are oblivious to how their actions affect others. They have spent too much time looking out for number one—themselves. In other words, their excuse is that they did not try, or they did not know. If they took the time to consider others they would see more clearly.

Get in the practice of silently asking yourself a few simple questions before you say or do things that will affect others. By doing so, you can figure out if your actions are in accordance with the law of unlimited love and kindness.

Recipe to be a GOOD WOMAN

Proverbs 31:23—The good woman's husband has the time and honor to be a ruler. She brings honor to her husband by the way she keeps his domain.

"Her husband is known in the gates, when he sitteth among the elders of the land."

Key words: *is known, sitteth*

Her support helped bring him to this place.

Letters from my Readers

Victory in Marriage

The story of how my husband and I first started out has shown me one thing: Despite your beginning, God will work miracles in your life if you put your faith in Him.

My husband and I started dating when I was 19 and he was 21. Soon after, I found out I was pregnant. My whole world changed and the years I fought against God just came to a crashing halt. My husband and I decided that we wanted to get married before we moved in together and our son was born. Despite some backlash in our family we knew it was the right decision and what God wanted of us.

There were second-guesses as to whether marriage was really the right choice. Again I was assured to walk in the ways of the Lord and not to stray from something He created. Based on how we started out, our marriage was designed to fail. We needed something to live for besides our own idea of what the world thinks marriage should be. Thankfully, God gave us the grace to follow Christ and to live for Him so that we were no longer just living for ourselves. Now He is the center of our marriage and we are not only accountable for ourselves, but to Christ.

Sometimes it's not how we start out that matters the most and determines our fate. Just look at the Apostle Paul. I doubt that he ever thought he would become the man Christ called him to be while he was killing Christians. By God's grace and our faith and obedience we cannot only become a new creature in Christ but our marriages will become new as well. 2 Corinthians 5:17 (KJV) says, "Therefore if any man [be] in Christ, [he is] a new creature: old things are passed away; behold, all things are become new."

Let's forget about how we may have started out and remember that through Christ our marriages can be victorious.

~ Brianna Hollenback

Letters from my Readers

Dear Erin,

Wow, this went straight to the heart of it for me! Erin, you sound exactly like me. My whole family and I struggle with this. I grew up in a fairly tidy home; but, like you, I never seemed to learn that habit myself. My husband grew up in a fairly messy home, and was never taught to put things away. So...our children also struggle. We are also surface cleaners...never blatantly dirty or messy, but lots of clutter.

I hope I can learn to be tidier...it's not for lack of trying. I just haven't quite got it yet. I would love it if you would write some posts on teaching your children to be tidier, because sometimes I want to tear my hair out trying to get them to pick up their stuff!

In Him,
Bethany

Dear Erin,

Excellent article! I am so tired of the "memes" that give women an excuse for having a dirty/messy home— "Your children are only little once; it's okay to have a messy home to play with your children," etc. Nine times out of ten, I doubt if the mothers are playing with the children! Love this statement: "It is just laziness on anyone's part if they cannot put things back where they belong. Training the kids to be organized is something that I have had to work on." Thank you for writing this. God bless you. P.S. I do admit I have paper clutter, but my closets and drawers are organized!

~Elaine

Chapter Nineteen
Virtuous Order

"She maketh fine linen, and selleth it;
and delivereth girdles unto the merchants."
Proverbs 31:24

The virtuous woman is organized. She not only makes a fine product, but she actively sells it, and executes its careful delivery. She is not sending her staff to do this job. She wants it done right. No messing around. There is an order to her operation. This fine linen was made from the flax grown in her fields that she carefully considered. She worked the land and harvested the crop. She was there feeding her maidens and her family, serving for all hours of the night to ensure nothing was glossed over. She had time to help others in her busy schedule. This woman was prepared when times got hard, and she patiently endured every storm with confidence. Her faith never wavered as she worked alongside her maidens to create the finest linen, and now she is ready to sell it. Every step along the way has been carefully purposed to ensure the success of her business.

There was a lot of burden on this woman, yet she did not skirt any responsibility nor shove her duties off onto others. She gave her all. When that fine linen is sold, she delicately hands over her prize to the merchants and gains the satisfaction of a job well done. Some of us would do well to follow her example and become organized. God is a God of order; let our homes reflect His glorious order.

Getting order in my home did not come naturally

Are you always ready for visitors to pop in unannounced? The answer for most women these days is NO. I know most ladies wait until about one hour before their husband comes home to tidy up the house. The rest of the day, the house is a pigpen. I definitely used to do this! I had to learn to have better housekeeping patterns. If I knew someone was coming soon, I would frantically run through my house, stuffing things into drawers, cupboards, and closets. These areas would get so cram-packed full, that if you would open a closet door, you were liable to get knocked over by the avalanche of my junk! My mother-in-law would purposely open my closet doors and chuckle at me, saying in mock surprise, "Oh! What is this?" It would drive me crazy. I knew she meant well, but it was just plain embarrassing to have someone finding out your hidden lifestyle as a hoarder.

My nickname was "The Clutter Queen"!

My hoarder story

I used to be a classic hoarder! My own mother knew it. When I was young, my mother would threaten to throw all my junk onto the driveway, which she actually did one time. I had to run outside around the back of the house and gather up my junk, hauling it back to my room, making fifty or so trips. My mother was taught to clean well by her mother who kept a fine home. I should have been better in my own home, since I learned from the best. When I talk to my mother now, she tells me how frustrated she was with my stubborn, slobbish tendencies. In fact, she had to keep my door shut just to keep from seeing it and allowing it to make her want to run me and my junk out of her home for good. When I first got married, she invited Mark and I to their home for a meal. When we pulled into the driveway, there sat what looked to be a caravan of plastic bins streaming fifty feet out from the back door.

She looked up at my tall, handsome husband and said, "She's your problem now!" Thankfully, my husband is not a pushover. He looked at me, dumped two of the tubs out and said with steadfast authority, "Okay, you have two bins. Whatever you can fit in these bins, you may keep. The rest is going to the dump!" All I could think was how merciful my dear husband was to allow me to keep a few of my special things.

I went through bin after bin of school papers, my dog's baby teeth (weird!), dolls I saved, rocks (really?), stuffed animals, and old worn-out clothes. I had saved everything. There were over forty bins, so it was a long, laborious afternoon—the afternoon the hoarder was caught red-handed. I love that my husband is strong for me when I am weak. I can tell you one thing, this was a purging which needed to happen in order for me to grow into a better homemaker. Today, I do not miss that trash. I cannot even remember what I threw away that day. For the few years after that, there would be more bonfires filled with trash purged from our closets. My transformation did not happen overnight. The habit of saving everything was a hard one to break.

Get this hoarder in order!

It frustrated my husband. He just hated all the clutter and especially hated how I would stuff his things frantically in places where only God would know to look. Going on a mystery treasure hunt right before he would leave for work was not a game my husband wanted to play. It embarrassed me when his mother would come for a weekend visit. She was not fond of me from the beginning, so it was a hard battle to convince her that I was worthy of her son. I wanted her to like me so badly. I wanted her to think I was a good wife and mother.

Finally, I did what most women would not dare to do…I asked my mother in law to help me organize my home!

One closet at a time, I let her pick through all my stowed-away messes, while she would ask me the dreaded questions: "Why would you keep this?" "Do you use this?" "Is this garbage?" Usually it was something that, uh, I should have thrown away! She taught me to put each thing in a certain place—its "HOME." When I was done using it, I had to return it to its "home." Wow, this went against my nature. It took years of training to get me out of some pretty bad habits of laziness. **Now I am known as "The Clean Freak"!**

There is hope

If I could learn new habits and train myself to be organized, then anyone can. My home is a place of order today, so you know there is hope. My home was never blatantly messy. I was a surface cleaner with stuff stashed under the beds and into the closets where no one could see it. My husband was not happy with my closets and drawers full of clutter and trash. I had to learn charity towards him in this matter. I had to love him enough to make his home a haven of peace and order. It makes him so very happy when he can find things. I have realized that it is unseemly behavior to cram things and lose things just because you feel there is not enough time to do things the right way.

I have special areas to store my husband's tools, his mail, his flashlights, etc. I make sure he has a shelf for his things. He still gets a little nervous when he is looking for something in a sparkling-clean room. He wonders if I stuffed it somewhere, because the memory of how I was is still vivid for him. I tell him right where I placed it—on his shelf with the other things that go together. Now, I can have people drop by and my home is in order. The kids help keep it clean, although I have to get on their case for stuffing things in the cupboards, and sometimes into their closets.

It is just laziness on anyone's part if they cannot put things back where they belong. Training the kids to be organized is something that I have had to work on. They are a lot more organized than I was when I was a kid. When you practice charity, you are ready to welcome people into your home at any moment and make them feel safe that when they open your closet, they will NOT risk their lives.

One drawer at a time

If you are a clutter queen like I was, every drawer, every closet, every cupboard is packed with junk. It is quite overwhelming to think of organizing the whole heap in one day. I recommend setting your goal for one drawer per day. It only takes thirty minutes at the most to organize one drawer, so that is doable, right? I used to have a "junk drawer" which I would stuff with all the miscellaneous items. Since then, I have stopped having a "junk drawer," because little by little I am less inclined to stuff junk into drawers. It does not happen overnight, but even us "old dogs" can learn new tricks if we put ourselves up to the challenge.

Teaching my children to be more organized

I get busy. I forget to keep tabs on the kids' bedrooms. Every once in a while, I make the long trek up the stairs to assess the damage, making sure everyone is doing their chores properly-that includes their bedrooms. Checking on them unannounced will cause the kids to keep their rooms tidy, just in case I come "like a thief in the night." As a parent, I want to give my kids a healthy concept of what it means to be ready, honest, and work with integrity in all things, even the hidden areas like drawers and closets.

- **First I walk into Miles' room...nice. Very nice and tidy, for a teenaged boy. WOW! Very impressive.**
- **Molly...Great room! Everything is in its place and it is very pretty.**
- **Megan...Very nice! What order she has in her room, very clean, and pretty!**
- **Mikey always has a clean room. He wakes up every morning, makes his bed, tidies his room, gets dressed and combs his hair. It is his routine. Great job!**
- **On to Junior's room...wow, what can I say? Looks like we have a child who takes after ME!!! His closet is overflowing with trash, dirty laundry, and who knows what else. My first reaction is to get mad. He had been checking off "TIDY BEDROOM, MAKE BED" on the chore chart. I had been paying him MOM BUCKS. It pays to check in on the jobs!**

What is a mother to do?

Instead of getting utterly disgusted, I chose to make a fun day out of teaching my little "Junior Hoarder" how to get organized again—how to OVERCOME! Junior was so excited. His attitude was absolutely precious. We started out by getting some old storage containers to organize all his Lego pieces that were sprinkled across the entire floor. With storage containers, you can fine-tune the organization. **Each storage bin, drawer, or container becomes a HOME for something.**

Sorting and giving things a new HOME

Sort by like items (everything that seems to have a similar purpose). They have a home and a family. They like to live together. Sort by:

- **Size**
- **Color**
- **Use**

We started by emptying all the Legos from every corner of the room. Junior found a nice set of organizing drawers and started to put the

Legos together by color or kind.

Keeper Tip #1

Storage containers = organizing items

After the Legos were tucked away, we unloaded the closet, under the bed, and all the dresser drawers. You could NOT see the floor at all. It felt overwhelming to Junior as it would to anyone. The mountain seemed too high to climb, but when you have a method by which you tackle that mountain, it is a snap…**chip away at the mountain and start sorting.**

Arm yourself with some options...

Keeper Tip #2

Trash Bag + Cardboard Box + Laundry Basket

= Organizing Clutter

Trash bag. Put all the garbage in the trash bag. When you organize any closet, drawer, or room, you will definitely find things that are either broken, never used, or if you are like I was, you have actual garbage (banana peels, crumpled papers, and other unmentionable trash). Junior had banana peels, orange peels, and toilet paper around his room. We gladly placed these items into a trash bag.

Cardboard box. Put all recyclable or giveaway items in the box. You may find something that is in good condition which you could give to a secondhand store. In Junior's case, the empty box was already in his closet (not sure why), so we used it for all the burnables. We have a wood stove, so any paper trash or cardboard can be burned.

Laundry basket. If you are cleaning a closet or bedroom, chances are you will find many soiled items of clothing which need washing. Junior had semi-folded, clean laundry under his bed and in his closet. I guess he forgot to put them away. Busy little boys do that.

Well, I must say, it is mostly my fault that things got this out-of-hand. I really need to spend extra time with Junior each day, helping him learn to put things back in their HOMES. Some children are just not geared to order. I was not geared to order at all. It took years of training myself to be orderly. I know it is possible because I have overcome this.

A child needs a parent to train them. Junior needs a daily assessment on his room and encouragement to keep it clean. I plan to give him extra MOM BUCKS for incentive. I will take MOM BUCKS away if I check and things are not put in their place. Junior often gets frustrated because he can't find anything. It is a daily situation. We hear him tromping through the house, searching. Many times there are accusations towards the other kids "taking his stuff." They shake their heads, saying they did not see his things. Sometimes there are fits and tears—yes, my kids have fits! All in all, it is time for a new positive direction.

This will teach him quickly that it is a win/win situation if he keeps his room tidy.

- **He wins because he knows where to find the things for which he is looking.**
- **He wins because he will earn extra MOM BUCKS.**
- **I win because I spend more time with my son.**
- **I win because I have a happier boy.**

Lessons in Etiquette
THE DAY GOBLIN

When trying to maintain your own order, you can easily see it is a good thing to observe others' time and schedule in their homes. In other words, you do not want to wear out your welcome. Let people have the time they need to keep order in their home. If you visit them every day, they will soon grow weary of you. You don't want that! There is a proverb about this very thing. I find it very interesting that God saw fit to give us this wisdom. It is alarming that someone could actually begin hating you if you are too often on their doorstep.

> *"Withdraw thy foot from thy neighbour's house;*
> *lest he be weary of thee, and so hate thee."*
> **Proverbs 25:17**

I have been enjoying reading a book about etiquette in the Civil War Era. As I was reading last evening, I came across a chapter on visiting. I thought, "Oh, I recently wrote about visiting etiquette. I wonder what the book has to say?" I was actually surprised at how close I was in my assumptions to what it would have been like a hundred and fifty years ago.

One thing struck me—the "Day Goblin"

Such a funny term that I had not yet heard, especially in a book about proper etiquette. I have to share this with you, it is so funny and yet so true…

"With respect to the first, be very careful that you do not acquire the charac-
ter of a day goblin. A day goblin is one of those persons who, having plenty
of leisure, and a great desire to hear themselves talk, makes frequent inroads
into their friends' houses. Though perhaps well-acquainted with the rules of
etiquette, they call at the most unseasonable hours. If the habits of the family
are early, you will find them in the drawing-room at eleven o'clock. It may be
they are agreeable and well-informed people; but who wishes for calls at such
a strange hour! Most families have their rules and occupations. In one, the
lady of the house attends to the education of her children; in another, domes-

tic affairs engross a portion of the morning; some ladies are fond of grading, others of music or painting. It is past endurance to have such pursuits broken in upon for the sake of a day goblin, who, having gained access, inflicts his or her presence till nearly luncheon time, and then goes off with saying, 'Well, I have paid you a long visit;' or 'I hope that I have not stayed too long.'"

~Louis Martine, 1866

I have been a day goblin. I have had day goblins in my home as well. On Sunday, I had a day goblin stop in—a daily occurrence with this person. Then, to flee the oppression of it, I became a day goblin to another lady. I tried to stay long enough at her home to be sure the day goblin who was at my home would be gone when I returned. A little selfish, I say!

Tea party at Shalom's

Shalom is one of the sweetest ladies you will ever meet and I am so blessed to have her for a friend. After church on Sunday, Shalom's daughter Gracie came up to my girls and invited them for tea. My girls told her that they could come after lunch. We went home and started to make some bean burritos by cooking and mashing canned pinto beans. It was a lovely lunch with our family. I knew we would be visiting Shalom's that afternoon so I thought about good visiting etiquette. I want to practice what I preach.

First, we made a batch of cookies to share. I found my grandmother's old 1950s cookie tin and carefully placed our warm gingersnaps in there. The girls were happily washing dishes while I baked the cookies. Thud, thud, thud…in walks our day goblin. He sits down and I quickly get him a glass of water and a cookie. He demands our undivided attention. I realized that the fellowship with my daughters was now over, and the attention must turn towards our guest. The guest whom we love and want to be helpful towards, but nonetheless, we could no longer engage in our sweet working conversation. I quickly gathered up some chamomile tea and a half-gallon of fresh milk and apologized for having to cut our visit short as the girls and I made our exit.

As I was driving down the road, I took time to explain why we were bringing these things to Shalom's: "When we visit for tea, it is good to bring a treat to pass so that we are not a burden but a blessing." Gracie greeted us very happily at the door while stating that her mother was taking a nap, and her father was out of town for that day. The littlest one had torn apart a box full of paper shavings and the sink was full of dishes. I asked her if it was okay for us to come in. She said, "Of course; Mama would not mind." Megan swept the mess off the floor while Molly helped tend to the little ones. I washed up all the dishes knowing that at one time I was a young mama and I would have loved an extra hand when I was tired.

I had brought my percolating teapot, so I made some tea for the children. I found some pretty cups and saucers, a creamer that I filled with the milk I brought from our family cow, and filled a bowl with our fresh baked cookies. I turned on some classical music and began a lesson on a proper tea party. I taught the little girls how to sit up straight with a good posture and ask politely for a cup of tea. "Would you care for a cup of tea, Gracie?" Megan asked in her best English accent. "Yes, please," Gracie responded, after my cue.

On and on we kept this tea party going. The phone rang and Gracie picked up the phone. She remained in a proper, lady-like manner on the phone and it was so cute. They clicked their cups together. The girls were learning how to be little ladies with good manners. Shalom woke from her nap and was so thankful for the cleanup and the tea party with her children. We sat down together, while the girls went into the other room to play. They were writing letters to each other. It was so adorable. There were these little mailboxes that they made into which they put the letters. Great girl fun.

I stayed to visit with Shalom while the children played. I could see that she had a headache, and was very tired. My first priority should have been to get out of her hair so she could rest, but I kept on talking. As I recall, I actually said twice, "Well, I should be going. You should rest. I do not want to overstay my welcome." Each time I would say this, I would find a chair and sit down and we would visit a little longer.

I am sure she did not feel like I was a bother, but I try to love my neighbor as myself, knowing if I were her with a headache, I would want to be lying down in my bed, resting and not trying to keep up a conversation. I do not want to acquire the name of day goblin!

After staying that long, I realized, even though she appreciated the tea, cookies and milk, she would rather have had more rest. I am constantly trying to observe what things I may be doing and how my actions may affect others—thus loving my neighbor as myself. I had a little check in

Keeper Tip...

Don't wear out your welcome.

- Know when to leave
- Don't stay too long unless invited
- Be courteous
- Think about others
- Consider their schedule

my spirit about wearing out my welcome, but it wasn't until I read that day goblin passage in the book that it became clearer to me.

It is interesting to read this book on etiquette. The author, who wrote this book over a hundred and fifty years ago, addressed all aspects of social etiquette in his era, including visiting, marriage, and dinner parties. He writes that if you are invited to a dinner party, it is customary to pay a follow-up visit in gratitude; it is called "a visit of ceremony." Knowing what time to come is crucial and also not staying too long—being sensitive to others' time and needs are important.

"Visits of ceremony must be necessarily short. They should on no account be made before the hour, nor yet during the time of luncheon. Persons who intrude themselves at unwonted hours are never welcome; the lady of the house does not like to be disturbed when she is perhaps dining with her children; and the servants justly complain of being interrupted at the hour they assemble for their noon-day meal. Ascertain, therefore, which you can readily do, what is the family hour for luncheon, and act accordingly.

Half an hour amply suffices for a visit of ceremony. If during your short visit the conversation begins to flag, it will be best to retire. The lady of the house may have some engagement at that fixed hour, and by remaining even a few minutes longer, she may be put to serious inconvenience. Do not, however seem to notice any silent hint, by rising hastily; but take leave with quiet politeness, as if your time were fully expired. When other visitors are announced, retire as soon as possible, and yet without letting it appear that their arrival is the cause. Wait till the bustle of the entrance is over, and then rise from your chair, take leave of the hostess, and bow politely to the guests. By so doing you will save the lady of the house from being obliged to entertain two sets of visitors."

~Louis Martine 1866

Good advice for today. Perhaps we could all use a refresher, myself included. The sad thing is that these are lost skills which our grandparents knew and practiced. Modern society is void of good teaching on etiquette. People tend to be out for themselves—what feels good to them. I think it is a good thing to consider others above ourselves. To truly love our neighbor as ourself is a teaching of Jesus. When we love our neighbor as ourself, we consider these fine details important.

"Let nothing be done through strife or vainglory;
but in lowliness of mind let each esteem
other better than themselves."
Philippians 2:3

"For, brethren, ye have been called unto liberty; only use not liberty for an
occasion to the flesh, but by love serve one another."
Galatians 5:13

Recipe to be a GOOD WOMAN

Proverbs 31:24—A good woman is a merchant. She makes, sells, and delivers quality goods.

"She maketh fine linen, and selleth it; and delivereth girdles unto the merchants."

Key words: *maketh, selleth, delivereth*

Letters from my Readers

The Things I Have Learned

As a child of God:

He sees past all of my flaws, fumbles, hard heart, and still loves and treasures me. He wants to be winner of my soul. Showering me with agapy (unconditional) love.
He gives me strength to deal with things in life that hurt deeply. That storm me and take my breath away.
He allows me to experience those things that I want to avoid. That show me what happens when I don't walk in step with Him.

As a wife:

He shows me His model of a heavenly relationship.
To be bound together, committed, to be forgiving, a peacemaker, an educator, a model of love, loyal.

As a mother:

He is allowing me to experience His actions of forgiveness to others, patients where I could possibly have no more, and a desire to know my children as His through His word.

As a friend:

He has taught me to speak less, listen more, and apologize when I make a mistake. He has placed in my life women; often older women, that are my role model to emulate for my time as wife and mother. They are God's gift to me.

Amen

~ Birdie Smith

Time-Tested Wisdom...
Generosity Amidst Poverty

"Out of the most severe trial, their overflowing joy
and their extreme poverty welled up in rich generosity."
2 Corinthians 8:2

This verse always stuns me...severe trial, extreme poverty...overflowing joy and rich generosity. Those phrases just don't fit together, do they? In God's economy they do. Here we live in the richest nation that has ever existed in the history of mankind and people grumble and complain about not having enough.

Our problems are due to our excesses—obesity, heart disease, sexually-transmitted diseases, etc., not due to our lack of anything. All of our needs are met, but not all of our wants, so there is deep dissatisfaction. Very sad...

Maybe our true lack is spiritual. People are running around trying to fill that emptiness with stuff, experiences, pleasures, food, etc., but it leaves them empty. God is the only one who can fill that emptiness. He makes all things new. When we have Him, we have everything. Let Him fill you up and you won't leave hungry or thirsty anymore. Out of you will flow rivers of living water so you can refresh others with true life, whether you are rich or poor materially.

You can also be generous with your food, time, and stuff even when you have very little, because you do reap what you sow. He wants us to be generous. He owns everything. He is our provider and sustainer. When we have little materially and we still are generous with it, that is when we see what an amazing provider the Lord is and how He keeps His promises.

"In everything I did, I showed you that by this kind of hard work we must help the
weak, remembering the words the Lord Jesus himself said:
'It is more blessed to give than to receive."
Acts 20:35

~Lori Alexander
From Blog: Always Learning

Chapter Twenty
Virtuous Joy

"Strength and honour are her clothing;
and she shall rejoice in time to come."
Proverbs 31:25

The virtuous woman is joyful. She has a good outlook on life. She rejoices in what is to come. She is not withdrawn. Others perceive her as strong and full of integrity. Her thankful spirit is written all over her face. She is not downcast or worried about tomorrow. She walks in grace, for her song is sweet and full of gladness.

Her strength of character is evident by the smile on her face. Life does not defeat her. She takes everything in stride. Every experience makes her stronger. This virtuous woman is steadfast. She sticks with the program. She does not faint or grow weary in well-doing. She knows she will reap a heavenly reward. She is optimistic.

Being optimistic

I have always been pretty optimistic. I see things differently. My husband says I wear "rose-colored glasses." I remind him how boring this world would be without people like me; we see things in a different light and get lost in a moment of pure bliss. When our soul is touched, we express it with smiles, with beautiful pictures, amazing stories of hope, music, dance, and loudest praises. For without our radiant perception, the beauty of God's creation would go misunderstood and unappreciated. There would be no fanfare, no triumphal entry, no beautiful songs, and no paintings to express his creative genius in us. We are made in His image. He is the Creator. We, being like Him, also create things.

$20,000 rose-colored glasses

While my husband sees things for what they are, I see them for what they could be. His glass is half-empty while mine is half-full. One evening as we snuggled in bed, I said, "Did you know that I won an award in high school for being the most optimistic?" He sat there thinking as I continued, "Did you know that I received a $5,000 scholarship for each year towards my college education?" Soon after, he piped up, "Wow, it pays to be optimistic. Your rose-colored glasses were worth twenty grand!" I think we giggled for a long time. Those are the moments I will always cherish. I guess we laughed more because I had a depression streak in there, with constant "pity parties"—somehow I must have pulled the wool over their eyes back then. Now, the joy is for real and I have turned those pitiful tunes into songs of loudest praise.

How to change pity to praise
Ask yourself, daily, "WHY…?"

WHY do you get to live in peace while others in this present world are in a war zone? How come God gave you a home, when He allows millions of others across the world to live in the streets? WHY do you get to eat while others have to starve today or find their food in trash cans? It is not fair that you get a shower and running water while many others have flies landing on their filthy skin from years of not bathing. They do not have a clean source of water like you do. WHY do you get the opportunity to get medical or natural healing, while thousands will die today because they cannot get the treatment needed? Many people are blind while you get to see. You get to hear your children's voices. WHY do you get to have multiple sets of shoes when there are people who have no legs? WHY do you get a nice bed to sleep in while others have been imprisoned for following Christ in other countries where there is no freedom to worship? If they are not being tortured, they sleep on a concrete floor. WHY do you get to keep your children when there are mothers who have to bury theirs? It is not fair. I protest. You have so many blessings compared to others. WHY do you get to have a husband who is faithful when other women have husbands that will molest their children tonight after getting drunk and beating them? How come you get to sleep with your husband, when other young women are trafficked and are forced to have sex with thousands of perverted men and beaten when they grow weary of it? How come you get to gather together freely to worship God, while other Christians have to fear for their lives and must meet in secret? WHY do you get to read your Bible when others are killed for having one in their homes? It is not fair that Christ died for your sins. You should have had to take that punishment. WHY should a perfect, sinless man, the Son of God have to die for you?

When you see how unfair it is that others must suffer while you enjoy so much abundance, you can count your blessings and thank God for all that you have. It is truly a gift of God that He died for your sins so that you could live abundantly and experience freedom from sin and shame. As long as you have salvation in Christ, you have EVERYTHING. Quit complaining—praise God, from whom all blessings flow!

> *"My brethren, count it all joy when ye fall into divers temptations;*
> *Knowing this, that the trying of your faith worketh patience.*
> *But let patience have her perfect work, that ye may*
> *be perfect and entire, wanting nothing."*
> **James 1:2-4**

Recipe to be a GOOD WOMAN

Proverbs 31:25—A good woman is known for her honor and strength of character. Her hard work and good attitude will pay high dividends. **"Strength and honour are her clothing; and she shall rejoice in time to come."**
Key words: *shall rejoice*
Not swayed or upset by circumstances, steadfast, valiant.

Chapter Twenty-One
Virtuously Kind

"She openeth her mouth with wisdom;
and in her tongue is the law of kindness."
Proverbs 31:26

The virtuous woman is kind. She does not get involved in idle chatter. Her words carry weight. They are well-thought-out and she has enough sense to say things to build others up. She will not be found gossiping and talking about things that do not matter in eternity.

She practices what she preaches. If she does not know something, she will not speak merely for the purpose of hearing her own voice. She will do her research and have a level of understanding before she opens her mouth to give advice. When she gives advice it is gentle and given with a heart full of love and compassion. She is not self-seeking or arrogant, so she is glad to offer thoughtful words of encouragement. This virtuous woman is not a "know-it-all."

"If you have nothing good to say, say nothing at all"

This is a very old saying but it still rings true. I tell my children these words all of the time. I try to thwart their efforts to share unkind words about each other. I remind them that they should think before they speak. If we take thirty seconds to think before we open our mouths, we would say far less negative things unnecessarily. I used to be impulsive with my mouth. I never thought first. One of my high school teachers announced that I had "diarrhea of the mouth" and "constipation of the brain." All my classmates roared with laughter. Yes, it is funny, but it was very true about my once loose-cannon of a mouth.

I used to be the opposite of the virtuous woman's rule over her tongue. I said the darnedest things. My husband helped me figure out how to temper that tongue. He said if I had to pay a dollar for every word I spoke I would quickly land myself in the poor house. It is only by the grace of God I do not say everything I think. Now I have my thirty-second rule. Most times I say silently to myself, "That is not really necessary to bring up." The only time you have to worry about me is when I am way too tired. When it gets past my bedtime, I get my second wind and the thirty-second rule goes out the window. You typically will not see me out past 8 pm. My husband guards me. He knows what happens. My brain just does not do overtired very well. I will actually fall asleep while people are talking to me. Do not expect any kind of wisdom to flow forth from my lips at that time of night.

Know-it-alls

I never want to come across as a "know-it-all" either. That kind of person is irritating to be around. They have the answer to everything, and half the time you feel they are pulling stuff out of the fluff in their imagination. Information without fact to back it up is a like a toothless person trying to take a bite out of an apple. Their words carry no purpose. You roll your eyes when they try to give you sound reason. When a person is accustomed to being a self-proclaimed expert on every topic, if they do finally have some kind of wisdom to impart, it falls on deaf ears.

Rather, I want enough sense to think deeply before I speak. I want to have gentle and kind words, making sure I have a pure heart towards others. Not self-seeking or with hidden purpose. The Bible says:

> *"He that handleth a matter wisely shall find good:*
> *and whoso trusteth in the LORD, happy is he.*
>
> *The wise in heart shall be called prudent:*
> *and the sweetness of the lips increaseth learning.*
>
> *Understanding is a wellspring of life unto him that hath it:*
> *but the instruction of fools is folly.*

The heart of the wise teacheth his mouth,
and addeth learning to his lips.

Pleasant words are as an honeycomb, sweet to the soul,
and health to the bones."
Proverbs 16:20-24

The hidden agenda

Why do so many women have this undercurrent going? I have yet to figure it out. Since I do not hold back a lot of what is in my heart from flowing out of my mouth, I find it mind-blowing that some women say one thing but mean something entirely different. What is up with that? I think it is because they do not want to look bad, so they cover up their evil thoughts with a half-hearted smile. They know what you want to hear. They say what your itching ears want to hear. They are two-faced. As soon as they get with someone else, the words start pumping out. And those words are not meant for anyone's good, especially not their own.

Words that are filled with guile are both evil and the opposite of kindness. They seek to ensnare the hearer. Their purpose is not pure.

"Where no wood is, there the fire goeth out:
so where there is no talebearer, the strife ceaseth.

As coals are to burning coals, and wood to fire;
so is a contentious man to kindle strife.

The words of a talebearer are as wounds,
and they go down into the innermost parts of the belly.

Burning lips and a wicked heart are
like a potsherd covered with silver dross.

He that hateth dissembleth with his lips,
and layeth up deceit within him;

When he speaketh fair, believe him not:

for there are seven abominations in his heart.

Whose hatred is covered by deceit,
his wickedness shall be shewed before the whole congregation.

Whoso diggeth a pit shall fall therein: and he that rolleth a stone,
it will return upon him.

A lying tongue hateth those that are afflicted by it;
and a flattering mouth worketh ruin."
Proverbs 26:20-28

Their own words will condemn them. They cannot fool God. I choose to use wisdom when I open my mouth, to encourage others, and embrace the law of kindness.

Recipe to be a GOOD WOMAN

Proverbs 31:26—A good woman studies and shares her wisdom and knowledge in order to help others. She uses her information in an agreeable and pleasant manner.

"She openeth her mouth with wisdom; and in her tongue is the law of kindness."

Key word: **openeth**

Discerning, thoughtful, gentle.

Requiring Husbands to Help Around the Home

My mom married my dad when she was 21 years old. Shortly after I was born, she had to leave her home and family to move to California where my dad was in medical school. She raised all three of us without any family or help from my dad. I have heard her admit how difficult it was to leave her family but I never heard her complain about my dad not helping her with the home or children.

We have a ton of appliances and items that make being a homemaker so much easier than it was for women many years ago. We have dishwashers, ovens, running water, hot water, vacuums, iron, electricity, lights, etc. that women of long ago didn't have. My mom had all of these modern conveniences and was very thankful. What has happened to women today?

I expected Ken to help me around the house and was often mad at him if he didn't. He was working and traveling many hours and days a year to make a living for our family and I still expected more from him. Why is that? How come we expect so much more from our husbands than our mothers and grandmothers did?

I believe it is the feminist movement that has tried to convince us that male and female roles are the same, that women should help with being providers and men should help with being keepers at home. Many women were convinced that working outside the home was more fulfilling, so they left the home and expected their husbands to help pick up the slack of being gone from the home so many hours a day.

God specifically commanded women to be keepers at home and to guide the home. Men are to be the protectors and providers of the home. This is His ideal situation. We must strive toward His ideal because His ways are always best. Yes, the years when the children are young are long and difficult, but God always seems to give us the strength we need for each day and for what He has called us to do.

Now, like I have said before, if your husband helps around the home and with the children, GREAT! If not, then love, serve, and please him anyway and thank him regularly for working so hard for you and your children. He has to work for many more years than you have to be a mother with children at home. The early years pass quickly and children want and need a peaceful home where Mom and Dad love each other deeply. Work hard giving this to them and be content with your ministry in the home. It is your high calling from God.

"She looketh well to the ways of her household,
and eateth not the bread of idleness."
Proverbs 31:27

~Lori Alexander
From Blog: Always Learning

Chapter Twenty-Two
The Virtuous Keeper

"She looketh well to the ways of her household,
and eateth not the bread of idleness."
Proverbs 31:27

The virtuous woman was also a keeper of the home. She was not idle; she looked well to every area of her home. It was not a pig sty. She did not have clutter and dirt built up from years of being lazy. She was on top of everything. Life can be wonderful for the keeper of the home. We get to cook meals that people enjoy. We get to have happy homecomings each day as our husbands walk through the door. We get to have a pile of children on our laps for story time, little ones who follow us as if we were the most glorious and important human in the world. We get to make our house a home with our special feminine touch. There is no greater calling for a woman than that of the homemaker. God gives instruction for women in the book of Titus:

"The aged women likewise, that they be in behaviour as becometh holiness,
not false accusers, not given to much wine, teachers of good things;
That they may teach the young women to be sober, to love their husbands, to
love their children, To be discreet, chaste, KEEPERS AT HOME, *good,*
obedient to their own husbands, that the word of God be not blasphemed."
Titus 2:3-5

The blessing of a clean home

Having a clean home makes a heart cheery. If my home is a mess I feel down and overwhelmed. I stare at the clutter and mess and wonder where to start. A clean home is a welcoming home. People feel at ease when they step into a clean and orderly home. It is a sign that all is well if the home is in order. A home filled with the love of Christ and a love for each other is paramount. Never put your clean home above that! Remember to keep everything balanced.

I have learned to like cleaning from my mother. She is the best cleaner I know. When you are in her home, it just smells clean. It is inviting and restful. Anyone can trust they will not contract a disease when entering her home. You can walk barefoot and not feel a crumb. My mother would teach me how to clean properly just as her mother taught her when she was growing up. And now, I am teaching my children the same. These skills are passed down from generation to generation. My grandmother ironed her sheets, bleached her babies' white shoes, and ironed and bleached the shoestrings. Everything had to be perfect. We live in a different time. I am not even close to that meticulousness. I have a very relaxed and joyful home. We all enjoy working, eating, playing, and fellowshipping together.

Dirty, happy homes?

I have heard the argument that a dirty home is a happy home. Some women will tell me that they would feel stressed and be nasty if they had to keep their home clean. My question is WHY? Why would cleaning a home make anyone stressed if they keep it up each day? I am a reformed slob. I know all the excuses. Now, I find cleaning to be very satisfying. If I have a dirty or cluttered home, I feel stress like nothing else. I feel unmotivated, lazy, and just plain overwhelmed when I look around at the mess. I get nasty and grouchy if my house is unclean. Once you have your home deeply cleaned, you can keep it up in a very short amount of time.

My husband loves a clean and orderly home. He works all day and truly enjoys coming home to a fresh environment. It sets the mood for a relaxing evening for him to unwind with his family.

Have some cleaning buddies.

I have five buddies, and my daughters are now even cleaning other people's homes. They get paid to help. Making money is very rewarding for them. They love cleaning. I started teaching them to clean when they were

Letters from my Readers

Dear Erin,

    The children and I are enjoying your posts on cleaning. We are getting the house in order one step at a time, little by little. We are having fun with it, which is more important than having a perfectly orderly home. I just wanted to tell you I had a realization the other day. I was trying to deep clean every time I cleaned and was becoming frustrated because it took sooooo long. I know it is really dumb but my mom worked and I had no one to teach me to clean. She was too busy and just didn't think about it, I guess.

    For instance, I would wipe down everything in the bathroom—shower, sink, toilet, shelves, cupboards, floors etc.—I mean everything! It would take forever and then I would have a sparkling bathroom, but the rest of the home would be in a shambles because I took so long on the bathroom. I could not believe I had been so dumb for so many years cleaning this way. Now when I clean the bathroom I do the toilet and the sink, wiping them down every day (I hate a smelly toilet) which only takes 5.52 minutes (I timed myself).

    On Saturdays, I sweep and/or mop the floor, and clean the shower and mirror. It is so simple and doesn't take much time at all. Thanks for sharing all you have been blessed with.

In His Love,
Heather

three years old and I guess I made cleaning fun for them. You can try that, too. It would not hurt. Some women also argue that they want to spend more quality time with their children. You can spend a lot of time cleaning with your children! That is a part of our family time. As soon as my kids could walk, they were my cleaning buddies. They learned early that cleaning was a part of daily living. It was not a mountain to climb, it was just a few short steps each morning. It brings a feeling of working as a team. We all live here, we all clean here! The more kids a person has, the more cleaning buddies. The older kids can buddy up with the younger children in their chores to pass on their learned skills. It is a win/win situation. Building relationships while creating a haven of refreshing beauty!

7 Days of Spring Cleaning:
Getting things deeply cleaned

Every home needs a good, solid cleaning once or twice every year. After the long, cold winter, you are ready to open up the windows to allow the light to shine in and the breeze to blow gently across the floors. The light reveals the dirt that has built up over the long time of hibernation indoors. The cold seasons are over, with all of their pesky germs. It is time to get on your apron and pull out the old mop. Get tough on your dirt.

It really feels like a huge task, but when you take it one day at a time, it is easily mastered. One closet at a time, one drawer, and one room at a time. You will feel so much better sitting in a clean home. I used to do marathon cleaning days. When I had no pain, I could spring clean my entire home in one day. I would start at 6 am and work up to 10 pm. It was a long day, but I loved to get it done. I realize not everyone is that crazy! I have to pace myself now, and I know it is good not to burn yourself out in the process. It is easy if you take it one step at a time. One room at a time.

To avoid frustration, try focusing on one particular cleaning task per day. It may help you organize your time better. I've created a series of checklists to help you get a good start this year. Finishing the large task of spring cleaning gives a good feeling of accomplishment. Every nook and cranny is decluttered, cleaned, and organized. I am ready for spring!

DAY 1 Freshen the Bedding:

- Wash all the sheets in the entire household. Make a fun day of stripping down each of the beds. This is a great job for little kids. They will feel like good helpers as they rip off the sheets.
- Wash the mattress pads.
- Wash the pillow coverings.
- Wash the quilts and pillow shams.
- Wash the pillows (make sure to observe the washing instructions) both decorative and regular head-pillows.
- Wash the bedskirts.
- **The mattress.** To freshen mattresses, which accumulate tons of dead skin cells and other dust and dirt, sprinkle baking soda over the mattress and then vacuum. I usually rent a Rug Doctor® to do mattresses, using the furniture attachment, which really does a great job at getting the sweat, grime, or pee from the occasional bed wetter's mattress. If you do not use a Rug Doctor®, use the wand attachment to your regular vacuum, or a shop vac. I love using my shop vac for things like this.
- For a really fresh scent, hang all bedding outside to dry. You can use the clothesline or try our handmade wooden drying racks—*the Homesteader* can fit either four quilts or two sets of sheets over it. It is huge.
- Wash the bedframe. Wipe down the entire bedframe to remove dust and dirt.

DAY 2 Wash the curtains and windows:

- There is a ton of dust that accumulates on curtains. You can take one down to see for yourself. The top will smell like dust and there will be a furry layer of dust. Take all of the curtains down in the entire home. Be careful to observe the washing instructions.

While the curtains are washing, get yourself a pail and I will give you the most amazing recipe ever for cleaning windows…

> **WINDOW CLEANING SOLUTION:**
> **2 gallons of water**
> **½ cup vinegar**
> **For a fresh scent, 2 drops of lemon essential oil**

I learned this recipe and window-washing technique from the Amish. It far outperforms any window spray cleaner, by a longshot. You need to have one rag for washing and one dish-drying towel for wiping dry.

Here are a few easy steps...

- Wash down the inside of the window with your wet rag. Then rub over it with the dry towel. You will see that is does not streak at all! It is amazing!

- Pop your window backwards if you have double-hung windows (which are handy) and repeat step one. If yours are not double-hung, then you can either pop the window out or wash the window from the outside. Be careful if you have to use a ladder!

- Vacuum the inside frame of the window and screen. Inside the window frame you will find all kinds of nasty things, from bugs to mold and dirt. The majority of these things can be vacuumed out using the wand of your regular vacuum or by using a shop vac.

- Wash out the frame using the same window-cleaning solution, and rub dry with a towel.

- Washing the trim: Using the same window-cleaning solution, wash the window sill and the top of the trim above the window. Dust will settle on any flat surface and you want to be sure to remove it all.

DAY 3 Freshen the Furniture:

- The furniture in your home is used on a daily basis so it is probably full of dust, old dead skin cells, oily residue, and dirt.

- **Fabric sofas and chairs.** You can bet these are one nasty cesspool of dust. If you pound your fist on the arm of the couch and it reveals a dust cloud, you have a situation! It is best if you vacuum the fabric furniture each week to maintain it, but if not, you will have to do some serious cleaning to remove the dust and grime. I like to rent a Rug Doctor® steam cleaner once a year for my furniture and area rugs. It will freshen them up nicely. If you can't rent a Rug Doctor®, you can use baking soda by sprinkling and vacuuming off. That will also deodorize and freshen. When vacuuming, do the dust cloud test to be sure the cushions are free of dust. If you pound on it and a dust cloud still forms, you need to vacuum that area again. For stains, either use the Rug Doctor®, or make your own cleaner...

> **FABRIC CLEANING SOLUTION:**
>
> **½ cup rubbing alcohol**
>
> **1 Tablespoon white vinegar**
>
> **Blot out stains and rinse well with water.**

- **Leather sofas and chairs.** Vacuum under and around cushions. Wipe the furniture down with a damp cloth and then with a dry towel. For oily grime spots, use a mixture of vinegar and water…

> **LEATHER CLEANING SOLUTION:**
>
> **1 cup water**
>
> **1 teaspoon white vinegar**
>
> **Gently cleanse area and wipe dry.**

- **Wooden furniture.** You will notice that dust settles on any surface that is flat, including below the chairs. Place the chair on a table so you can examine the dust that has settled beneath the seat. Make your own furniture polish to brighten wood and make it shine again…

> **WOOD CLEANING SOLUTION:**
>
> **1 cup olive oil**
>
> **½ cup lemon juice**
>
> **3 drops of lemon essential oil**

- Wipe over wood and then, using a towel, rub in and dry off excess oils.

DAY 4 Walls, Ceiling, Fans, and Trim:

- The walls get dirty! Especially if you heat with wood. We have some black soot on our walls and ceiling.
- Vacuum all cobwebs around the corners of the rooms and around the ceiling. You will find more than you think when you are actually looking for them.
- Dust all running boards, which is the trim around the floor.
- Wipe down the walls, one room at a time. You can get wall and ceiling

mops that will make the job easier.

- Wash down ceiling fans because they collect a lot of dust. If you run your ceiling fan without washing the dust off, you will have that dust blow around your room.
- Wash light fixtures. Ceiling light fixtures usually fill up with dust and bugs.
- Dust shelves and the tops of doorframes. Don't forget the doorknobs!
- Vacuum off lampshades and dust lightbulbs to reveal more light.
- Tough scuffs on walls or trim can be effectively removed using rubbing alcohol. It works really well. Be careful; if you rub too hard, you can remove paint. I like to rub gently and rinse with water. I have just figured this out after my son drew on our dry-erase board with a permanent marker. I washed it all off with rubbing alcohol. It is like a miracle cleaner for hard-to-remove stains.

> **WALL WASHING SOLUTION:**
> 2 gallons warm water
> ½ cup white vinegar
> 4 drops of lemon essential oil + a squirt of dish soap

DAY 5 Kitchen:

- The kitchen is a room that really needs a good spring cleaning. Cooking will cause grease to settle on every surface in the kitchen, so it is imperative to give the kitchen a good once-over.
- **Cabinets.** Wash all cabinet faces and drawers off with this great degreaser. Don't forget the knobs and handles. Every surface the human hand touches has germs and bacteria, oils and residue.

> **DEGREASING SOLUTION:**
> 1 gallon hot water
> ½ cup white vinegar
> 2 drops lemon essential oil + 1 Tablespoon dish soap

- **Inside drawers and cabinets.** Empty out drawers and vacuum. Wash with the degreasing solution and put items back into the drawer in a more organized fashion. Make sure all like items are together in one place.

- **Refrigerator.** Take everything out. Toss out all outdated and spoiled food or condiments. Wash the outside of any containers. Vacuum out drawers and wash with degreaser (make a fresh batch: 1 gallon hot water + ½ cup vinegar + 2 drops of lemon essential oil + 1 teaspoon dish soap). Wash the outside of the refrigerator as well as the handle. When putting items back into the refrigerator, make sure to have food sections to further organize your groceries. Have a section for dairy, one for meats, one for veggies, and one for fruits. That way you will always know right where to find the food you need when you need it. Don't forget to clean off the top of the refrigerator. Move the refrigerator out so you can clean underneath and behind it. There is a lot of dirt, grime, and dust that accumulates in those areas.
- **Stove.** Make a fresh batch of degreaser:

DEGREASING SOLUTION:
1 gallon hot water
½ cup white vinegar
2 drops lemon essential oil + 1 Tablespoon dish soap

Vacuum out the stove drawer and inside the stove. If you have burners, vacuum out under the burners and take off the grills. Wash the grills and the oven racks. Using the degreaser, wash out the entire bottom and inside walls of the oven. After it is clean inside, work on the outside. Wash off the knobs by removing them and wiping down behind where the knobs sit on the stove. Wash the top and the outside of the door with the handle, until it shines. I do not use aluminum foil much, but a good use is to layer the bottom of your stove with foil to catch food that boils over or drips down. It will save you a ton of cleaning time in the future. Whenever the foil looks disgusting, just throw it out and replace it with another clean piece. If you have let your stove go, you may need to pull out the big guns. That essentially means you have to be very careful because you may need to use harmful chemicals. I used ammonia. (Never use ammonia with bleach, it is a deadly combo.) Make sure to have a well-ventilated area. Leave the ammonia to sit on bad spots, cover to trap fumes and work off with non-abrasive scouring pads. **Be careful.**

- **Sink.** The sink is a yucky place. It is good to bleach out the sink if it is white porcelain. If you scour it with baking soda it could leave scratches. I have always just filled up my sink with a mixture of water and about one cup of bleach. I let it soak and the stains come off really well. If they are tough stains, dab pure bleach on them and they will come off within a few minutes time. If you have stainless steel, you could use the same degreasing solution or a scrubbing paste made from baking soda and enough vinegar to make it wet like toothpaste. Use an old toothbrush to get the grime off around fixtures and around the sink base with your paste. Rinse with water and dry for a nice bright shine.

> **SCOURING PASTE:**
> ½ **cup borax + a little white vinegar**
> ½ **cup baking soda + 1 teaspoon course salt**
> **2 drops lemon essential oil**

- **Decorations.** Wash all decorative items. Using the degreasing solution, rub off all knickknacks and wall-hangings. If you have silk flowers or plants, you should bring them outside to shake out the dust before you wash them. Wash them in water and allow them to drip-dry. They will look bright and fresh all over again.

DAY 6 Bathrooms:

- Bathrooms are a dirty place to begin with. Most people neglect the bathroom. I do not. I clean my bathrooms almost every day. With many people using the toilet, there are lots of germs and bacteria. Some people's bathrooms smell like a man's urinal. I cannot stand that smell, so I routinely clean up after others each day. Here are some tips for spring cleaning the bathroom…

- **Sink.** Clean the sink with the same degreasing solution or a scrubbing paste made from baking soda and enough vinegar to make it wet like toothpaste. Use an old toothbrush to get the grime off around fixtures and around the sink base with your paste. Rinse with water and dry for a nice bright shine. For marble use ½ rubbing alcohol + ½ water in a spray bottle.

- **Mirror.** Wash the mirror and dry with a towel to reveal the perfect shine of your reflection. Wipe dry until streak-free.

> ### MIRROR CLEANER
> **2 cups water**
> **2 Tablespoons white vinegar**
> **2 drops lemon essential oil**

- **Tub and shower.** Use the degreaser and scrub all dead skin cells from the walls of the shower. For granite or marble tile, use ½ rubbing alcohol + ½ water in a spray bottle. After the fixtures are clean and walls are rinsed down and wiped clean, dump all the baking soda cleaner down the drain along with the vinegar mixture. It will act as a drain declogger as well.
- **Toilet.** Use a scrub brush to clean the inside of the toilet bowl with vinegar and baking soda. Make sure to get all of the scum off. Wipe down the entire toilet (the seat top and under the seat, the rim of toilet, behind the seat where the hinges are, around the base of the toilet, the top of the toilet as well as the flushing handle).
- **Rust.** If you have rust in the tub and toilet, I recommend using an entire gallon of vinegar and let it sit overnight. The vinegar will break down bacteria, neutralize odor, and break down mineral buildup. For severe buildup of hardened mineral deposits, I recommend CLR® (the big guns).
- **Floor.** Sweep the floor and wash the floor. Make sure to get around the bottom of the sink and toilet.
- Wash the shower curtain. If you have a white shower curtain, take it off. You can soak it in bleach water in a pail for about ten minutes and then rinse out. It will take off all the soap scum and make it look fresh and new again. Hang it back up.
- Wash all the towels that are hanging around. Lay out all fresh towels for a brand new start.

FREE DAY...

Take a day off when you need to :) Kick back and enjoy the outdoors.

DAY 7 Floors.

- The last thing you do is all your floors.
- Shake out or vacuum all rugs and sweep under all of the furniture.
- Move everything including the refrigerator, stove, laundry machines, and other furniture. You will be surprised how many things collect under the couch, behind the fridge, and under the beds. Wow, it is like Christmas all over again. You will find a zillion lost treasures. Even though I am a clean freak, I still find things under my furniture that I never thought were possible.
- Mop under everything. I like to have an old sock hanging over my mop pail so I can easily grab it to power off tough grime spots. I use it around the edges and corners. You could never possibly get the edges and corners clean with a mop. This is a good practice.

> **WOOD + LINOLEUM FLOOR SOLUTION:**
> **1 gallon hot water**
> **½ cup white vinegar**
> **2 drops lemon essential oil**

- Wash small area rugs in the washing machine if they are washer-safe. If not, bring them outside and give them a flush of the hose to get the ground-in dirt out. Hang out to dry. If you have a lot of carpets, now is the time to rent the steam-cleaner for carpets. Steam-clean all your area rugs or carpeting. They will look so fresh.

Keeping up with things is easy!

Once you have everything deeply cleaned you can keep it up in a short amount of time. Create a system you can stick with. A schedule can help you look well to the ways of your home. There is no reason you should get overwhelmed and behind. Maintenance is key.

Letters from my Readers

Dear Erin,

    We have a nice-sized home with cement floors and a few rugs. Everyone is supposed to sweep or vacuum the room they are cleaning for chores, but the mopping is left for weekly cleaning. Problem is, we didn't always get around to it, being very busy with other things. So, our floors would be dirty, even though they looked clean. We have dark cement floors and a sweeping would make them look like they were clean. But the kids would end up with black on the bottoms of their feet from walking around barefoot. Yuck! The mop bucket we have is this massive commercial one on wheels and a nice big mop to go along with it. But it sat idle in our closet way too often... it seemed like such a chore to get it out, fill it, clean the mop... sometimes it would sit there with dirty mop-water for days. :P Another Yuck!

    An idea came to me to assign a child to prepare the mop water in the morning during chore time. I liked to add lemon Lysol because it smells so good. But you could add whatever you like for your floors. Anyway, the mop bucket would stay in our utility/laundry room all day. As each child finishes cleaning the room for which they are responsible and has it swept, they go get the mop, squeeze it out and in a matter of minutes they can have their room mopped. No more black feet from dirty cement floors! Yay! At the end of the day, before my husband comes home from work, that same child empties the mop bucket, rinses it, and rinses the mop. It is really very simple and very doable. Another plus is that when there is a spill, it's no biggie because the mop is ready to go! Even after the bucket is empty, the mop is still damp for the evening, so we can run it over the kitchen floor after supper. I have two heads for the mop, so I can alternate and wash often.

You get what you inspect, not what you expect.

Have a great day!
~ Jeanne Tate

Here is our Daily Schedule:

Simple Daily Schedule	
TIME	**ACTIVITY**
6:30 am	Get up, Make Beds, Get Dressed
7:00 am	Eat Breakfast
7:30 am	Chore Time
8:30 am	School Time--Math, Spelling, LA, Reading
10:00 am	Break Time
10:15 am	School Time--Writing, History, Science
11:45 am	Prepare Lunch
12:00 pm	Eat Lunch
12:30 pm	Chore Time
1:00 pm	Free Time--Naps, Outings, projects
4:30 pm	Prepare Dinner
5:00 pm	Eat Dinner
5:30 pm	Chore Time
6:00 pm	Free Time--Relax, Read, Visit, Play Games
7:45 pm	Get Ready for Bed--Bathe, Teeth
8:00 pm	Go to Bed--Mom & Dad Time

Many of you reading this book may have your children in a public or private school, which gives you a lot more flexibility. If you are used to the education of a brick-and-mortar school, with their eight hours of structured teaching each day, it may shock you when you see my schedule with homeschooling. Do not be alarmed. They get everything they need to learn in a shorter amount of time, because they have a private instructor there to help them. I am right there at their fingertips. All their assignments are done, they understand, and they enjoyed learning. If we get behind, we adjust the schedule in order to accommodate with more time for completing school subjects.

You can take the general concept of my simple daily schedule and apply it to your unique situation. The object of the game is to maximize your time by finding a way to organize it. Your schedule may look completely different than mine and that is okay. We all have different goals.

Being productive with your time

If a person sleeps 10 hours, they are awake for a total of 14 hours. I typically sleep 7 hours so I have 17 hours of time each day. What do you do with your time? If you feel overwhelmed with all that you have to do in a day, it is time to make yourself a schedule. Schedules organize our time so we can do all the things we set out to do. If you already have control over your environment, it is easy to keep it up. Cleanup should take no more than 30 minutes after each meal if you have each person doing their own share.

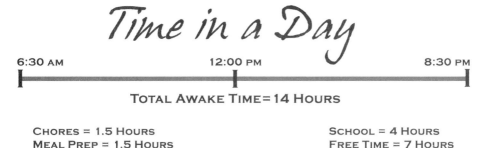

Time in a Day

| 6:30 AM | 12:00 PM | 8:30 PM |

TOTAL AWAKE TIME = 14 HOURS

CHORES = 1.5 HOURS
MEAL PREP = 1.5 HOURS

SCHOOL = 4 HOURS
FREE TIME = 7 HOURS

Teamwork

First thing after breakfast, we break away to do our share of the work. We all live together so we all work together as a team. I buy a spray bottle for each of the kids, a broom, and some other cleaning tools to go in their own cleaning caddy so they can do their jobs efficiently. I will share our typical morning which is a piece of cake for TEAM HARRISON (the kids and I) who rent a 4,000-square-foot home…

- **Junior** (my nine-year-old) has bathroom duty. Each bathroom takes five minutes. There are four bathrooms. First, he sprays the counter top and sink and wipes it clean (1 min.). Then he sprays the mirror and shines out all the water spots (1 min.) He dumps a little vinegar into the toilet and brushes it clean (20 sec.). Then he takes the bag filled with garbage out of the trash can and takes it outside to the garbage bin (15 sec.). He sprays down the toilet seat and around the outside of the toilet and wipes it down (30 sec.). Lastly, he sweeps the floor (1 min.). He finishes out the other three bathrooms with the same routine. He only puts in about 30 minutes of total work time.

- **Mikey** is my ten-year-old boy. He feeds and waters the chickens and gathers the eggs (10 min.). When he comes back into the home, he goes into the living room to pick up items that have been left on the floor and returns those items to their proper places (5 min.). He then gets his broom and starts sweeping the living room (5 min.). Then he gets our handy spray mop and mops over the living room floor (5 min.). In his remaining five minutes, Mikey dusts the living room.
- **Megan and Molly** work on the kitchen together. While Molly is clearing the breakfast table, Megan is rinsing the dishes. Typically, it takes about ten minutes to clear all the countertops, put away any leftover food, and wipe off the countertops. It takes another ten minutes to wash the breakfast dishes. The remaining ten minutes are for rinsing, drying and putting away the dishes.
- **Miles** is the cow-milker (we live on a little hobby farm). It takes him about 30 minutes to get the milker ready, milk the cow, dump out the milk, and wash out the milker.
- **Mom:** While they are working, I am also busy working alongside them. I start a load of laundry and fold a load that is dry (10 min.). I wipe down the faces of the cupboards in the kitchen while the girls are washing the dishes (5 min.). I sweep and mop the kitchen (10 min.). If needed, I help any of the kids with their work. I sweep my home office and tidy it up.

Preventative cleaning

In a short amount of time, our home is completely clean. I call this "preventative cleaning" because it prevents us from having to deeply clean once a week. When you clean up messes right away, the grime and filth will not have a chance to take over and set in. When you maintain a clean home each day, you have more flexibility to do other things.

We have about a half-hour before we typically start school, so it feels very relaxed. If our chores take a little longer, we have that extra time. We all like finishing our work quickly so we have time for other things. If we are in a summer vacation time, during the normal school hours we will do other projects. Projects like gardening, canning, sewing, building forts, mowing grass, or most days, just enjoying more playtime with friends.

Schooltime

Once school starts, I am busy teaching and helping the kids when they need me. We usually start with math because I need their minds as fresh as possible. Miles, Molly, and Megan are older so they open their math books and get to work. I usually work with the younger boys because they have a lot of questions. We work on some spelling, language or grammar, and reading.

After about an hour and a half, I find it is a good time to take a little recess. The kids enjoy running outside for a game of four-square or coloring a picture. When they come in it is time for fun! I really enjoy teaching history and science. The kids love it because I love it. I might show them a documentary or read a story about some kind of ancient civilization. Oftentimes we will paint a picture or make a storybook about all that we learned. I let them set up ancient villages after we do the research on a civilization. We reenact, make recipes from the time period, download some music from that time (if relevant), and just enjoy the whole experience. After they have learned all they can about that particular civilization, I have them write a paper about it. I teach them grammar, punctuation, and how to effectively communicate an idea, as well as how to prove a point with writing and how to make their writing more interesting. We look forward to learning each day.

I teach history on Mondays and Wednesdays. On Tuesdays and Thursdays I do science. We enjoy doing experiments and watching science shows on YouTube. I still give out quizzes or tests and we also enjoy going on adventures outside to explore nature and make our own findings. I have taken the kids to planetariums, nature centers, museums, or just to our backyard for a geological dig. You can find all kinds of minerals, rocks, and even fossils out in your own dirt!

When it is time for meal prep, I let the kids out for some playtime. I make something simple and call them in for lunch. We sit down, thank God for our day, and eat together. While we are eating we are talking and having great fellowship. Cleanup after lunch is a snap. Since the entire home was cleaned first thing in the morning, there are really only some minor things to clean up. If there was a messy school project, we would tidy that up at this time. The rest of the afternoon is free time. The kids can play outside if it is nice, or read, make crafts, build things, practice an instrument, sewing, baking, play board games, or anything they like doing. This is a time for them to find something of interest to pursue. It is all learning. Life skills are also great to master.

While the kids are having free time, I can do things that I need to take care of like business or correcting schoolwork. I feel like I have a lot of time. Being productive helps me stay motivated. I gain momentum as the day goes on and I just keep plugging away.

People come to visit and they look around and say, "You must clean all day long." No, I actually do not need to clean very much because we keep it up. Some moms say, "Well, you have a bunch of kids to help." If you do not have a bunch of kids, you have a lot less mess. Less dishes to wash, less food to prepare, less people to teach, so it is all relative. If you have 20 kids, you have 20 people to team up and tackle the jobs. If 20 people worked a solid 30 minutes each, you would have the equivalent of 10 hours of work. And it is all done at the same time.

Wow. Let's do the math…

20 people   x   30 minutes   =   10 hours

When I work with my five kids, we actually put in a total of three hours of cleaning in the morning. Here is the math equation…

6 people   x   30 minutes   =   3 hours

30 minutes is nothing to one person when they have 14 hours a day! The more members in the home, the less time is required out of each individual. I like to give my kids schedules where they can check boxes off. It is good to see what is expected of each person. It feels good to check things off your list.

Chore Chart Example #1

Below is an example of one chart I made when my son, Mikey was only six years old.

Each day of the week he could check off his simple list. Most things on the list were five-minute jobs or less. I picked jobs that he could easily accomplish. I would help him with anything that was a bit more difficult. You can make a chore chart on your computer. I have charts, schedules, recipes, and other printouts at *www.KeeperoftheHomestead.com*

Mikey's Chores

Chore	Mon	Tue	Wed	Thu	Fri	Sat	Sun
Make bed							
Eat							
Living Room							
Dining-Hall							
Chickens							
Tidy Room							
English, Math							
Set table							
Lunch							
Dishes							
put away							
Teeth, Bath							

Chore Chart Example #2

I have been reaping the benefits of the MOM BUCKS system in my home. The kids are enjoying earning, saving, spending, and even bartering with bucks among each other. The results for me are…

- **My home is always clean.**
- **I am always happy.**
- **My home is peaceful.**
- **Most importantly, my kids are productive.**

Here is another idea that is easy and very practical. It is the dry-erase chore chart that I created. I bought this dry-erase board about a year ago at Wal-mart for a couple of dollars. They sold extra magnets as well. I thought the magnets would be a fun touch.

Using a permanent black marker, I carefully printed out their chores and then traced the magnets to make a circle area for the magnet to be placed. Each of my children has their own dry-erase chore chart with their specific responsibilities. When they complete the list of jobs, they simply place a magnet over the circle and move on to the next job at the next time slot. Now, I have them turn in magnets for MOM BUCKS. It works great and if you use the permanent marker, you do not have to rewrite your list each day. I periodically change up the chore lists by cleaning my board with rubbing alcohol. I have different schedules in the summer versus fall or winter when school is in session.

Chore Chart Example #3

I also designed little cards that keep tracks of their jobs and the MOM BUCKS.

You get the idea. These are just a few examples of chore charts for the kids. Everyone knows what needs to be done; I find our home runs more smoothly when we have it all spelled out. When your time is organized, you can fit more into your day. **When the kids know what to expect they feel a good sense of security.**

Use your creativity and make some of your own schedules hand-tailored to suit your lifestyle.

Mom Bucks
TIME CARD

$	Job description	√
$1	Make bed/tidy bedroom	
$2	Sweep/vac/mop/window	
$2	Wash dishes/rinse dishes	
$2	Dry dishes/put away dishes	
$2	Kitchen countertop/table	
$1	Tidy room/dusting	
$2	Outside chores/garbage	
$2	Feed and water animals	
$2	Haul wood/stack wood	
$2	Milk cow/gather,wash eggs	
$2	30 minutes exercise	
$1	Schoolwook per subject	
$2	Laundry wash/fold/put away	
$4	Organize drawer/closet	
$2	Cook/bake/shower/teeth	

Name:

Keeper of the **Homestead**

Recipe to be a GOOD WOMAN

Proverbs 31:27—A good woman is conscious of responsibilities. She does not waste her time or other people's time.

"She looketh well to the ways of her household, and eateth not the bread of idleness."

Key words: *looketh, eateth not*

Duty-conscious, reliable, not idle.

Will the REAL Mama Please Stand Up?

Just because you happen to be the birth mother of a child does not make you THE mama of that child. If you hurriedly get up in the morning and rush your little one off for someone else to dry his tears, feed him lunch, and read him a book, please do not call yourself his *mama*. That child is being "adopted" out every day, with the added insult of being yanked around from one adopted mama to another. In order to bond properly and grow up emotionally stable, a small child must spend the vast majority of his time with his one, true, permanent mama, whom God has ordained to daily pour knowledge and love into that little life.

Daddies are different from mamas in many ways. They provide security that is so vital to a child's emotional health, but no dad can take the place or fill the need that only the feminine personality can supply. A mother's constant presence—the same comforting, nourishing breast, the same room, the same blanket, the same sippie cup, and the same toys—makes a child feel secure. You cannot jerk a child around from one babysitter to another and expect him to be secure and well-balanced at four years old. But you *can* expect a child raised in that manner to *not cherish* his mother later when he is 8, 10, 15 or 25 years old, just when she begins to need some cherishing herself! If your child is to later cherish you, you must cherish him every day, every hour of his development. There are no neutral moments in a child's life. Every moment is a time of continuous need and development.

For a moment, if we skip forward in the list of commands in Titus 2:5, we read that women are to "**love their children**" and to be "**keepers at home.**" There is a context in which we are to love our children *to the max*, and God says it is when we are **keepers at home**. Consider this your fair warning. You cannot improve upon God's design. In life, there are a few things that must be done right the first time around.

~Debi Pearl

Chapter Twenty-Three
Virtuous Mothering

"Her children arise up, and call her blessed;
her husband also, and he praiseth her."
Proverbs 31:28

The virtuous woman was a good mother. Her children appreciated her. They lived with her their whole lives, observing her character. Rising to the call of duty from her loving example, these kids were sure to be successful. She set the tone from working willingly with her hands to showing love in her every deed. Kids are good judges of character. They can see when a parent is hypocritical. This woman is the real deal. She maintains her integrity. Her husband takes notice of her virtues. They call her "blessed" because she was a blessing to her family and to everyone she knew.

I want my children to rise up and call me blessed. I want my words and actions to flow from a pure heart. I want to prove that my love is real by how I treat them and their father. Many times women act so sweet when they are in front of others, but when they are behind closed doors they show their true colors. Mothers usually treat their own children and husband worse than other people, which is sad. The reason for this is because you know your kids and husband love you unconditionally. They will still love you just because you are their mother. You did not have to earn that title. If you fail to be a good example and train your children to have integrity, you will have children that will add to the world's problems.

"...a child left to himself bringeth his mother to shame."
Proverbs 29:15

Too much freedom

One of my cousins has a couple of children. When they were little she would hire me to babysit them while she would go out to the bars. Every Friday and Saturday evening she would stay out late, so I usually spent the night. By the time her children were 4 to 6 years old, she had already fallen out of love with their father and moved out to live in her own place. She relinquished her custody of the children to their father. Their father had a good job but harbored a secret drug addiction. When the two kids were just getting into their teen years, he died from a drug overdose. The kids were torn out of their home and the school they attended, and placed with their mother.

I became close to her children because I was with them every weekend. I did not have the sense then to see what was going on and how it would shape their entire future. My love and care for them was not enough to save them from their destruction because I was not their mother. What they desperately needed was more attention at home. They were offered every luxury and freedom their mother could afford, and there was no supervision at all. Soon they started hanging around bad influences at school while their mother was busy working and living her life. They could hang out with their friends in old barns doing who-knows-what. Eventually they started using and dealing drugs. Both of her children ended up in prison, each with a three-year sentence, by the time they were 20 years old. Her son has three children born out of wedlock with two different women. Her daughter is in prison for the second time. The first time she was incarcerated, she gave birth to her first child, and could not see him unless her mother carried the child through the metal detector at her prison facility. When she got out, she went back to live with her drug dealer boyfriend and they had another child. After getting into the drug scene once again, she landed right back in prison. Because the mother *enables* her children by picking up after their messes, the cycle keeps repeating. It is extremely sad.

This mother now raises her imprisoned daughter's children and leaves them with babysitters half the time because she works full-time. Kids need their mother. As you can see, these two misguided souls may have turned out better if their mother would have invested her time raising them instead of pushing them off onto others much of the time.

Not enough freedom

On the opposite end of the spectrum, I have seen Christian families fail just because they held on too tightly. They offered almost no freedom at all. Some parents see the 18 years of their child's life as the entire picture. They lose themselves in their own form of perfect Christianity and abandon the idea that their children may have to face the rest of their adult life in a world that is without their protection.

I knew a family that never told their kids about sex. They would turn the magazines around in the checkout aisle of the grocery store so their children never saw immodest women. Going to the beach was out of the question because they would have to look at half-dressed women. If they received a magazine in the mail, they would feverishly take a black marker and blot out everything with which they did not agree. The kids were not allowed to watch television, play video games, watch movies, or use a computer. The parents believed everything was a doorway to Satan. The kids could not play after church because the other families at church were way too liberal-minded. The kids had each other, after all—the mother gave birth to all the playmates they would need to become social. These kids were like perfect little statues, little clones of dear Mommy and Daddy. They wore outdated, over-sized clothing, with their hair all parted the same. The girls wore long dresses and the boys always wore long pants and long-sleeved shirts. If you asked them what they believed, you could tell it was their parents' faith and not their own. It was more of a prison camp than a home.

Their super-policed lifestyle did not give them the room to make life choices for themselves. Without free will we are nothing more than cogs in a system. God gave us free will and an instruction manual (the Bible). We read that manual and make choices whether or not to follow His divine counsel. When we follow instruction we reap the blessing. When we make wrong choices we live with the consequences and learn from them. Free will is a gift.

To their utter disappointment, when the kids were old enough to think for themselves, they ran to the farthest extreme. Their son got heavily addicted to porn and alcohol after joining the service. He went from a Christian family bubble right into the real world. He did not know how to handle the things that others were showing him because he had no knowledge. Just like Adam and Eve wanted to know all things, the curiosity overtook him, to his own destruction. He ended up in a drunk-driving accident which landed him in jail. Had he been armed with a healthy knowledge of good and evil growing up, he would have known where those paths would have led.

Their daughter ended up shacking up with the first guy that payed attention to her. On went the tight pants, thick makeup, and a wild hairstyle. Once she knew she was desirable she wanted to be noticed and out there to get attention from men. She was sick of being hidden behind the bars of her prison-like home. When she was young, her mother did not realize she was sneaking around, as she was good at lying and pretending to be perfect. Little things like sneaking cookies and eating them in the bathroom became an art. She became good at finding loopholes because she knew if there was any infringement upon the law in their home, it was dealt with by long religious scoldings that to her were void of meaning. They did not have any friends or family because they felt all were bad company. They wanted to protect their children from the corrupt world.

The parents never showed affection in front of the kids because that would be inappropriate and lustful. The end was a lack of real love and joy. They forgot that their kids are people, too, with the same drives and passions they once had.

Finding balance

I have illustrated two opposite extremes and where they led. What is interesting is that they both produced the same end. The kids who were allowed too much freedom and little supervision ended up just as bad off as the kids who were not allowed any freedoms at all and were under constant supervision. I have been there and experienced both sides. Being raised in a secular world with all its trappings I wanted to jump to the furthest extreme as I raise my precious children. I found out that I could not create walls thick enough to shield my children from the evil of this world. I saw how some families were completely liberal and I did not like that. I could not understand the point of raising kids to be just like everyone else in the world. I felt that kids having too much freedom would be a mistake. Anyone would get accustomed to a life filled with ways to follow their flesh.

My brother and his wife chose the mainstream path. Their kids are glued to devices all the time, and because they get so much instant gratification, they tend to be bored easier and less interested in things of God. They are nice people but they never eat around the table as a family. The girls are top-notch cheerleaders in their high school. They are very seldom at home, having unlimited time with friends, and as a result they do not have close relationships with their parents.

I also noticed that conservative families, when in constant fellowship with people of a looser lifestyle, will cause discontentment in their children. They will say, "So-and-so is allowed to play video games, and they are Christians." The children will slowly become less and less conservative because they want the freedoms their peers enjoy.

I could not find like-minded people who practiced our same standards and I knew that kids need to have some peers so they can learn to relate to others. I thought if we joined a conservative Amish community, that would be the perfect thing. I learned that the Amish kids were smoking, cussing, and behaving in a more disrespectful way than the kids who were not even churched. We dressed the part and even had a horse and buggy. The Amish kids still found our kids different even though they looked the same. Our kids had to face rejection from the Amish kids. Eventually, they hated living among them, being a spectacle, and just wanted to be normal.

After getting off of my high horse, I could see that I was causing them more damage by forcing them to be something they were not than if I just left them to their own devices. I could see kids turning out better raised in non-Christian homes who were public school educated. I had to find balance for their sake and for the survival of our family.

So many families are somewhere in-between. We have found a healthy balance. We are actively engaged in raising our children to love the Lord and teaching them how to make good choices. We try to provide a good example and good instruction. We work hard and balance it out with lots of fun activities as well. Our kids have become our best friends. We feel comfortable around each other and talk freely about anything. We accept them for who they are, and love them with the abundance of love we have received from God. We quit trying to fit into a mold and started trusting God with our family.

Worldly-wise

Children need to be prepared to live their own lives. They need to know what is out there in the world, giving them a healthy perspective from which to learn. Telling them about porn and what it leads to will give them information to make better choices when they are faced with an illicit image popping up on their computer screen. If they are never told about it, when it comes up they will be shocked and curious. If you tell them about cigarettes and what happens to people if they get lung cancer, when someone offers them a smoke, they know what could happen. It is not as appealing as they remember the images I showed them of black, tar-filled lungs. They see the holes in the cheeks of those who have used chewing tobacco and what happens after you get cancer of the mouth. I show them documentaries of drug lords and gang shootings, as well as videos that show people talking about the scars of killing someone from drunk driving.

We do not turn the magazines over in the aisle of the grocery market. We do not make a big deal out of it. If they pick one up, we talk with them about it and make it a teaching moment. We let them think their own mind about things while giving them sound instruction. Someday they may be faced with something not so pure, when you are not there to give instruction. When someone says a cuss word, we tell them what that word means and that it is a word people use, but it is inappropriate.

We do not avoid people, because the world is filled with people. They have to learn to deal with other people. No two families raise their kids exactly the same way. Some kids have more freedom. You teach your kids how to balance their passions only by allowing them to exercise some judgment on their own. When you are there leading them, talk out the choices and make sure they understand the consequences; if they do make a bad choice, you are there to give them direction in the future. You should view their bad choices as a good teaching moment in their lives.

If you feel that a particular child is a bad influence, you can moderate the time spent with them. Some of these kids are your best teaching tools. You can talk about why the parents have problems with that kid. When they experience a crafty liar first-hand, or a selfish brat, they learn how NOT to be like that. As long as you are there to discuss freely with them each encounter they have, it works great. You should never just let them run unsupervised with another kid who has a habit of making bad choices, because chances are, your kids will follow them into sin.

Arm your children with the truth and the truth shall set them free. They need to know what is out there so they can make better choices. No person can survive in a vacuum. Build trust in your children by always giving them the facts. You do not want them to grow up saying, "They never told me!" Pour the words of God into their lives.

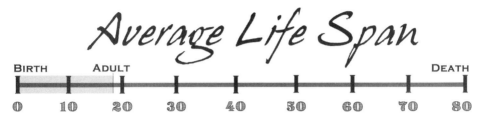

LIFE SPAN OF AVERAGE PERSON = 80 YEARS

CHILDHOOD= 18 YRS

ADULTHOOD = 62 YRS

The importance of investing in your children

Compared with the average life span of roughly 80 years, childhood is very brief. What you invest in that short space of time matters. You can fill their formative years with the ugliness of being critical and depressed or with an overflow of joy and love. When they see real joy and gladness, they will learn contentment. The time we have with them is so precious. We need to make it count, like the virtuous woman long before our time.

Each child is given to us as a blank slate. We begin writing into those pages. Our words either build them up or tear them down. If we break promises they will learn not to trust. If we shove them aside they will feel like they do not matter. When we talk disrespectfully to our husbands, they lose respect for us. Small children have a great amount of faith and trust in their parents. They believe in us like we believe in God. We are their source of life and love. The more we let them down by our lack of faith, our disapproval, and our long list of woes, the more they will learn to just give up.

In contrast, if we continually point them to Christ because our faith does not waver, they have reason to believe. If we kiss their daddy in front of them and show them what true love looks like, they learn how to love. They learn to be unselfish when we stretch forth every ounce of ourselves to help others. When we smile often, they learn to be happy. When the storms of life come and they see us stand strong, they learn to stay the course. If we exemplify peace, the law of their tongue is kindness. If they observe us being honest and taking pride in our work, they learn good business. We can make or break our kids just by our example.

"To every thing there is a season"

"To every thing there is a season, and
a time to every purpose under the heaven:
A time to be born, and a time to die; a time to plant,
and a time to pluck up that which is planted;
A time to kill, and a time to heal; a time to break down,
and a time to build up;
A time to weep, and a time to laugh;
a time to mourn, and a time to dance;
A time to cast away stones, and a time to gather stones together; a time to
embrace, and a time to refrain from embracing;
A time to get, and a time to lose;
a time to keep, and a time to cast away;
A time to rend, and a time to sew;
a time to keep silence, and a time to speak;
A time to love, and a time to hate; a time of war, and a time of peace."
Ecclesiates 3:1-8

I love these verses because they remind me that every season in life is important. God uses each one of them in our lives to teach and grow us. I endeavor to learn, grow, and then share what I have learned with others.

The full season

There is a full season in life when your children are little. They need every ounce of you. You pour love, attention, smiles, training, reading, teaching, diapering, wiping tears, tucking in, and holding them in your loving arms. You still their cries with soft lullabies and hold their hand when they cross the street. Every piece of your heart is woven into each of these moments. Your rewards are their big eyes looking back at you with smiles that say, "I love you."

You sometimes grow weary in your continual labor and you feel the need to have a friend to keep you company. This is the busiest season. The work never seems to be done and you keep pouring and pouring into their little dependent lives. They need you so much and sometimes you just feel like you have given all you can give.

As they grow, your children become less dependent upon you. They can go to the potty on their own, tie their own shoes, and they do more things to help and work by your side. They understand things at a more mature level. Conversation deepens. Life changes. You feel less need to leave your home. Contentment sets in and you enjoy your family time.

When they reach adolescence, they become more independent. They have their own ideas and dreams. They start forming convictions and standing on what they believe to be true. More and more you see them as their own person and not your little baby anymore. They are getting ready to plan for their future and you are there to see what life holds for them.

It can be a challenge in this season if you did not spend the time investing in their childhood. They could rebel against you—if they do not feel loved or accepted by you, they will find someone else who will. If you have not trained your children to have self-control, you will reap the fruit of it. They will talk back and snarl at you when you do not submit to their will. If they were a demanding, strong-willed child, they will be a completely ungrateful, self-serving teen.

One by one the children grow up and move on to live their own lives. They go to live out their dreams and start their own families, and the nest is empty. When the house is quiet you feel lonely. You long for days of busy children underfoot. When little grandchildren come running to climb into your lap, you feel needed all over again. If you do things God's way, you can reap the benefits of good relationships with your married children.

Investing in your children will always be worth it! It is the only thing we have worth anything in eternity.

CHILD TRAINING 101

Here are a few steps on training your little child how to listen and be a good helper. You reap great fruit and a wonderful relationship if you invest some time into training your children when they are young.

1 **Lead them.** Do not ask them what they want to eat or what they would like to wear today. Lovingly tell them, "We are having eggs for breakfast" or "This is what you are wearing today." When small children are given options they feel less secure. You are forcing them to make decisions far before their minds are capable. That is why a small child will choose one thing, and then quickly change their mind. They are not secure with making so many choices. It is far better for them if you lead them. God did not give you thinking and reasoning adult minds when he gave you your newborn baby. If that were the case, they would not need parents to lead them.

2 **A time for everything.** Children thrive on a schedule. It gives them security if they know what is expected of them and what they will be doing next. I always told my small children, "It is time to eat now," "It is time to get dressed," "It is time for your nap," "It is time to clean up," or "It is time for a snack." If you ask them if they would like to go to the potty, you will almost always have "no" for an answer and a mess on your hands. Some people wait until their children are "ready" to be potty-trained instead of gradually getting them used to going on the potty.

3 **Listen the first time.** Always mean what you say and say what you mean. If you say you will take their toy away if they do not stop hitting another child with it, take it away if they do not stop. Do not give them 25 opportunities to disobey before you get serious about stopping them. Someone could get hurt, and what's worse, your child is learning that your words means nothing. If they are not taught to listen to your command, it could be very dangerous. One mom, who did not teach her child to listen to her first command, ended up having to bury that child. She had a philosophy of counting to three before she would give a time-out. The child knew that he had three chances to disobey before Mom got angry. When he was crossing the street by their schoolyard, the mother saw a big truck coming, and told her little boy to stop. He

was not used to obeying the first time, so he started crossing the street and she said stop the second time. Because he did not ever listen at the second command he kept walking across the street. He was hit and killed instantly by the truck. It pays to train your kids to listen the first time.

 Be consistent. No matter what rule or instruction you have established in your home, stick with the program. In the real world the law is not bent when you steal something; you still have to go to jail. If the children know that rules are made to be broken, they will have a life full of disappointment. They will feel that the law is not just and that criminals should be allowed to do as they feel is right. Stand by your word. When you say "no cookies," do not give in to their whining. If you give them a cookie after they lay on the floor kicking and screaming, you have just taught them that kicking and screaming gets them a cookie. That will be a hard habit to break later in their life. They will learn that they can manipulate any situation to get their way.

 Build relationships. Take time to enjoy their creations and talents. Read them stories and be their buddy. Experience life with them. Do not shove them off when you have too much to do; instead, let them help you. It makes more mess having a two-year-old help wash the dishes, but you are teaching them to be your cleaning buddy in the process. When you involve them in your life, they will involve you in theirs as they grow.

 Nurture and admonition. When your child does something they are not supposed to do, you need to give them a consequence and then teach them how to do better in the future. If you just punish bad behavior, they do not know how to make better choices next time. They need instruction. Teach them daily how to love their neighbor as themselves, and how to be kind and merciful by your example. Teach them how to appreciate their life by showing them how others live across the world. Give them a healthy perspective from which they can grow. They need lots of love and affection. Take time to sew seeds of truth and joy into their hearts.

Health and wellness. Feed your children nutritious foods that help their bodies grow properly. Do not give them an abundance of sugar and other junk foods that can cause unwanted behavioral issues. Help them have moderation when they eat. Do not encourage overeating. Give them plenty of water to drink; it is important for your child to stay hydrated. Make sure they get plenty of exercise and activity. Keeping their body fit and active will help them grow strong. Make sure they bathe frequently. Do not bring your kids into public looking like poor children from a refugee camp. When you go places, comb their hair, wash their face, and put clean clothing on them. It is a bad witness to others when your kids look dirty. Teach them to brush their teeth daily and clean under their nails properly.

 Ministry mindset. Do not just bring your child to church to show them how to be a spectator. Christianity is not a spectator sport. Instead, show them how to minister to others and how to reach out to the lost. Equip them with the knowledge and let them watch you minister to your fellow man. More is caught than taught.

"And, ye fathers, provoke not your children to wrath: but bring them up in the nurture and admonition of the Lord."
Ephesians 6:4
"Train up a child in the way he should go: and when he is old, he will not depart from it."
Proverbs 22:6

Child-centered parenting

Child-centered parenting is when a parent wants to center their whole life around their child, making that child feel they are the most important person in the world. When a child grows up in an environment where everything is handed to them, where they always get their way, and they get an award each time they do the right thing, they become self-centered when they are grown. They also feel like they deserve things that they did not earn. It is healthy to have a good relationship with your child, and be happy with them when they succeed, but I have seen people ruin their child by trying to make the child's life perfect.

I knew a family who wanted their kids to know they were special and the best at everything. We would go to their home for award ceremonies. They would recognize each of their children for all their amazing qualities. They took pride in their kids and bragged about them to everyone. At first, I thought it was a nice form of public affirmation. Later, when I tried to talk with their oldest son, I found out that the affirmation went straight to his head. He got so full of himself that you could not even carry on a conversation with him. He didn't care what anyone else said; he loved hearing his own glorious words. In his mind, he was the best, the smartest, the best-looking, most talented person on this planet. It was actually annoying and somewhat revolting to hear him brag about himself like he did.

After three hours of listening to him rant about all his grand ideas and excellent qualities, I did an experiment. I tried to tell him one of my ideas to see what he would do. While I tried to hijack the conversation and keep the ball in my court, he rolled his eyes, he became agitated, and he gave a few sighs of discontentment. He was not used to listening to others or caring about what they had to say. I told this "Me Monster" about my experiment and I tried to help him realize that if he wanted to have good relationships with people, he needed to take his focus off himself and listen to what others say. In essence, treat others as he would want to be treated. If he likes others to listen to him, he needs to listen to them.

He had learned a lifestyle of being selfish and self-centered. Had his parents eased up on the affirmation and grand fanfare, he would be a pleasant person to be around. Balance is key. Encourage your kids in their strengths while teaching them to love their neighbor as themselves.

Recipe to be a GOOD WOMAN

Proverbs 31:28—You will know a good woman by how much her children and husband appreciate her and truly enjoy her company.

"Her children arise up, and call her blessed; her husband also, and he praiseth her."

Key words: *arise, praiseth*

She reaps her pleasant fruits.

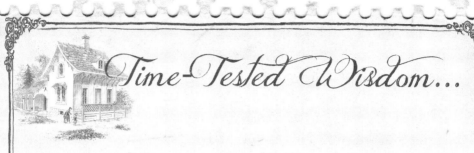

A Lesson Learned

There are times in life when we learn from the regret and mistakes of others. Such was the case, when a friend of mine told me about a lady who was a successful hairstylist. She had a four-year-old daughter whom she loved dearly. Frequently, her daughter would ask with a smile, "Mommy, will you dance with me?" "Yes, we can dance later," her mother would reply.

One day while she was videotaping her daughter, she again cheerfully asked, "Mommy, will you dance with me?" As usual, she replied, "Yes, a little later." The day came when her daughter was almost fifteen years old and the mother came across the video. As she watched it, tears came rolling down her face realizing that not once did she ever dance with her daughter.

The precious days of her daughter's childhood had passed by, never to be regained again. The mother regretfully said she recalled some wonderful times with her daughter, but mostly she recalled the busyness that filled her days.

This story has stayed with me through the years and frequently reminds me to stop what I am doing even when I can legitimately justify my workload. I have to choose what I fill each day with and when to accomplish them. I am always asking myself, "What are my priorities?" Industry and domestic duties surely are necessary, but what will our children remember about their childhood?

Daisy Farrales

Letters from my Readers

He Got His Wife Back

In the fall of 2008 I was transplanting fruit trees with our Suburban truck, pregnant with our 8th child. I looked for our 17-month-old, Joshua, and saw that he was away from the vehicle. I pulled forward to get the next tree. In a panic, I realized what had happened. I ran over our Joshua. I lived the next hour nonstop in my brain for the next 8 months.

My husband, Barry, followed an ambulance home from work that day. Joshua died before he got there. I lived in Hell on earth. I woke up every morning and functioned. But just barely. I wanted to die. I read in my Bible, "Abel's blood crieth to me from the ground." The next day I read, "hands that shed innocent blood." I stopped reading my Bible. "Oh, God, Help me!" was all I could pray and I prayed it without ceasing. My husband was dealing with losing his son and his wife. I was gone. Checked out. Unavailable for conversations or reality. If someone said Joshua's name I had to leave the room.

I thought of the accusations I would have thrown at Barry if the situation had been reversed. I knew what would have happened if Barry ever said anything like that to me. I was so fragile and had totally lost my will to live. I would have just curled up and died. He never did. He never even hinted at anything like that. He was strong. He just loved me.

A couple of months after the rest of the world resumed a normal life, Barry read John 6:16-21. The disciples were in the boat, and in the next verse "they were on the other side." God showed Barry that He would get me to the other side. I would be healed. Barry didn't tell me. He just kept silently and gently loving me. On Mother's day weekend, God healed me. I can't explain it other than He re-wrote the bad coding in my brain. He took the ruts in my brain that had been running that same movie in my mind and filled them with His Spirit. The movie stopped. I wanted to live again. I was with my family again. I could hear Joshua's name and I could talk about him again. My sweet husband, through his patience, love, and faith, got his wife back. My respect for this man soars when I think of how strong he was when I needed him most.

Kim Plath

The Virtuous Woman is to be Praised

Proverbs 31:29—God describes a virtuous woman as one whose own hard work proves her value. She has won the right to be where she is and to have what she has acquired— honor, appreciation, esteem, and love. **"Many daughters have done virtuously, but thou excellest them all."**

Key word: *excellest*

Day-in and day-out, in-season and out, she puts forth her creative labor; for that effort, she was named the most worthy of all.

Virtue means "acting power." It has the strength to affect or improve that which is around you.

Proverbs 31:30—A good woman is not caught up in looking good. She is conscious of the fear of God in her life. She has lived every day as though she believes she will reap what she has sown. **"Favour is deceitful, and beauty is vain: but a woman that feareth the LORD, she shall be praised."**

Key word: *feareth*

Fear of God is the beginning of wisdom.

Proverbs 31:31—A good woman reaps what she has sown, and it is good fruit. The enterprises and business ventures to which she has put her hand are profitable. The crafts, goods, and clothes she has made are known to be of excellent quality. Her dwelling and her services are well-managed, efficient, and tidy. Her children are honorable and seek God. Her husband has the time and heart to invest in other people's lives because she is a good help meet. A good woman has lots of good fruit. **"Give her of the fruit of her hands; and let her own works praise her in the gates."**

Key words: *give, let*

Praiseworthy, complimented, approved, deserving, admired, applauded, worthy.

"A gracious woman retaineth honour" (Proverbs 11:16).

~Debi Pearl

Chapter Twenty-Four
Virtuously Praised

"Many daughters have done virtuously, but thou excellest them all.
Favour is deceitful, and beauty is vain:
but a woman that feareth the Lord, *she shall be praised.*
Give her of the fruit of her hands;
and let her own works praise her in the gates."
Proverbs 31:29-31

The virtuous woman has excelled in every way. She enjoys the fruit of a life lived in service to God, her husband, her family, and her people. Many women do virtuously, but she rises above them. Most women will get caught up in gossip or give themselves over to a worrysome heart. She just does not waver. She holds true to her convictions, her faith, and her purpose for life. The healthy fear and reverence she has of the Lord has given her much wisdom. Even if no one praised her, if her virtue went unnoticed, she would not cease from doing what she knew was right in her heart. Flattery is deceitful and she is not swayed by it.

God describes a virtuous woman as one whose own hard work proves her value. She has won the right to be where she is and to have what she has acquired—honor, appreciation, esteem, and love. Beauty is only skin-deep and will fade with the passing of years. She does not pursue the vanity of outward adorning. Her beauty springs forth from within. God has blessed her with the fruit of her hands. Her virtue and victory are known in the gates. She does not have to tell people she is good. It is evident by how she conducts herself and how she loves her neighbor as herself.

Living Virtuously

God created us to be a help meet to our husband, a mother to our children, and a keeper of the home. Beyond that, he endows us with different dynamic personalities, interests, and gifts. We are all each unique but have a similar purpose.

Living Virtuously does not mean perfection. You can do all the right things and totally miss the point of this book. Victory and virtue are not awards that are given because you ran the furthest; they are gifts given to those who persevere on their own journey that God has given them, no matter what life may bring. Virtue involves learning contentment, choosing joy, and being teachable. The Lord is calling us to be virtuous in our marriages, in our mothering, in our homemaking, in our relationships with others, and in our faith. We have victory when we live life to the fullest; it is in our investment toward the things that have eternal value. Our homes could be spotless, but if within the walls of our homes there is bitterness, jealousy, selfishness, anger, or pride, we are fighting a losing battle. It is no different than a whitewashed tomb full of dead men's bones. There is nothing more important than a clean heart—a heart that has been washed by the pure blood of Christ. Only with Christ, and Christ alone, can we have a life filled with virtue and victory.

I have heard it said a thousand times that if everything is right on the inside, nothing on the outside matters—God only sees the heart. God does see the heart but in his Word, he tells us that out of the heart our mouth speaks. Whatever is in the abundance of our heart will come out in our actions and our words. I say rather, if the heart is right, everything matters! How we love and serve our husband matters. How we teach our children by nurturing and admonition matters. How we treat our neighbor matters. Being teachable matters. Being kind matters. How we outwardly dress or present ourselves matters. How we spend our money matters. How we eat matters. How we spend our time matters. What we listen to or watch matters. How we keep our home matters. It all matters.

In this book, I have endeavored to share some things I have learned on my journey. If we are going to get anywhere we need to put our faith in something. You could put your faith in this book, reading each word and applying it to your life; but it may not endure. You can put your faith in yourself, set the book down and decide you can figure things out on your own. Or you could simply put your faith in Christ, the finished work of the cross, and trust that He will lead and guide you as you submit to His will for your life.

I am not a scholar. I am not an aged woman. I do not have it all figured out. What I can tell you is that I am a willing vessel. I want the Lord's will in my life each day. I have made many bad choices and have had bitter thoughts, but because I have always taken the stance of learning from my mistakes, God has been able to work some pretty great miracles into my life. I am convinced that by having a willing heart and by putting your trust in Christ, you can overcome anything in your life.

You all have a story hidden in your heart with pages of it yet unwritten. I am not asking you to rip out the former pages and throw them away. I am asking you to search those pages, and learn to use those things to grow in Christ. That is what I have done. You can make a choice today how the story ends. You can choose to continue writing pages filled with woe and dread or you can choose to fill those pages with thankfulness and contentment. What about a happy ending? A happy ending is not having everything work out the way you want it to, it is living a life for Christ, learning to find joy and peace in all circumstances, knowing you will be with Him one day. We shall all stand there in front of the judgment seat of Christ, answering for how we spent our days, the days he gave us here on earth. Let us fill our days with gladness and a thankful heart.

Let us live a life full of integrity, a life full of love and virtue. It is the only way we can experience true joy and victory!

"Thanks be to God, which giveth us the victory
through our Lord Jesus Christ."
1 Corinthians 15:57

For other materials by Erin Harrison contact:
Homesteading Productions LLC
homesteadproductions@gmail.com or visit
our online store at www.Homestead-Store.com
For more helpful articles, visit Erin's blog: www.KeeperoftheHomestead.com

Homesteading for Beginners DVDs

Journey with this city gone country
family as they share some basic
homesteading skills that anyone can
master. In these videos you will learn
such skills as raised bed gardening,
milking the family cow, making butter,

cheese, kefir, bread, canning produce, sewing, woodworking, raising
livestock, and so much more. Highly educational and entertaining for the
entire family. 9 discs total. Over 12 hours of lessons. Homesteading DVDs
can be purchased at www.Homestead-Store.com

Handcrafted Drying Racks

Erin's husband handcrafts these wonderful drying racks
that are great for drying clothing, cloth diapers, towels,
blankets, sheets, rugs, and much more. They are the
sturdiest and highest quality on the market. The wooden
drying racks come in four sizes.
Go to www.Homestead-Store.com

Keeper of the Homestead Blog

Erin writes an encouraging blog for women. In her blog she continues
to share the truth she holds in her heart as well as practical insights to
keeping your home with natural recipes as well as tutorials on cleaning.
New posts each week with a following of nearly 30,000 people from around
the world. Visit her blog at www.KeeperoftheHomestead.com